SEMANTICS

The Language & Thought Series

SERIES EDITORS
JERROLD J. KATZ, THE GRADUATE CENTER, CITY UNIVERSITY OF NEW YORK
D. TERENCE LANGENDOEN, THE GRADUATE CENTER, CITY UNIVERSITY OF NEW YORK
GEORGE A. MILLER, PRINCETON UNIVERSITY

Readings in Philosophy of Psychology
    Ned Block
    Editor

Semantics: Theories of Meaning in Generative Grammar
    Janet Dean Fodor

The Language of Thought
    Jerry A. Fodor

Propositional Structure and Illocutionary Force
    Jerrold J. Katz

An Integrated Theory of Linguistic Ability
    Thomas Bever, Jerrold J. Katz, and D. Terence Langendoen,
    Editors (Distributed by Harper & Row, Publishers)

SEMANTICS:
Theories of Meaning in Generative Grammar

JANET DEAN FODOR

Harvard University Press
Cambridge, Massachusetts
1980

To my family, up-, down-, and sideways,
but most of all for my mother.

CONTENTS

PREFACE

A preface is where one makes excuses for all the books one might have written but did not. My first excuse is that research in semantics would not stand still while I was writing about it. In other words, this book is not, and really could not have been, an absolutely up-to-the-minute, stop-press report of what is being said about semantics in the latest research journals. The last chapter does sketch some of these present concerns, but the main body of the book reviews the debates and conclusions of roughly a decade, beginning in 1963 when the study of meaning was first broached by generative linguists. Some of the results of this work seem likely to be of lasting value. Other proposals I have included because they are there. Though their weaknesses are beginning to show through, they are a common heritage of linguists now working in semantics. And also, of course, seeing what was wrong with earlier moves is a large part of seeing how to get it right next time.

My intention, then, has been to write a textbook, a book which lays out the major preoccupations of the field, indicates why these have been the major preoccupations, and outlines the theoretical conclusions that have been drawn and the arguments on which they rest. In down-to-earth terms, this book is designed to be a basic text for semantics courses for graduates and advanced undergraduates in linguistics who already have some training in generative syntax and general linguistic theory.*

I hope the survey of semantic theories presented here will be a useful guide to students who are new to semantics and who have to cull from the contradictory and often heated discussions in the literature both some idea of what has been claimed and some idea of what is true. It may also be a convenient source of background material for more advanced students who are already exploring the latest research and beginning to contribute to it. And, though it was written mainly with linguists in mind, it may perhaps

*With sufficient application, it may be read alone. But class discussion is strongly recommended, since keeping a clear head in semantics is always easier with a little help from one's friends. In either case, it should ideally be read in conjunction with the original books and articles referred to in each chapter.

offer a relatively painless way for those in other disciplines to find out whether the kinds of things linguists have had to say about meaning are relevant to their own concerns.

I must stress that this is a book about theories. A different book, and a useful one for students of linguistics, would have been a compendium of semantic *data*, drawing on the detailed and sometimes quite elegant descriptive studies of the meanings of particular words, the complex interactions of quantifiers and negation, the mysterious properties of opaque constructions, the varieties of presupposition and so on. In a sense, the data of semantics are readily accessible to us all. But some facts are more significant than others, and to identify those which are revealing of the underlying principles of semantic organization is a very important task. But, for better or worse, the data base for early theoretical work in semantics tended to be very narrow. The emphasis was on devising SOME formal treatment for certain quite obvious and basic facts about meaning. It is only relatively recently that there has been attention to spare for a wider array of semantic phenomena, and that more subtle semantic distinctions have been brought to bear on the problem of choosing between competing theories.

The fact that there are disagreements about the proper treatment of meaning within a generative grammar has made this a difficult area of study. It has seemed to me, and to students I have taught, that there is now an urgent need to bring together the different theories among which linguists have divided their allegiance, and to try to clarify them and their relations to each other. Despite the obvious difficulties, this may be as good a time as any for such a project. Generative linguistics operates on a compressed time scale all its own, and by this standard we have recently passed through a rather stable (stagnant?) period, and seem to be emerging into another period of rapid change and reorientation. We do agree at last on some things. On others, opinions are diverging even more radically than in the past, and new concerns are beginning to take the place of the more traditional ones which occupied semanticists for many years.

Though I have not explored them in detail, some of the reasons for these developments are hinted at in the chapters that follow. In part they explain what would otherwise be a peculiarity in a textbook on linguistics. I have devoted one long chapter to issues about meaning which, until recently, have been discussed almost exclusively in the philosophical literature. This chapter is one of those that grew rather alarmingly in the course of being written. During those months of writing (more of them than I could have wished), it became increasingly clear that these topics are far from being of merely academic interest to linguists with an interdisciplinary bent. They are an important source of new insights and new demands on linguistic theories.

Finally, I must say something about my own attempt at impartiality in the face of the controversies that abound in semantics. My own opinions inevitably show through in places. But this is not a manifesto on behalf of one theory to the exclusion of the others. I have tried to keep to a rough principle of equal, and equally critical, representation. For the proponents of the various theories to press their claims forcefully is natural, and it is also quite proper, since a clash between opposing theories very often leads to scientific progress. But if linguists as respected as Chomsky, Ktaz, and Lakoff can sincerely differ in their views, beginning students must surely be exposed to all sides of the debate and encouraged to make up their own minds. Then they will be in a better position to help us resolve our disagreements. There would be no point to an undigested summary of contradictory claims, but I have at least tried to restrict my evaluative comments to specific points and not to prejudge the major issues.

Some of the linguists whose views are represented here may nevertheless feel that I have criticized them unfairly, but I have had to follow my own judgment, such as it is. If I have not expounded on the merits of their theories as energetically as they would have themselves, space limitations can take much of the blame. But for downright misrepresentation there is no excuse, and I can only apologize for any errors this book contains.

Noam Chomsky, Jerry Fodor, Jerrold Katz, Ray Jackendoff, Jacqueline Schachter, Richmond Thomason, Katherine Watson, and some anonymous reviewers have read all or part of various drafts of the manuscript, and I must thank them for their generosity and for their helpful comments. If I had been able to incorporate more of their suggestions, I would have fewer excuses to make. Mary Ellen Elwell and Irene Cretella typed and retyped and corrected my corrections with such good will that mere thanks are quite inadequate.

SEMANTICS

1
Semantics and Generative Grammar

Semantics has been claimed at various times by a variety of disciplines, among them anthropology, psychology, philosophy, and linguistics. It has been held to be invaluable, worthless, impossible, trivial, the salvation of mankind, a harmless hobby. This book takes semantics to be a serious and difficult area of study, and takes its goal to be the construction of a theory of meaning and meaning-related phenomena in natural languages. This theory must specify the general characteristics of a precise formal description of the semantic properties of the expressions of any given natural language, a description which can stand as part of a complete formal description, or grammar, of that language. Semantics, as we shall be concerned with it, is thus an area within linguistics, and the study of semantics exhibits the dual goal common to all linguistic research. We want to uncover the properties of particular languages in order to gain some insight into the nature of human language in general, and we want to develop a general theory in order to organize and explain the properties of individual languages.

Although alternative theories of language have been developed, the approach that is known as generative or transformational grammar can plausibly claim to be the most successful to date in achieving these goals, and we shall confine ourselves here to the study of semantics within this framework. But it must be remembered that transformational linguistics, despite its successes, is only about twenty years old, and that of all its subdisciplines semantics is by far the youngest. Chomsky's *Syntactic Structures* was published in 1957 and it was not until 1963 that the question was explicitly raised, by Katz and J. A. Fodor, of how semantic phenomena could be treated within a transformational grammar. Even then, semantics remained the concern of a very few linguists and received much less attention than either syntax or phonology.

This has changed in the last few years. The study of semantics has become as widespread and is taken as seriously as the study of syntax and phonology. This may be due in part to the judgment that at least the fundamentals of syntactic and phonological structure are now understood so that attention can usefully be directed elsewhere. But even the most optimistic linguist could not claim that we know all there is to know about phonology and syntax, and the growing interest in semantics is attributable at least as much to the realization that further progress in syntactic theory demands some understanding of semantics. Whether or not semantic and syntactic phenomena can be clearly distinguished and separately described has been the subject of much recent debate, and we will discuss it at length later in this book. But even if it should turn out that a grammar must contain quite distinct semantic and syntactic components, the evaluation of hypotheses about the syntactic component will necessarily involve an investigation of its place in the total grammar and hence of the nature of its interaction with the other components of that grammar. Many significant questions about syntactic structure thus presuppose an adequate theory of semantic structure.

From having been the poor relation of syntax, semantics has become a topic of urgent concern. It has also brought linguistics into a closer relationship with philosophy, which has long been interested in questions about the nature of meaning. But with all the attention it is now being given, and with all the help linguistics is receiving from other disciplines, the problems are enormous and progress is slow. Several theories, which we shall discuss in later chapters, have now been formulated with some degree of precision, and several particularly significant and revealing semantic phenomena have been identified and at least partly described. But in many respects we are still at the stage where just to specify what the problems are, and which are the fruitful questions to ask, must be regarded as an achievement. We have no final and comprehensive account of the semantic properties of natural languages. And though we dignify our suggestions by calling them theories, we are even further from having any EXPLANATION of why it is these properties and not some others that natural languages exhibit.

Still, we have gotten somewhere, and this book is intended to show where. So let me begin by indicating some minimal requirements on a linguistic theory of meaning, in the form of a preliminary sketch of how a semantic description of a natural language can be expected to fit into a complete formal grammar.

A sentence of a natural language, whether spoken or written or tapped out in Morse, has a certain physical form, and it also has some characteristic communicative or expressive function—it is used to make a statement, ask a question, give an order, to comment, exclaim, greet an acquaintance, and so on. The relation between the form of a sentence and its expressive function or content is obviously not a random one. Except where the normal correlations are deliberately flouted (as in the use of a code), a sentence such as *What is the time?* is not used to make a statement, and a sentence such as *It is chilly today* is used to make a statement but not, for example, the statement that simultaneous equations are difficult. At its most general, the goal of a linguistic description of a language is to correlate, by means of some well motivated and precisely stated principles, the physical forms of expressions of the language with their contents, i.e., with their meanings.

Two general characteristics of this correlation should be stressed. One is that, since there is no principled limit to the number of sentences in a natural language, the mechanisms that effect the form-meaning correlation must be quite general and capable of pairing form and meaning for an infinite range of sentences. This argument is exactly like the familiar argument for recursiveness of the syntactic rules. Like the assignment of syntactic structures to sentences, the assignment of meanings to sentences cannot be effected by a mere list. For even if a list were illuminating, which it is not, it could never be complete.

A second point is that, as it turns out, to state the form-meaning correlation directly is prohibitively difficult. More generalizations can be captured, hence the principles expressing the correlation can be simpler, if the correlation is established in a number of separate stages. By and large, the phonetic form of a sentence can be determined without reference to its meaning; it can be predicted solely on the basis of the phonological properties of the morphemes in the sentence and certain information about the syntactic configurations into which these morphemes are combined. The phonological rules which assign phonetic properties to sentences can thus be separated off as an independent component of the grammar, a component whose input is the output of the syntactic rules but which does not otherwise interact with either the syntactic or the semantic rules of the grammar. And once this component is separated off, the task we are left with in semantics is stating the correlations between the meanings of sentences and the syntactic structures that are input to the phonological component; we can ignore the correlations between the input to that component and its output.

What we cannot ignore in assigning meanings to sentences is either the morphemes they contain or the way in which these morphemes are combined syntactically. It is patent that sentences containing the same morphemes in different syntactic configurations can differ in meaning. Compare sentences (1), (2), and (3).

    (1) The hunter trapped a wounded bear.
    (2) The wounded hunter trapped a bear.
    (3) The hunter wounded a trapped bear.

It is even more obvious that structurally similar sentences containing different morphemes[1] can have different meanings.

(4) The cat sat on the mat.
(5) The boy stood on the deck.

This is a point to which we shall return again and again—the meaning of a sentence is a function of the morphemes it contains and the way in which those morphemes are syntactically combined. Clearly, then, sentence meanings must be correlated by the rules of the grammar with sentence structures and lexical content. But this task too can be broken down. Indeed it is the fundamental insight of generative grammar that to attempt to give a direct one-stage account of the syntactic properties of sentences is not productive. There are generalizations about sentences that are missed entirely, or can be captured only very uneconomically, by traditional 'taxonomic' or 'immediate constituent' grammars which assign only a single syntactic structure to each sentence. Such a grammar can capture, for example, the fact that if a noun phrase consisting of an article and a noun can appear in a certain context then noun phrases with other internal structure can appear there too; it is traditional to give independent characterizations of the contexts in which noun phrases occur and the internal structure of possible noun phrases. But there are other generalizations that a taxonomic grammar will miss, for example, the generalization that if there is a grammatical sentence in English of the form NP_1 V NP_2 NP_3 then there will also be a grammatical sentence of the form NP_1 V NP_3 $Prep$ NP_2 containing the same verb and noun phrases.

Harris (1952) stated such equivalences between sentence types simply as equivalences. But Chomsky observed that among a set of sentential structures related in this way, some are more 'basic' than others—they can be described more simply, and they contain more information. For example, the second of the two structures in the preceding paragraph, the one that contains the preposition, is more basic in this sense than the other. The prepositional constructions (6) and (7) contain extra information in that they exhibit a contrast between *to* and *for*.

(6) Mary gave some reprints to him.
(7) My mother baked a fruitcake for me.

---

1. Incidentally, note that though we must be able to identify different morphemes, we need not do so in terms of their phonological characteristics; for the purposes of semantics we could in principle just as well use numbers or other arbitrary symbols to identify morphemes. For a morpheme is standardly defined as the smallest meaningful unit of a language, which is a way of saying that the form-meaning correlation for morphemes is not systematic, that the internal phonological structure of a morpheme is irrelevant to its meaning.

This contrast is not made explicitly in the related nonprepositional constructions.

    (8) Mary gave him some reprints.
    (9) My mother baked me a fruitcake.

Also, the prepositional constructions can be generated by rules already needed in the grammar to account for sentences like (10) and (11), though these have no counterparts of the form *NP V NP NP*.

    (10) I put three ashtrays on the table.
    (11) Joe wrapped a bandage around his knee.

By contrast, to generate directly the double noun phrase constructions (8) and (9) would require including in the grammar a phrase structure rule used only for this type of sentence. For these reasons it is simpler and more revealing to generate only the prepositional construction directly, and to derive the double noun phrase construction from it by a rule, a TRANSFORMATION, that interchanges the two noun phrases and deletes the preposition.

    A sentence like (8) must therefore be assigned at least two syntactic structures, one a DEEP STRUCTURE of the form *NP V NP Prep NP*, the other a SURFACE STRUCTURE of the form *NP V NP NP*. In fact, other transformations must also be applied in the generation of (8)—a transformation making its verb agree with its subject, a transformation assigning the appropriate cases to its noun phrases, and so on. So (8), like the majority of sentences, actually goes through several derivational stages between the level of deep structure and the level of surface structure.

    It is the surface structures of sentences that determine their pronunciation and hence constitute the input to the phonological component. (Though accepted for many years, this statement has been challenged. See Bresnan, 1971. But for our purposes it is a convenient simplification.) So our goal in semantics can now be more precisely stated as the characterization of correlations between surface structures and meanings. But part of this task is performed by the syntactic transformations, which effect correlations between surface structures and deep structures. For it turns out, in many cases if not in all, that sentences which have the same deep structure also have the same meaning. We have seen, for example, that the sentences (6) and (8) have the same deep structure and are differentiated only by the application of one transformation (the Dative transformation). The passive sentences below also have the same deep structure as (6) and (8).

    (12) Some reprints were given to him by Mary.
    (13) He was given some reprints by Mary.

These sentences differ respectively from (6) and (8) only in the application of the Passive transformation. So these four sentences, which mean the same, all have the same deep syntactic structure. Rather than formulating principles to relate each of the four surface structures independently to their common meaning, we can define a single correlation between their common meaning and their common deep structure. The syntactic transformations will correlate the deep structure with the four surface structures. So now we have broken down the relation between form and meaning into three subrelations; we can ignore the relation between phonetic and surface syntactic structure, and the relation between surface structure and deep structure, and restrict our attention to the relation between deep structure and meaning.

This is the picture that guided most of the early research in semantics within the theory of generative grammar and it will serve as a framework for further discussion. But I should point out now that this conception of the place of semantics in a grammar has been called into question recently in a number of ways. There are linguists who object to the extrapolation from examples like (6), (8), (12), and (13) to the conclusion that sentences with the same deep structure ALWAYS have the same meaning, so that semantic rules can completely ignore the effects of syntactic transformations. There are also linguists who maintain that the semantic component of a grammar, as I have characterized it, is empty and that the deep structures of sentences themselves constitute adequate representations of meaning, so that the relation between deep structure and meaning is simply that of identity.

These claims and others we will examine in detail in later chapters. But the rough sketch that we have developed so far is sufficient to indicate what we should require of a semantic theory. It must make available some format for the precise representation of meanings, both of lexical items and of phrases and sentences (as syntactic phrase markers are a format for the precise representation of syntactic structure). It must specify the nature of the rules that will relate the meaning representations of phrases and sentences to representations of the meanings of the lexical items they contain and of the syntactic configurations in which they appear (as syntactic theory specifies, at least ideally, the properties of syntactic transformations). And we can also expect it to provide formal definitions of meaning-dependent properties of expressions (e.g., anomaly, self-contradictoriness) and meaning-dependent relations between expressions (e.g., the paraphrase relation, the entailment relation, the relation between a question and its possible answers). And, of course, we will value such a theory more highly the more narrowly it constrains these semantic representations and rules, for it will then embody a more detailed and informative characterization of the nature of human language. Semantic theory is no different from other areas of linguistic theory in this respect.

None of this is easy. To start with, we have a serious data problem. In studying meaning we have to contend with the fact that meaning is even more indirectly related to the measurable physical properties of utterances than are phonological and syntactic structure; we have to rely even more heavily on intuitions that are even less confident and less reliable. Also, when it comes to formalizing these intuitions, we find that while it may be hard to devise any representation system at all for some aspects of meaning, for many others there is an embarrassment of apparently distinct alternatives. Deciding which are genuine alternatives, and finding good empirical reasons for choosing between them, are very important tasks. If we were content to accept just ANY representation of a semantic phenomenon, and if we were content to adopt a new descriptive or theoretical principle every time we met a phenomenon not yet accounted for, we would end up with a theory so eclectic and amorphous that, though it might technically meet the goals set out above, there would be both little reason to believe it was true and little chance of falsifying it. We may also note that there is a connection between this goal of motivating and constraining the semantic theory and the goal of developing a theory which can contribute to the prediction and explanation of psychological facts about the ways in which people learn and use their language. But there is as yet very little really informative psychological data about meaning, and what there is has rarely been appealed to by linguists, even though the general question of how grammars and psychological processes relate to each other lurks not far below all linguistic research.

The study of meaning has a long history. What is original about recent linguistic approaches to the subject is the conjunction of formal description with a concern for the special peculiarities of natural language. As we have seen, this permits the formulation of some quite specific research goals. As we shall see in later chapters, the proper way of meeting these goals is still far from clear; more than one semantic theory has been developed within the framework of generative grammar and still thrives at least by default. In this book we will review the major contenders and will compare and to some extent evaluate them with respect to a number of issues. This will involve at least a cursory consideration of a variety of semantic phenomena. But before embarking on all of this, we should take a step back from contemporary linguistics and consider some quite ancient and fundamental questions about the subject matter of semantics—questions about the nature of meaning.

2
Theories of Meaning

2.1. WHAT IS MEANING?

Semantics is the study of meaning, but what is meaning? This question has been repeatedly asked, and variously answered, throughout the history of philosophy and related disciplines. Along with problems about free will, the nature of time, and so on, it has seemed one of the ultimate metaphysical puzzles. And the apparent lack of a satisfactory answer has led many people to be sceptical about semantics as a legitimate field of study. Since this is a book about semantics, it is obviously committed to the rejection of such scepticism. But I do not pretend to be able to refute the sceptical position by providing a definitive answer to the question of what meaning is, or even by proving that it has an answer. My concern in this section will be with the various ways in which the question has been construed, with what KIND of answer it has been taken to be a demand for. In subsequent sections of this chapter we will examine some of the answers that have been given.

General theories of meaning have typically been developed by philosophers rather than linguists, and it might be wondered whether they have any significance for linguistics at all. There is obviously plenty of basic descriptive work to be done, and surely this does not depend on the answers to any more fundamental questions. Lexicography, after all, has never been held back by lack of a theory of the nature of meaning.

But to draw this moral from lexicography would be an oversimplification. Even the most 'purely descriptive' statement about meaning inevitably presupposes some idea of what meaning is and is not. Suppose, for example, it is asserted that the meaning of a certain word changed in some fashion during the sixteenth century. This statement will be unjustified if the data on which it is based are faulty, or if the data do not support the inference that a change occurred, but also if what changed about the word was not its meaning, but, say, its frequency of use or its inflectional paradigm. Hence, if the question "What is meaning?" is construed as a question about what constitutes a semantic phenomenon, we can hardly shrug it off as irrelevant to linguistics.

This point is easy to overlook because in practice we are fairly confident about what to include and what not to include in an account of the meaning of an expression. I simply took it for granted, and surely I was right, that an observation about frequency or pattern of inflection is not an observation about meaning; changes in these properties might be associated with a change in meaning but they certainly do not, by themselves, constitute a change of meaning. But how, in the absence of a general theory of meaning, could one justify claims such as these?

Katz (1972) has listed a number of phenomena which, according to our 'pretheoretic intuitions,' are semantic. These include, among others: synonymy, antonymy, meaningfulness, meaninglessness or semantic anomaly, redundancy, semantic ambiguity. Any fact about an expression that is relevant to the description of these phenomena thus has a *prima facie* right to be regarded as a fact about the meaning of that expression. And any theory that did not bear on all or at least many of these phenomena (and, ideally, make clear why it did not bear on the others) would be suspect as a theory of meaning. Of course there is no guarantee that our intuitively constructed list of semantic phenomena is exactly correct; but if it is not, we can hope to discover this in the course of our work, since any attempt to construct a unified theory of a fundamentally disparate set of phenomena is bound to fail. Hence, it looks as though, if we have to, we can proceed with research in semantics without waiting upon a theory of the nature of meaning.

Indeed, Katz has argued that a theory of meaning is the goal, not a prerequisite, of research in semantics, that a theory of meaning just IS a theory of the various semantic phenomena: "a theory of the underlying principles that will interrelate and thus organize the empirical facts within the domain of semantics" (Katz, 1972, Chapter 1). Katz contends that the question "What is meaning?" has too often been misconstrued as a request for a simple, direct answer (e.g., "The meaning of an expression is that to which it refers") when it is really a request for a highly articulated system for describing, generalizing, and predicting a wide range of specific semantic observations. He argues that an answer of the form "Meaning is this or that" will be of value only insofar as it is a condensed form of a fully developed theory of this kind, just as the answer "Electricity is the property of electrons and protons by virtue of which they exert force on one another over and above their gravitational attraction" is simply a condensed form of a highly articulated theory of electrical phenomena.

This view presents a theory of meaning as essentially similar to a theory of grammaticality. Linguists do not puzzle over the question "What is grammaticality?" in the abstract. Instead we set about devising grammars for particular languages, which distinguish grammatical from ungrammatical expressions; and we then set about formulating generalizations about the proper vocabulary and form for such grammars. Having done all this, we may say that grammaticality is the property of being generated by the grammar of a language. But this answer by itself is quite unilluminating. What is illuminating is the grammars, and the general theory of grammars, that have been constructed; it is these that give content to the definition of grammaticality.

But the analogy with grammaticality also makes it clear that while an unelaborated definition is insufficient, it is fruitless to elaborate a definition that can be shown, on quite general grounds, to be wrong. Grammaticality used to be attributed, in effect, to all and only those expressions actually uttered by members of a language community. Reasoning from the infinity of a natural language, we can see that this is incorrect, that grammaticality must be explicated in terms of general rules which a speaker 'knows' and which he could in principle employ in the production and comprehension of an infinite range of expressions, most of which he will never in fact either utter or hear. And this conclusion has had as much impact on current theories of language as have specific observations about the kinds of syntactic devices that natural languages employ.

The same can be expected of semantics. There are no fixed rules governing the order of research, and there is no reason why we should not close in on an adequate semantic theory by developing some very general lines of argument about what meanings could and could not be, as well as by describing and systematizing particular semantic observations. For example, a general hypothesis about the nature of meaning should provide a principled basis for deciding which phenomena are semantic; though we may achieve the same end by a process of trial and error in theory construction, this would be an unnecessarily laborious way to proceed if the answer were derivable from the kinds of general consideration that philosophers of language have been concerned with.

In fact, though it may not have been the only or even the major goal of philosophical theories of meaning, predictions about some of the semantic phenomena that interest linguists do follow directly from these theories. If, for example, the meaning of an expression is said to be that to which the expression refers, it follows that an expression will have a meaning just in case it refers to something, and that two expressions will have the same meaning (will be synonymous) just in case they refer to the same thing. Other implications follow about linguistic universals. For example, the theory that meanings are behavioral responses to verbal stimuli implies that we should formulate and seek to explain universal cross-language semantic similarities in terms of universal laws relating stimuli and responses. The theory that meanings are ideas implies that the compositionality of meanings should be accounted for in terms of the compositionality of ideas.

Without too great a distortion, then, we can regard theories of meaning in philosophy as having, at least in part, the same goal as semantic theories in linguistics. In fact some recent philosophical discussions of meaning stress the need for recursive rules to assign meanings to expressions, and the integration of these rules with what is known about the syntactic structure of sentences, in a way that is very familiar to linguists. (See, for example, Davidson, 1967). But we can also distinguish at least two other questions to which philosophical theories of meaning have traditionally been directed.

The first we have already touched on. It has seemed obvious to some (though equally obviously false to others) that a theory of meaning which was simply a systematization of available semantic data would leave unanswered the question of what meaning REALLY IS. This is like the situation in mathematics. Mathematics is a more advanced discipline than linguistics, and has achieved goals whose counterparts we are only just beginning to identify. A recursive procedure for specifying the natural numbers can be given, and many theorems about numerical relations are known. But despite the existence of this highly articulated theory, the answer to the question "What is a number?" remains obscure. There is disagreement over whether the question is a coherent one, and very little understanding, if it is, of even the general shape of its answer. Notice that the answer is not uniquely determined by the axioms of number theory. But an ontological theory of numbers certainly WOULD constrain number theory, since the axioms of the theory must express true propositions about numbers, whatever it is that they turn out to be. Similarly, if it should be possible to say something sensible about what meanings really are, this could be expected to determine the answers to many descriptive questions about semantic phenomena, semantic universals, and so on.

The other persistent concern has been the question of how meanings relate to speakers and to the world. We say that the English word *bachelor* means 'unmarried man,' but what is the nature of the connection between the word and unmarried men? The connection is not an inevitable one. Onomatopoeia does exist but its domain is very limited; the overwhelming fact is that different languages use different words to express the same meanings. We must allow for the 'arbitrariness of the sign.' It is natural, therefore, to look to the language USER for the connection between an expression and that to which it applies. Thus it might be hypothesized that the word *bachelor* means what it does because speakers are conditioned to utter it when they see an unmarried man, or because it is associated in their minds with an idea of an unmarried man, or because they have internalized conventions for using it in various sentential contexts to make statements, promises, predictions, etc., about unmarried men.

Whether or not we can accept these particular answers, they are nevertheless answers to an intelligible and important question, a question that is only partially answered by a linguistic theory of meaning, and which constrains the construction of one. To put it in contemporary terms, one demand on a theory of linguistic competence is that it should make possible an adequate theory of linguistic performance; an account of what meanings are, or of the properties they exhibit, cannot be correct unless it is compatible with an account of the way in which the meanings of expressions make it possible for speakers to use their language to talk about the world.

These three overlapping concerns should be borne in mind as we examine the theories of meaning that have been developed in response to them. With total disregard for their subtleties they may be summarized thus: someone who wants to know what meaning is may be asking for a highly elaborated account of specific semantic properties and relations; he may be seeking the 'essence' of meaning which underlies these particular manifestations; or his interest may be in how meanings make it possible for people to communicate information about the events and objects around them.

2.2. MEANING AND REFERENCE, IDEAS, BEHAVIOR

This section is devoted to three theories of meaning—the referential, the ideational, and the behavioral. These theories are inadequate or perhaps even downright false, but people have been tempted by them for centuries and it is important to understand why they will not do. If we cannot establish what meaning is, we can at least establish some things that it is not.

We have no space here for a detailed historical account of the forms in which these theories have been held at different times, but a broad characterization will suffice for our purposes. However, in connection with the different questions about meaning that we distinguished in the last section, we should consider a stronger and a weaker form of each theory. Let us begin with the stronger form, in which these theories are IDENTITY theories. The meaning of an expression is said to BE what the expression refers to, or the idea associated with it in a person's mind, or the stimuli which elicit utterances of it and/or the behavioral responses it evokes. In this form, these theories are intended as answers to the second question, the question about what meaning really is. They answer it by identifying meaning with something else. The desire to make this move is understandable, especially when what meaning is identified with is something relatively familiar and unproblematic.

The meaning of an expression, for example of the word *apple*, has often seemed to be something abstract, obscure, mysterious. But if the meaning of a word can be identified with what the word refers to, the meaning of *apple* will be no more obscure or mysterious than apples themselves. A similar demystification of meaning should follow from its identification with observable, measurable sensory stimuli and behavioral responses. Even if meanings are identified with ideas, something seems to be gained, for though ideas are themselves obscure entities they are at least something which scientists, psychologists, are concerned to describe; the problem of meaning is thus reduced to another familiar problem.

But whatever the temptation, these identifications are untenable. Meanings are not apples. Apples can be eaten but meanings cannot; meanings can be learned but apples cannot; the meaning of *apple core* contains, in some intuitive sense, the meaning of *apple*, but apple cores do not contain apples. And meanings are also not stimuli or responses. An utterance of the expression *Help!* is typically provoked by danger of some kind and the typical, or at least charitable, response is to rush to the aid of the speaker. But the meaning of *Help!* is not danger, or being in danger, or a rescue mission. Danger can be mild or acute, the rescue of someone in danger can be willing or reluctant, but meanings can be none of these. Similarly, the meaning of a word cannot be an idea, at least in the familiar sense of idea, for ideas can be charming or vile, clever or silly, stable or fleeting, but the meaning of a word does not have these properties.

These theories thus do not give correct answers to the question of what meaning is. But they might nevertheless at least specify the identity conditions on meanings, i.e., tell us when the meanings of two expressions will be identical and when they will be different. This would be a partial answer to the first kind of question about meaning that we distinguished; that is, it would be a contribution to a descriptive account of the semantic properties and relations that expressions exhibit. It would undeniably be a retreat, for if ideas, for example, determine the identity conditions on meanings without actually BEING meanings, we can still wonder what meanings are and why they correlate with ideas in this fashion. Though identity is too strong a relation to posit between ideas and meanings, mere accidental correlation would be quite unrevealing. However, a principled connection could perhaps be established indirectly; we might say, for example, that to know the meaning of a word is to have a certain idea associated with it, or, on the behavioral theory, that to know the meaning of a word is to be conditioned to respond to utterances of it in a certain fashion. So developed, these theories of meaning would have some bearing on our third question, the question about how meanings relate to speakers and the world.

But even in this weaker form, these three theories are inadequate. Frege's refutation of the referential theory is well known (Frege, 1892). The phrases *the morning star* and *the evening star* both refer to the same thing, the planet Venus. But they do not mean the same. If they did, the sentence *The morning star is the evening star* would mean the same as *The morning star is the morning star*, yet the latter is analytic and uninformative while the former expresses an unobvious empirical truth about the universe. So two expressions with the same referent do not necessarily have the same meaning; identity of reference is not a sufficient condition for identity of meaning.

Nor is it a necessary condition. An expression like *this book* can be used on different occasions to refer to different objects but it is not true that *this book* has a great many different meanings, if only because this would imply that my being able to understand a sentence containing this phrase when used to refer to one book would be no reason at all for assuming that I could understand the same sentence used on a different occasion of a different book. But of course we do not (and it is hard to imagine how we could) learn the meaning of a phrase like *this book* afresh each time it is used to refer to a different book.

The morning star and *this book* are at least expressions of the kind that can be used to refer, even though their referents do not in fact covary with their meanings. But there is a vast range of perfectly meaningful linguistic expressions that cannot plausibly be said to refer at all. Even a noun like *book* presents problems. *This book* can be used to refer to a book, but *book* by itself cannot. Its connection with reference is that it can be combined with certain other elements to form noun phrases which do have referents, but this is different from saying that *book* itself has a referent. So even common nouns like *book* seem to demand a significant weakening of the basic tenet of this theory, that an expression has a meaning if and only if it has a referent.

A standard response to this problem has been to say that the referent (or the EXTENSION) of the common noun *book* is the set of ALL books. If this move is made, additional principles must be given to explain why the set of all books is not what is referred to by noun phrases like *this book*, *your books*, *few books*. But these principles will of course require an account of the meanings of the words *this*, *your*, and *few* in such phrases, and it is far from clear that the meanings of THESE words can be captured by appeal to their referents. It takes even more ingenuity to fit verbs, adverbs, prepositions, conjunctions, and the like into the referential mold. Verbs might be implicitly nominalized; we might say, for example, that the meaning of *knit* is the act, or the class of all acts, of knitting. But what about *although*, or *under*, or *not*? Any candidates for the referents of these words will be at least as obscure and even more dubious than meanings themselves.

As has often been observed, the paradigm examples for a referential theory of meaning are proper names, which, by no accident at all, are words that can stand alone as noun phrases; noun phrases do have referents. All that needs or can be said about a name like *Rome* is that it is the name of a certain city. The program is then to assimilate all words and expressions to names like *Rome*, but it is a very curious program. For what is characteristic of proper names is precisely that they have no meaning. (Some names, for example *London Bridge*, do develop out of meaningful expressions, but the more they function like names the less relevant their meanings are; London Bridge did not change its name when it was moved to Arizona.) A theory of meaning based on expressions that have no meaning would certainly, if it succeeded, make short work of puzzles about meaning, but it could hardly be expected to succeed. (Note: More sophisticated versions of the referential theory are discussed in Sections 2.4 and 2.5, and the end of Chapter 6.)

Let us now consider whether ideas provide the identity conditions on meanings. What suggests this theory is something like the following. I have a thought or an idea, I formulate a sentence, I utter it to you, and when you hear it you come to have the same thought as me. This may be a crude picture of the way language is used but it is not an obviously false one. As a theory of meaning it says that an expression has a meaning if and only if it is associated (universally? standardly?) with some idea, and that two expressions have the same meaning if and only if they are associated with the same idea. Notice how this avoids the defects of the referential theory: the morning star is identical with the evening star, but an IDEA of the morning star need not be identical with an IDEA of the evening star.

The truth of an ideational theory inevitably depends on what ideas are taken to be and how the associative relation between expressions and ideas is defined. But the ideational approach to meaning has traditionally been combined with a very simplistic notion of ideas as mental pictures or images (as, for example, in Locke, 1689). As such it is simply false. Mental imagery is shifting and arbitrary, and differs both in extent and kind from person to person and from occasion to occasion. On one day the word *tablecloth* may conjure up in me the depressing thought of the laundry that needs to be done, on another it may make me think of an elderly aunt who sends the same gift every Christmas, for someone else *tablecloth* may be associated with a party game, and yet another person may have no image associated with it at all. There simply is no stable correlation between imagery and the meanings of expressions heard or uttered. And there are probably no images at all which would serve to explicate the meanings of words like *how*, *despite*, *to*.

For an ideational theory to be plausible it would therefore have to be integrated with a much more sophisticated idea of an idea, one which is applicable to all types of expression and which is not at the mercy of the vagaries of mental imagery. But as we refine the theory in this direction it becomes more and more doubtful that we have a theory at all. Since there is no mental picture or image standardly associated with the word *how*, we posit some more abstract kind of idea associated with it. But how do we identify this idea? Is there really any way of specifying it other than as that idea present in the mind of a person understanding or meaningfully using the word *how*? At worst this specification would be empty, if there is nothing that meets this description; at best it would be circular, since it defines ideas in terms of understanding and hence of meaning.

We might try giving a more sophisticated account of the modes of combination of ideas into complex ones than the traditional empiricist theories provided. Then, perhaps, we could say that *how* has a meaning not by virtue of being associated with some particular idea but by virtue of its contribution to complex ideas associated with expressions in which *how* occurs. But again, we have no way of characterizing these complex ideas and no way of characterizing the contribution that *how* makes to them. And again this raises the deeper worry that our inability to identify the ideas that would explicate meanings is not simply a matter of the practical inaccessibility of ideas, or of the lack of an adequate psychological theory, but of the need to refer to the identity conditions on the meanings of linguistic expressions in giving the identity conditions on ideas. If this is so, meanings may serve to identify ideas but ideas cannot serve to identify meanings.

It may be observed in this connection that Katz's theory of the semantic component of a generative grammar (which we will discuss in detail later in this book) assigns CONCEPTS to expressions as the means of specifying their meanings, but this is not intended as an explanation of the nature of meaning. Katz openly identifies concepts with meanings, and hence concedes that the identity conditions for the one are no less obscure than those for the other. (See Katz, 1972, Chapter 2.) In this respect (though not in respect of the structural representations and computational processes ascribed to language users), the mentalism of much of the current linguistic research in semantics is not a working part of the theory but simply reflects the anti-behavioristic conviction that there ARE ideas, that they do play a significant role in human activities and language use, and that when we eventually achieve an adequate theory of meaning, meanings and ideas will turn out to be closely interrelated.

Finally let us consider behavioral theories of meaning. Since ideas seem to be as ungraspable as meanings themselves, many philosophers and psychologists (and until recently many linguists, e.g., Bloomfield) have eschewed all talk of ideas and mental processes in favor of talk about physical stimuli and behavioral responses to them. The meaning of an expression is said to be the stimulus situation that evokes its utterance, and/or the response which it elicits from the hearer. This cannot serve as an account of which expressions HAVE meaning, for a nonsense word is presumably evoked by a stimulus and elicits a response as much as any meaningful expression is and does. But the theory does predict that two expressions mean the same if and only if they are evoked by the same stimuli and/or elicit the same responses.

This theory goes the same way as the ideational theory. Either it is simply factually false, or else it must be so elaborated to deal with the empirical data that it loses all empirical content. If we interpret 'stimulus situation' and 'response' in a natural and straightforward way, what people say in different circumstances and what they do in response to things other people say is just not uniform enough to support the proposed correlation with meaning. I may utter *What a nice party!* in a situation consisting of a nice party but I may also not utter it in that situation; identity of stimulus situation does not guarantee identity of linguistic behavior. I might also utter *What a nice party!* in a situation consisting of a dreary party given by my boss; differences between stimulus situations do not invariably correlate with differences of linguistic behavior. And I may even say *What a nice party!* to my toes in the bath, though no party-related change in my stimulus situation has occurred at all (except of course my thoughts, which to a strict behaviorist are inadmissable data).

Responses fare no better than stimulus situations. You may respond to my comment on the party by shaking my hand, by pulling a wry face, by changing the subject, or by saying and doing nothing at all. And each of these responses could be your response to some quite different utterance of mine. So there is no hope of identifying THE response evoked by a given expression. And if we were to try explicating meaning in terms of a RANGE of possible responses, we would have to contend with the virtual infinity of the range and the enormous overlap between the ranges for different expressions.

One irremediable defect of any behavioral theory would appear to be that, apart from cases of genuinely conditioned verbal behavior such as saying *Ouch!* when hurt, someone could willfully refute any account of the stimuli and responses associated with an expression simply by uttering it in a situation, or responding to it in a fashion, not predicted by the theory. To avoid such deliberate refutation, the theory must be framed in terms of 'normal' or 'appropriate' behavior, or, as has often been proposed, in terms of behavioral DISPOSITIONS. Your actual response to my utterance of *What a nice party!* could be anything or nothing at all. But if you wanted to be polite you might reply with *We are delighted you could come*, if you were shy you might simply smile, if you were hating the party yourself you might raise your eyebrows, and if you wanted to refute a theory of meaning you might say *Three blind mice*. Although actual responses do not correlate uniquely or uniformly with the meanings of expressions, the hope is that dispositions to respond in certain ways DEPENDING ON OTHER ASPECTS OF THE CIRCUMSTANCES might so correlate.

The trouble with this refinement of the theory is that each expression of the language will now have to be associated with a more or less infinite class of propositions of the form "If in such-and-such state, the hearer will do so-and-so." But this association can be achieved only on the basis of some stable property of the expression from which this vast range of predictions can be derived by general principles. And it is highly likely that the critical property of the expression will turn out to be none other than its meaning. If so, we can hardly claim that behavior provides an entry into the study of meaning. Undoubtedly there is some correlation between behavior and the meanings of expressions, just as there is some correlation between ideas and the meanings of expressions, but these correlations are complex and indirect, and a theory of them will almost certainly require an independent characterization of meaning.

2.3. MEANING AND USE

We now turn to some more sophisticated theories of meaning, which characterize the meaning of an expression in terms of its use. As everyone knows, it was Wittgenstein who said "the meaning of a word is its use in the language" (*Philosophical Investigations*, 1953). He also said, "Don't ask for the meaning, ask for the use," which can be construed as a warning against talking of meanings at all. But it has also, at least as often, been taken as a recipe for specifying meanings.

What is common to both interpretations is that it is a serious (as well as silly) mistake to regard meanings as ENTITIES that stand in some special relation to expressions. This mistake may be what lies behind the identification of meanings with referents or with ideas, criticized in the previous section. The meaning of an expression is thought of as like the father of a friend—to specify the meaning is to identify a thing (whether concrete or abstract) and say what that thing is like. But in fact, the meaning of an expression is more like the weight of a table—to specify the meaning is to specify the 'value' of the expression (to use a Saussurian term) in the system of which it is a part.

Wittgenstein emphasized not just the role of an expression within the language, but the role of language in human life. Language is integrated into our behavior and our interactions with others in an intimate way. We USE it, to give commands, to answer questions, to greet each other, to argue, and so on. Language should be viewed not as an abstract calculus but as a tool, and just like a hammer or a can opener, the proper characterization of a linguistic expression must include an account of how it is used and what it is used for.

A can opener might be used as a bookmark, and there are also nonsystematic uses of linguistic expressions, such as shouting a word loudly out of context simply to startle someone. To exclude such cases and capture the CHARACTERISTIC roles of different expressions, the theory of meaning as use is usually cast in terms of rules, rules which determine the standard or conventional uses of expressions. Unlike the theories of meaning discussed in the last section, this has a familiar ring about it to the generative linguist. A grammar consists of rules governing the pronunciation of expressions, the combination of expressions into more complex ones, the superficial realizations of basic grammatical relations, and so on. So the rules-for-use approach to meaning promises to integrate naturally with the linguist's approach to language description.

Another immediate advantage of the use theory is that it appears not to exclude any class of meaningful expressions. Words like *if* and *for* and *the* have no referents and evoke no mental images or characteristic responses, but they do have a use. The notion of a 'use' is broad enough to cover, for example, the use of *the* in the formation of noun phrases, as well as the use of *the brown cow* to refer to a particular cow and the use of *The brown cow is sick* to report the news from the farm. In fact the danger of this theory is that it might be too broad to be useful. If it is to serve as the basis for a theory of meaning, the notion of a use must be constrained in some way. In listing what the Englishman eats, one should say *fish and chips, roast beef and Yorkshire pudding*, not *chips and fish, Yorkshire pudding and roast beef*. Here is a rule governing the use of words that does not bear on their meanings, for *fish and chips* surely means the same as *chips and fish*. There are also social rules (don't use four-letter words to your mother-in-law), practical rules (don't use fourteen-letter words to children), and stylistic rules (don't keep saying "and then"). Even some clearly linguistic rules, such as number agreement, do not appear to have any connection with meaning. So if we are to characterize meaning in terms of rules for use, we must specify much more precisely just what kinds of rules for use we have in mind.

Meaning and verification

"Stating the meaning of a sentence amounts to stating the rules according to which the sentence is to be used, and this is the same as stating the way in which it can be verified (or falsified). The meaning of a proposition is its method of verification" (Schlick, 1936). The verificationist theory of meaning deals in the meanings of whole sentences; the meanings of other expressions are characterized indirectly in terms of their contribution to the meanings of the sentences in which they appear. In particular, the theory is restricted to the meanings of declarative sentences, since it relates the meaning of a sentence to its use in stating something true or false about the world.

The identification of meaning with method of verification leads to absurdities. The meaning of *It is raining* is not putting one's hand out of the window, or calling the weather bureau. The meaning of a sentence in the future tense is not, as Schlick suggests, a matter of waiting for the occurrence of the event it describes. Even as an account of the identity conditions on meanings, verificationism fails. The meaning of the sentence *This solution is acidic* did not change when litmus paper was invented, nor will it change if someone hits upon a novel method of verification tomorrow. Also the sentences *This swimming pool is 25 yards long* and *If this swimming pool were five yards longer it would be 30 yards long* do not have the same meaning, though both can be verified by measuring the pool and determining that it is 25 yards long.

Nevertheless, there clearly is some essential relation between declarative sentences and the making of statements, and between the making of statements and the notions of truth and falsity. Where verificationism goes wrong is in forcing the further connection between truth and falsity and the practical methods by which truth or falsity can be established. No list of actually available methods of verification will serve as a specification of meaning, for the list will change as science and technology advance, and there can be meaningful sentences for which we have as yet no practical or even theoretical method of verification at all. As an explication of meaning, a 'method of verification' must therefore be some much more abstract relation between a sentence and the world, the most plausible candidate for which is a general specification of the conditions under which the sentence would be true and the conditions under which it would be false. If we are concerned with epistemology, with how we can KNOW whether some statement is true, we might then feed a specification of truth conditions into a body of scientific principles to determine which consequences of a statement could be empirically tested and how. But it is the truth conditions, not the practical methods of verification, that will be revealing of meaning.

Verificationism was the product, indeed the major tool, of logical positivism, whose goal was to rid science of metaphysics by unmasking metaphysical statements as simply meaningless; only those statements which permit of empirical verification or falsification were to count as having a meaning. (Logically true or false statements might be allowed in by analyzing them as statements about linguistic expressions.) There are problems with this program, for as we have seen, some principled distinction must be drawn between statements that are unverifiable for merely scientific reasons and statements that are unverifiable because they are meaningless. But the program is in any case of marginal interest to linguistics, because its conception of meaningfulness is a special-purpose one. The sentence *God is good* may have no place in a scientific theory, and *I have a yellow after-image* may have to be supplied with some sort of corrective analysis, but these are perfectly respectable sentences of English and they ARE meaningful in the sense that is relevant to an empirical description of a natural language.

Meaning and speech acts

Even if it succeeded for declarative sentences, verificationism has nothing to say about the meanings of imperative sentences, interrogative sentences, sentences like *I swear I won't touch it* or *I warn you I'll leave*. The theory of speech acts, developed originally by Austin (1962), is explicitly concerned with sentences of all these kinds. Austin's program was to characterize the kinds of act that can be performed in or by uttering sentences, and it has been argued that to specify the speech act(s) for which a sentence is standardly used is to specify the meaning of that sentence.

What is a speech act? Austin distinguished three kinds. A LOCUTIONARY act is an act of uttering a sentence with a particular sense and particular referents for the terms it contains; it is an act OF saying something. An ILLOCUTIONARY act is an act of asking a question, giving a warning, making a prediction, etc.; it is an act performed IN saying something. A PERLOCUTIONARY act is an act of persuading someone to do something, of annoying someone, of bringing someone to his senses; it is an act performed BY saying something. Austin illustrated these informal definitions with an example.

Locution
He said to me "Shoot her!" meaning by "shoot" shoot and referring by "her" to *her*.

Illocution
He urged (or advised, ordered, etc.) me to shoot her.

Perlocution
He persuaded me to shoot her.

Austin's characterization of locutions implies that two sentences can be used to perform the same locutionary act only if they have the same meaning (sense). We can turn this around and conclude that two sentences have the same meaning if they can be used to perform the same locutionary act.[1] But despite this connection, neither Austin nor anyone else has offered locutionary acts in explication of meanings, for the obvious reason that with locutionary acts defined in terms of meaning, the theory would be narrowly circular. We are left with illocutions and perlocutions.

Perlocutions are also not tempting as a basis for characterizing meanings, but in this case, it is because perlocutions involve too much else besides meaning so that the required correlations simply do not hold. For example, continuing with the illustration above from Austin, someone might achieve the perlocutionary effect of persuading me to shoot someone by uttering *Shoot her!*, but he might also do so by uttering *If you don't shoot her, she'll spill the beans*, or *Shooting her would please Mother*. Yet these sentences do not mean the same. Conversely, the speaker might fail to persuade me to shoot by uttering any or all of these sentences.

There is, however, a theory of meaning which, though it does not fit very neatly into Austin's classification, is in some degree a perlocutionary theory. Grice (1957, 1968) has argued that to say that a speaker *A* MEANT something by an utterance of an expression *x* is to say something like: *A* intended the utterance of *x* to produce some effect (typically a belief or an intention to act in a certain way) in his audience. To say WHAT *A* meant is to specify the intended effect. An important condition (designed to exclude certain kinds of interaction which intuitively do not involve meaning) is that the effect produced in the hearer should be at least partly ascribable to his

1. Note that this may omit some cases of sameness of meaning. Austin apparently intended that sentences containing different words cannot be used to perform the same locutionary act. But they can, of course, be synonymous.

recognition of the speaker's intention to produce that effect. In fact, the theory has been considerably elaborated since the early sketch, to provide a more delicate discrimination between genuine acts of meaning and superficially similar cases which do not qualify; recent versions of the theory refer to higher-order beliefs and intentions, possibly *ad infinitum*—e.g., the speaker intends the hearer to believe that the speaker intended the hearer's (primary) belief to be based on his recognition of the speaker's intention to induce that belief.

We cannot do justice here to the intricacies of this theory, but it is interesting to see how it avoids the defects of the crude perlocutionary theory that we rejected above. First, only certain effects in the hearer are stipulated as relevant. For example, in later versions the primary effect characteristically associated with an indicative sentence is merely that the hearer should believe that the speaker believes what he says to be true. Austinian perlocutions are typically more robust, e.g., persuading the hearer of the truth of what the speaker said. Secondly, and more importantly, SUCCESS in the production of these effects it not presupposed; Grice rests his analysis on the intentions with which speakers utter sentences.

As I have outlined it so far, Grice's theory is a theory of 'utterer's meaning,' of what it is for someone to mean something by an utterance. As such it bears on the third broad question about meaning that we identified in Section 2.1. It contributes to an account of what it is to use a sentence to make an assertion, give an order, and so on. It is concerned with the role of meaning in the use of language for communication. Indeed, Grice has based on it a detailed theory of how we so often succeed in meaning more than we actually say. He has outlined certain maxims of conversation, cooperative principles which we abide by and expect others to abide by to facilitate communication. Violation of one of these maxims may give rise to an 'implicature,' an inference by the hearer about the speaker's beliefs or intentions, which is needed to understand why he said what he did or the manner in which he said it. One of Grice's simpler examples concerns the maxim of relation (viz., "Be relevant"). This is violated by someone who responds to a casual inquiry about a friend by observing that he hasn't been to prison yet. The implicature is that the friend is potentially dishonest, though of course the speaker did not explicitly say this and what he did say might well have been quite true even if what he implicated was not. (Grice's long awaited *Logic and Conversation* will be the standard source for readers interested in pursuing these matters. Grice (1975) is an extract from this longer work.)

For our purposes, however, the important question is whether Grice's theory of utterer's meaning offers any explanation of what it is for a SENTENCE or other linguistic expression to have a meaning. Grice has proposed a derivative account of sentence meaning—the meaning of a linguistic expression x is a matter of what effects speakers intend to bring about in hearers by uttering x. The consensus, however, is that here the theory is less successful; the major complaint is that it throws no light on the conventional or the compositional aspects of meaning. What a linguistic expression means is a matter of the conventions in the language community and is not, typically, determined by a particular speaker's intentions—however relevant his intentions are to his having uttered it meaningfully or to what in particular he meant to convey by it. Conceivably, linguistic convention could be accommodated by the theory by appeal to some sort of social contract between speakers of the language, by which we agree on certain correlations between sentences and the communicative intent with which we shall utter them. But there is still the problem that the meanings of all the sentences of a natural language could not have been agreed on, even implicitly, one by one. They must be the consequence of the meanings of individual words and the ways in which they are put together. Some theory of the compositional mechanisms underlying sentence meaning thus seems to be presupposed by an account of utterer's meaning, rather than explained by it. What are the intentions with which I use the words *shoot* and *her*, and how do they combine to form the intention to communicate my desire that she be shot? These objections are similar in spirit to those which have been brought against illocutionary theories of meaning, to which we now turn.

The most familiar attempt to illuminate the nature of meaning by reference to speech acts is founded not on locutions or perlocutions but on illocutionary acts such as warning, asking, ordering, exclaiming. Do meanings correlate suitably with illocutionary acts? Certainly they do not correlate with any PARTICULAR illocutionary acts, for acts are specific, dateable events and it is irrelevant to the meaning of *I'm hot*, for example, that it was uttered by John Smith at noon on the third of January, 1957. It is illocutionary act types, not tokens, that the theory must appeal to. But even act types are not general enough. Austin associated with *Shoot her!* a variety of illocutionary acts including urging, advising, and ordering, but *Shoot her!* is surely not three and more ways ambiguous; we don't think of it as having multiple meanings in the same way as sentences like *They are flying planes* or *Every girl kissed one boy*. (We might concede that it is 'speech act ambiguous,' but this just shows that speech act ambiguity differs from ambiguity of meaning.) To relate each type of illocutionary act that a sentence can be used to perform with one meaning of that sentence would thus be empirically incorrect.

In fact, the identity conditions on meanings correlate with the identity conditions not on illocutionary act tokens or on illocutionary act types but on RANGES of illocutionary act types. *Shoot that old lady!* differs in meaning from *Shoot her!*; the meaning of the former is more specific. And this correlates with the fact that it can be used for a narrower RANGE of illocutionary acts. (It can be used to order someone to shoot an eighty-year-old but not, properly, to order someone to shoot an eight-year-old.) *I order you to shoot her* is also more specific in meaning than *Shoot her!* and is also associated with a narrower range of illocutionary acts. (It can be used to ORDER someone to shoot Mary or to ORDER someone to shoot Jane, but not to ADVISE or URGE someone to shoot Mary or Jane.) On the other hand, *Shoot!* is LESS specific in meaning than *Shoot her!* and can be used for a WIDER range of illocutionary acts, (to order someone to shoot John, for example). *The moon is full* is totally unrelated in meaning to *Shoot her!* and the ranges of illocutionary acts for which these two sentences can be used do not overlap. *Hit her with a bullet from a gun!* means the same (more or less) as *Shoot her!* and this is matched by identity (more or less) of the ranges of illocutionary acts with which these sentences are associated. Thus, the relation between the meanings of two expressions does seem to be parallelled by the relation between the ranges of illocutionary acts for which they are standardly used.

The program of characterizing the meaning of a sentence in terms of the range of illocutionary acts standardly associated with it (i.e., its ILLOCUTIONARY ACT POTENTIAL, Alston, 1968) has not been totally unsuccessful. Austin, and others since, have catalogued and defined 'performative verbs', i.e. those verbs which can be used (in the first person and simple present tense, sometimes with *hereby*) at the beginning of a sentence to make explicit its illocutionary force—verbs like *promise, warn, advise, beg, propose, denounce,* and so on. They have also begun to specify the conditions under which an utterance of a sentence of the appropriate form would be 'felicitous,' i.e., would qualify as a genuine act of promising, warning, advising, etc. (See, for example, Searle, 1965, 1969.) Though much descriptive work remains to be done, a theory of this kind WOULD constitute a theory of the meanings of performative verbs and thus of a significant aspect of the meanings of sentences containing them. Of course not every use of a verb like *promise* is a performative use, but nonperformative uses are also illuminated indirectly by the speech act analysis. The sentence *I think John will promise to leave* is used not to promise but to express an opinion about a possible promise, but an account of its meaning obviously must involve an account of what it is to promise; we need to indicate what it is that the speaker is saying he thinks John will do or say, what beliefs or intentions are expected to prompt John's doing or saying it, what obligation John would thereby put himself under, and so on.

But a theory of the meanings of performative verbs, even including their nonperformative uses, is not a general theory of meaning. The notion of illocutionary force illuminates the semantic contrast between *I promise to leave* and *I warn you to leave,* and indirectly the contrast between *I think John will promise to leave* and *I think John will warn you to leave,* but it does not tell us anything about the semantic difference between *I promise to leave* and *I promise to stay.* These two sentences have the same illocutionary FORCE in the broad sense that they are both used to make promises. Their difference lies in what is promised. So to identify sentence meanings fully we need a way of distinguishing illocutionary acts not only by the broad categories of illocutionary force but also, within these categories, in terms of their PROPOSITIONAL CONTENT. We must distinguish among an infinite set of distinct possible promises and associate each one with the sentence or sentences that can be used to make it. And we must do so without recourse to the notion of meaning, or else the illocutionary theory, like a locutionary theory, will be simply circular. It is here that the theory comes to grief.

At the very least, the theory must provide a way of deciding which among the infinite set of sentences in the language can be used to perform the same illocutionary act. Consider the act of promising to leave, which can be performed by uttering (in appropriate circumstances) the sentence *I promise to leave*. Which other sentences can be used for this? *I promise to go* can; *I promise to stay* cannot. As speakers of English we know this intuitively, but how could a formal theory of illocutions establish it? Only, as far as anyone can tell, by first establishing that *I promise to go* means the same as *I promise to leave* and that *I promise to stay* does not. The identity conditions on illocutions can be stated by reference to the identity conditions on meanings, but no one has yet given a meaning-independent account of them.

It might be proposed that in order to identify an infinite set of distinct illocutionary act potentials for assigning to sentences, the theory should include a recursive device similar to the one we outlined in Chapter 1, a body of rules taking as input the syntactic structure and lexical items of sentences and recursively generating representations of their illocutionary act potentials. But if this device is to make genuine use of illocutionary notions in explicating meaning, then the meanings of lexical items to which it appeals must themselves be specified in illocutionary terms. As we have seen, the meanings of a handful of words, like *promise* and *warn*, may be specifiable in terms of the institutions of promising and warning. But nonperformative verbs like *leave* and *stay* have no special illocutionary role, nor do nouns, prepositions, etc. These words, the greater part of the vocabulary of a language, are used in the making of promises, the giving of commands, in exclamations, exhortations, in the performance of illocutionary acts of all kinds.

But perhaps we should not give up on word meanings yet. Though there is nothing in common at the level of promising, warning, exclaiming, between all occurrences of the verb *leave*, we might be able to analyze these illocutionary acts into constituent acts of referring, predicating, and so on, which are equally a part of promising, warning, exclaiming, and all the other 'sentence-sized' illocutionary acts. At this level of analysis, the meaning of *leave* could perhaps be UNIFORMLY characterized in terms of the predication of a certain act (of a subject). But this program also fails. Taking predicating to be a distinguishable act presents some puzzles (I can't just stand up and predicate); but in any case the identity conditions on such acts as predicating are just as difficult to specify without reference to meaning as the identity conditions on the sentence-sized acts of promising and warning. Which verbs in English have the same predicative use as *leave*? *Go* does; *stay* does not. But we do not know how to establish such equivalence classes over the infinite range of predicates in the language, any more than we do for the infinite range of sentences, without relying on a prior notion of sameness of meaning.

Alston (1968) has said, "the performance of an illocutionary act involves relating oneself in various ways to extra-linguistic conditions and states of affairs." The WAY IN WHICH a speaker relates himself to a state of affairs is presumably a function, in part, of the ILLOCUTIONARY FORCE POTENTIAL of the sentence he uses; and, as we have seen, the theory of speech acts does deal with this relation and its connection with sentence form and content. The state of affairs TO WHICH the speaker relates himself is presumably a function, in part, of the PROPOSITIONAL CONTENT of the sentence he uses, and it is about this that the theory of speech acts has nothing to offer. Rather, a theory of meaning which connects sentence meanings with these states of affairs is needed to complete the theory of speech acts. The theory of meaning that we shall turn to next is of this kind (though it was not developed in this context). But it should be observed that the working parts of this theory are notions such as truth and entailment, not illocutionary notions. We will attempt to put the two sets of notions back together again in Section 2.7.

2.4. MEANING AND TRUTH

To say what a sentence means, we must specify its illocutionary force potential and its propositional content, but we as yet have no way of characterizing the latter. Let us temporarily take a backward step and consider only declarative sentences, and in particular only those declarative sentences that are standardly used to make statements or assertions. How would we set about specifying the content of an assertive declarative sentence such as *It is raining*?

From the speech act theory of meaning we can draw the insight that the meaning of such a sentence cannot be explicated without reference to its use for the making of statements. While rejecting the verificationist theory we can retain the insight that it is of the nature of statements to be true or false. To MAKE a statement or an assertion is to commit oneself to the truth of a proposition, to claim that it is true, to claim that some state of affairs obtains (whether or not one believes that it does). To UNDERSTAND an assertion is to know that the speaker is claiming something to be true and also to know what he is claiming to be true; and to know this is presumably to know what the world would be like if it were true, under what circumstances it would be true and under what circumstances it would not. In short, it is no accident that a difference in meaning between two assertive sentences, such as *It is raining* and *It is snowing*, correlates with a difference between the conditions under which each would be true.

Considerations of this kind suggest that the propositional contents of assertive sentences can be individuated and characterized by reference to the truth conditions on the statements they are standardly used to make.[2] If so, our goal of recursively characterizing the meanings of the sentences of a language becomes that of recursively characterizing the truth conditions on its sentences. And this is a project that we already know a good deal about, for it has been a major concern of logicians and philosophers for many years. (See Tarski, 1944, for the classic statement of the program.) A specification of the truth conditions on the formulae of a logical system is in fact what logicians call "giving the semantics for the system." If a system is defined only by giving its formation rules (which determine the well-formed formulae), its axioms and its inference rules (which determine derivability relations between formulae), then it is merely an uninterpreted calculus. Whatever interesting formal properties it has, it obviously cannot be used to say or prove anything ABOUT anything until its formulae are assigned an interpretation, that is, until they are related to objects and situations in the world by a specification of their truth conditions.

The formulae of a logical system constitute an artificial language, and for such a language the truth conditions are of course simply stipulated. The logician is free to interpret the language in any way that is of interest for some purpose; or, more generally, he may be interested in the properties of all of its possible interpretations. For a natural language such as English, the truth characterization must be responsive to antecedently given facts. The sentence *Snow is white* is true just in case snow is white, and not, for example, just in case the moon is made of cheese; a theory that said otherwise would be false. Nevertheless, the kinds of technical mechanisms developed for STIPULATING the semantics for artificial languages can be adapted quite naturally to the task of DESCRIBING the semantics for natural languages. (This is not to say that every construction of every natural language has a 'translation' in some logical system for which a semantics has already been given. For some kinds of construction it is still an open question how, or perhaps even whether, existing principles can be extended to cover them. We will return to this point shortly.)

2. In what follows, I shall talk of the truth values, truth conditions, and entailments of SENTENCES. This is inaccurate, since sentences can be ambiguous and can contain terms whose referents are not fixed. What has a truth value is not the sentence *I am a bachelor*, but the proposition expressed by this sentence or the statement that it is used to make by a particular speaker on a particular occasion. Since linguists deal primarily in sentences, observing these distinctions makes for cumbersome exposition. But I do not mean to minimize their importance.

The best way of explaining the nature of the semantic rules given for artificial languages is by illustration, and we may begin with a simple case, the semantics for the standard propositional calculus (that is, for one of many distinct but equivalent formulations of it). The vocabulary of this language contains sentential variables (p, q, . . .); a negation operator ($\sim$); and three sentential connectives ($\wedge$, v, and $\supset$, corresponding roughly with English *and*, *or*, and, *if-then*, respectively). There are also parentheses to indicate the internal structure of complex formulae. The formation rules of the system constitute its syntax, and specify what counts as a well-formed formula (wff) as follows:

(2-1) (i) Each sentential variable is a wff.
     (ii) If A is a wff, then $\sim A$ is a wff.
     (iii) If A is a wff and B is a wff, then $(A \wedge B)$ is a wff, $(A \text{ v } B)$ is a wff, and $(A \supset B)$ is a wff.

Thus for example, the set of wff's contains the expressions on the left below; it does not contain those on the right.

$$p \qquad\qquad (p$$
$$(p \text{ v } q) \qquad\qquad (p \wedge \text{ v } q)$$
$$((p \wedge q) \supset \sim r) \qquad\qquad \supset p$$

The truth conditions on the simple formulae of the language, those consisting of solely a sentential variable, must simply be listed. Thus it might be specified that p is true if and only if snow is white, that q is true if and only if the moon is made of cheese, and so on.[3] The real work of the semantic rules for the language is in showing how the truth conditions on its infinitely many complex formulae are constructed from those of its finitely many simple formulae. This is specified as follows:

(2-2) (a) If a formula A can be analyzed as $\sim B$, then A is true if and only if B is false (not true).
     (b) If a formula A can be analyzed as $(B \wedge C)$, then A is true if and only if B is true and C is true.
     (c) If a formula A can be analyzed as $(B \text{ v } C)$, then A is true if and only if B is true or C is true.
     (d) If a formula A can be analyzed as $(B \supset C)$, then A is true if and only if B is false or C is true.

Many readers may be more familiar with these principles in the form of truth tables, which chart the dependencies between the truth values of complex formulae and the truth values of their constituents. (T = true; F = false.)

---

3. p, q, etc. are thus more naturally regarded as sentential CONSTANTS, but the distinction between variables and constants has no real significance for this language.

(2-3)

B	~B
T	F
F	T

B	C	B ∧ C
T	T	T
T	F	F
F	T	F
F	F	F

B	C	B ∨ C
T	T	T
T	F	T
F	T	T
F	F	F

B	C	B ⊃ C
T	T	T
T	F	F
F	T	T
F	F	T

Principles (a)–(d) are quite simple and straightforward, and between them they assign truth conditions to every well-formed formula of the language. But the language is a simple one, very much more simple syntactically than any natural language. Natural language sentences can be translated into it only if we are prepared to ignore much of their semantically significant structure. Negation is treated, but other sentential operators such as *probably, unfortunately, apparently*, etc. are not. *If*-clauses are handled, but clauses introduced by *although, because, after*, etc. are not. Moreover, it is very doubtful that the principles (a)–(d) for ~, ∧, ∨ and ⊃ do justice even to the semantics of negation, conjunction, disjunction and conditionals in natural language. Principle (d) is the most obviously questionable. Applied to *if-then* constructions in English, it would predict that a sentence such as *If Smith was at the meeting, nothing was accomplished* would be true as long as Smith was not at the meeting. This certainly does not accord with the judgments of most English speakers. For English conditional sentences, therefore, condition (d) must be replaced or supplemented by some further condition; and it seems likely that that condition will turn out to be considerably more complex than any of those given above.

Another limitation (for the purposes of describing a natural language) of the simple semantic principles given so far is that they take the SENTENCE to be the smallest unit of analysis. A simple sentence like *Snow is white* must be rendered as a unit, by a single sentential variable; nothing is said about the way in which its truth conditions depend on the words from which it is composed and the manner of their combination. We suggested in connection with the verificationist theory in Section 2.3 that the meanings of words might be regarded as their contributions to the meanings of sentences in which they appear. We must now be more explicit about this. That is, if we are to pursue our construal of sentence meanings as truth conditions and at the same time be realistic, both linguistically and psychologically, we must make clear how the truth conditions for a sentence can be built up on the basis of its lexical and syntactic structure.

Now this is precisely what we did for *and, not*, etc. Principle (b), for example, makes explicit the contribution of the word *and* to the truth conditions of sentences in which it occurs. But when we turn to words like *snow, is* and *white*, we see that the nature of the problem has changed. It is no longer a matter of building up truth conditions out of other truth conditions, for nouns, verbs, adjectives and other nonsentential constituents are not the sorts of things that HAVE truth conditions (since they are not the sorts of things that can be true or false). Rather, we must identify some other relevant properties of these constituents and show how truth conditions can be constructed out of these.

As before, the basic machinery for doing this has already been developed by logicians, this time in connection with the predicate calculus (quantificational logic). I will not attempt here a full formal presentation of the syntax and semantics for this system. This can be found in standard textbooks of logic (e.g., Thomason, 1970). But the fundamental ideas are as follows.

Consider the sentence *Nelson D. Rockefeller is rich*. Obviously the truth definition for English should specify that this sentence is true just in case Nelson D. Rockefeller is rich, and it should specify this on the basis of some properties of the constituents *Nelson D. Rockefeller, is* and *rich*. *Nelson D. Rockefeller* is a name, and the fact about it that is relevant to the truth of this sentence, and of others in which it appears, is that it is a name of Nelson D. Rockefeller. What we must do for names, then, is to associate with each one the individual to whom it refers, i.e., assign to each name its extension.

What is relevant about *rich*, on the other hand, is that it expresses a certain property. A standard move (whose validity we will consider shortly) is to construe properties extensionally, i.e., to individuate them by reference to the set of individuals which have the property. Then what we must do for an adjective like *rich* is to associate it with the set of all and only those individuals who are rich. Once again, what we assign to the expression as its semantic value is its extension, though for predicative expressions that extension will be not a single individual but a set.

Finally, we may take the function of the copula verb *is* to be that of indicating that the referent of the noun phrase has the property expressed by the adjective, i.e., that the individual which constitutes the extension of the noun phrase is included in the set of individuals which constitutes the extension of the adjective. Thus the sentence will be true just in case Nelson D. Rockefeller is a member of the set of things that are rich.

Other types of sentence can be handled in basically the same kind of way. A relational expression such as *richer than* in *Nelson D. Rockefeller is richer than Howard Hughes* can also be assigned its extension, where this is taken to be the set of ordered pairs of individuals such that the first member of the pair is richer than the second. The sentence will be true just in case the ordered pair of Nelson D. Rockefeller and Howard Hughes is a member of this set. A sentence such as *Someone is rich*, which contains a quantified noun phrase, is specified as true just in case the set of individuals which is the extension of the predicate *rich* has at least one member, i.e., just in case it is not the null set. *Everyone is rich* is specified as true just in case every individual (strictly speaking every person—the range of the quantifier must be appropriately restricted) is a member of the set of individuals which constitutes the extension of the predicate, i.e., just in case this set is the universal set.

Adjective-noun constructions are handled in terms of set intersection. Thus, *Jean-Paul Belmondo is a French actor* is true just in case Jean-Paul Belmondo is a member of the set which is the intersection of the extensions of *French* and *actor*. Similarly, *Someone is rich and happy* is true just in case the intersection of the extensions of *rich* and *happy* is not the null set. (Notice that this sentence does not have the same truth conditions as the sentence *Someone is rich and someone is happy*. It therefore cannot be assigned its truth conditions by principle (b) above which applies to *and* only when it appears between two sentences.)

These examples show that a semantics based on the assignment of extensions to subsentential constituents can successfully derive truth conditions for a variety of sentence types. Nevertheless, there are other natural language constructions which present problems of various kinds and various degrees of seriousness. These include other quantifiers such as *most*; generic noun phrases such as *shipowners* in *Shipowners are rich*; 'attributive' adjectives such as *large* in *Large fleas are smaller than small elephants*; and mass nouns like *snow* (is its extension an individual? a set of individuals? a part of an individual?). Problems also arise in extending this kind of system to the treatment of complement constructions, adverbs, counterfactual conditionals, and other natural language phenomena.

Though it is still programmatic in many areas, some linguists have recently become sufficiently interested in this approach to semantics to borrow the semantic mechanisms developed by logicians where these are successful, and to try to help with the task of refining them and extending them to other types of sentences. The borrowings are not always exact, for the semantic principles must sometimes be modified to make them mesh with the special syntactic properties of natural languages. (For example, certain time references are typically carried by verb tenses and others by temporal adverbs. A tense logic may disregard this distinction, but it is probably an important one for linguistics.) Nevertheless, the fact that some borrowing occurs may suggest that linguists accept, at least in practice, that the study of meaning in natural languages CAN legitimately be reduced to the study of truth and reference along the lines sketched above.

In actual fact, most linguists believe that there is considerably more to meaning than merely conditions of truth and reference. Though more inclined than in the past to acknowledge that these matters are a necessary part of semantics, they still do not consider them to be sufficient. Having seen what a formal specification of truth for a language would be like, at least in outline, we must now return to the general question of the extent to which this would constitute a specification of meaning.

To simplify discussion, let us begin by restricting ourselves again to the meanings of whole sentences. We are considering the hypothesis that (declarative) sentence meanings can be construed as truth conditions. And we may interpret this claim as saying that from any correct characterization of truth conditions, of the form "Sentence *S* is true if and only if *p*," we can derive a correct characterization of meaning, of the form "Sentence *S* means that *p*."

Immediately a problem arises. The "if and only if" in these statements of truth conditions is standardly taken to express MATERIAL EQUIVALENCE, and a statement of material equivalence is true just in case the sentences that flank the "if and only if" have the same truth value. Thus given the fact that (quibbles aside) snow is white, and hence that the sentence *Snow is white* is true, then the truth conditions for that sentence can be correctly expressed by the statement: "The sentence *Snow is white* is true if and only if snow is white." But given the fact that grass is green (same quibbles), the truth conditions on *Snow is white* are also correctly expressed by the statement: "The sentence *Snow is white* is true if and only if grass is green." Now as part of a theory of truth, this is just fine. But once we attempt to construe the theory of truth as a theory of meaning we are in trouble. For then we would be committed not only to the true claim that *Snow is white* means that snow is white, but also to the false claim that *Snow is white* means that grass is green.

It is clear that the problem is not restricted to this particular example. As long as what we are concerned with is only truth conditions, ALL true sentences could in principle be assigned the same truth condition (e.g., that grass is green), and all false sentences could be assigned the same truth condition (e.g., that grass is pink). But not all true sentences MEAN the same, and nor do all false sentences. The point is that a theory of truth for English which acknowledged only two distinct truth conditions would not for that reason be an incorrect theory of truth, but a theory of meaning for English which acknowledged only two distinct meanings would *ipso facto* be an incorrect theory of meaning.

The moral of all this is that even if meanings can be identified with SOME truth conditions, they cannot be identified with just ANY truth conditions. There is an infinity of meanings, but so far our conception of a truth condition has been so unconstrained that truth conditions may stand in a one-to-one correspondence with truth VALUES, and there are only two of those. This problem is very like that which afflicts the identification of the meanings of noun phrases with their referents. This theory is incorrect, because the meanings of noun phrases do not stand in a one-to-one correspondence with their referents—the phrases *the morning star* and *the evening star* have the same referent but different meanings (see Section 2.2).

Frege explicitly identified these two problems by taking sentences to have referents, and their referents to be their truth values (the True and the

False).[4] Then for both noun phrases and sentences, the problem is that meanings cannot be fully individuated in terms of referents (extensions). And the same is true for predicate expressions too. If all and only those individuals who are rich are happy, then the extensions of *rich* and *happy* will be identical. But it surely doesn't follow that *rich* and *happy* will be synonymous.

For these reasons, the kind of semantics that has been provided for the standard predicate calculus is bound to be inadequate as an account of the meanings of the corresponding sentences of English and other natural languages. As we have seen, the values which are assigned to words and phrases by these semantic principles are their extensions, and differences of extension provide too coarse-grained a classification of expressions to capture all differences of meaning.

When Frege rejected the theory that the meaning of an expression is its referent, he put in its place the theory that the meaning of an expression is "the manner in which it designates its referent." This theory obviously promises a finer-grained discrimination of meanings. We are to understand that the phrases *the morning star* and *the evening star* designate their common referent in different ways, as do the sentences *Snow is white* and *Grass is green*. In subsequent sections of this chapter we will examine some refinements of the truth condition theory of meaning which suggest how this somewhat metaphorical notion of manner of designation might be given substance.

2.5 MEANING AND NECESSITY

Snow is white means that snow is white and not that grass is green. Therefore, as we concluded in Section 2.4, if meanings are to be identified

---

4. Treating truth values as objects to which sentences refer may seem strange, but Frege was interested in developing a recursive theory of reference as well as a recursive theory of meaning. And sentences exhibit analogies with noun phrases (the standard example of expressions which have referents), which this move enabled him to capture.

The referent of a complex noun phrase is determined by the referents of simpler expressions that it contains. For example, we cannot determine the referent of the phrase *the sister of Jim's teacher* until we have determined the referent of the phrase *Jim's teacher*, and we cannot do this until we have determined the referent of *Jim*. Also if we substitute for part of a complex noun phrase a different expression which has the same referent, the referent of the whole noun phrase remains unchanged. Thus if Jim's teacher is Martha's husband, the phrase *the sister of Martha's husband* will have the same referent as the phrase *the sister of Jim's teacher*.

Like complex noun phrases, sentences too can contain referring expressions, and the referents of these expressions are relevant to the evaluation of the sentences in which they appear. In particular, they are relevant to the determination of TRUTH VALUE. We cannot determine whether the sentence *Jim's teacher is fat* is true until we know who the phrase *Jim's teacher* refers to. Also, substitution of a phrase in a sentence by another with the same referent with truth conditions at all, not just any truth conditions will do. We must find a way of picking out from among all the possible truth condition specifications some favored subset which includes "*Snow is white* is true if and only if snow is white" but which excludes "*Snow is white* is true if and only if grass is green." One approach to this is the following.

The fact that *Snow is white* is true if and only if grass is green depends on two quite different kinds of consideration, considerations about meaning and considerations about the way things are in the world. It depends on meaning since, if *Snow is white* meant that ants can talk, it would not be true if and only if grass is green. It depends on the world since, if snow were purple or if grass were pink, *Snow is white* would again not be true if and only if grass is green. Now it is clear that to a theory of meaning, only the first kind of consideration is relevant. This suggests that the way to pick out the special subset of truth condition specifications which are correct as specifications of meaning is to require them to be independent of the way the world happens to be (except, of course, insofar as this includes the way the language happens to be). In other words, the truth conditions we want are those which would be correct WHATEVER the world happened to be like, i.e., they would be GUARANTEEED to be correct.

Two sentences that have the same truth value are said to be materially equivalent, to materially imply each other. Two sentences that NECESSARILY have the same truth value, i.e., that would have the same truth value whatever the world happened to be like, are said to logically imply (entail) each other, to be logically equivalent. In Section 2.4 we concluded that MATERIAL implication is too broad a notion for the proper characterization of meaning, for it would allow us to say, falsely, that all sentences with the same truth value have the same meaning. The suggestion to be considered in this section is that the narrower notion of LOGICAL implication WILL permit an adequate account of meaning. The proposal is that all and only sentences which NECESSARILY have the same truth value have the same meaning, that a sentence S means that p just in case NECESSARILY S is true if and only if p.[5] (For subsentential constituents, the proposal is that two expressions have the same meaning just in case they NECESSARILY have the same extension.)

This theory correctly predicts the nonsynonymy of *Snow is white* and *Grass is green*, *the morning star* and *the evening star*, and other extension-

---

preserves the TRUTH VALUE of the sentence. If *Jim's teacher is fat* is true, and if Jim's teacher is Martha's husband, then *Martha's husband is fat* is also true.

Thus, Frege's suggestion that we take truth values to be the referents of sentences makes it possible to extend to sentences the compositional principles of reference independently needed for noun phrases.

5. Some care is needed here. What we want to capture is that, the English language being what it is, it is necessary that *Snow is white* is true if and only if snow is white. But we DON'T want to say that it is necessary that the English language is such that *Snow is white* is true if and only if snow is white.

ally equivalent pairs. For though these HAPPEN to have a common referent, given the way the world is, they COULD, in other states of affairs, refer to different things. It thus comes much closer than the unrestricted truth condition theory to capturing basic intuitions about sameness and difference of meaning. As we shall see shortly, it does not come close enough, for there are other nonsynonymous expressions that it fails to distinguish. But even apart from its empirical inadequacies, this theory has been criticized. It must not be forgotten that our ultimate goal is to say what meaning is. And it has been argued by some that the shift from truth to necessary truth as the basis for characterizing meaning is a shift from an independently clear notion to one which is itself as obscure and in need of analysis as meaning is.

Those philosophers who are sceptical about necessity doubt that there is any principled dividing line between necessary truth and mere contingent truth. Quine, for example, has maintained that there are no necessary truths at all, no statements that must be held to be true no matter how the world might turn out to be. In place of a simple dichotomy of statements into those that are necessarily true or false and those that are contingent, Quine argues for a complex field or network of interrelations between statements. Some statements are close to the periphery of the system; in the face of new discoveries about the world we might very well revise our opinion of their truth values. Other statements are more central in the network; revision of these is less likely since it would not be a local matter but would have extensive repercussions elsewhere in the system. But still these statements are considered to be in principle revisable, and they would be in fact revised in return for a sufficient gain in the overall simplicity of the system. This is asserted even of the laws of logic, which are regarded as statements on the same footing as all others but simply more central in the network (see Quine 1953a).

If no appeal can be made to a notion of necessity, then either the theory of meanings as truth conditions must be abandoned altogether, or else we must find some substitute for necessity in its role of narrowing down the class of truth conditions to those which correctly capture meanings. Davidson (1967) has offered an epistemological principle for this purpose. He says that pairing the sentence *Snow is white* with the truth condition that grass is green

> . . . is acceptable, if it is, because we are independently sure of the truth of 'Snow is white' and 'Grass is green'; but in cases where we are unsure of the truth of a sentence we can have confidence in a characterization of the truth predicate only if it pairs that sentence with one we have good reason to believe equivalent. It would be ill advised for someone who had any doubts about the color of snow or grass to accept a theory that yielded [this pairing], even if his doubts were of equal degree, unless he thought the color of the one was tied to the color of the other.

This proposal bears some similarity to the one with which we began this section, viz., that though not EVERY correct account of truth conditions for a language will be a correct account of meaning, at least every DEPENDABLE account of truth conditions will be, i.e., every account which is guaranteed to be correct even if the world should change. There is a reliance here on a distinction between what MUST be the case in the world and what might or might not be, and we interpreted this to be a dependence on the notion of logical necessity. Davidson, on the other hand, tries to make do with a distinction between what we are sure of and what we may have doubts about, and with some notion of facts being "tied" to each other. But this will not work.

For one thing, it still leaves *Snow is white* paired with *Grass is green*, and with all other sentences whose truth we ARE sure of. Indeed, the more facts we discover about the world, the closer we will approach the situation in which there are only two distinguishable sets of truth conditions and hence only two distinguishable meanings. Meaning distinctions would break down as science progresses.[6]

The proposal also makes the wrong predictions in some cases where we are ignorant of truth values. Suppose I know (no matter how) that John either has red hair and green eyes or has grey hair and brown eyes, though I do not know which is the case. Then I have "good reason" for believing that the sentence *John's eyes are green* is true if and only if the sentence *John's hair is red* is true. These two sentences certainly do not mean the same, but Davidson's approach does not explain why they do not. Notice that the problem remains even if we suppose that the truth values of the two sentences are "tied" to each other by a law of nature relating green eyes and red hair. What this shows is that not every tie between the truth values of sentences will support a claim of synonymy. And to distinguish those that do from those that do not, it looks very much as if we would have to appeal to some notion of necessary truth. Davidson's epistemological principle thus does not substitute for the notion of necessity, but must itself be explicated in terms of it.

Let us turn now to a different approach to the problem. Suppose it could be shown that a theory of truth which assigned *Snow is white* the condition that grass is green could do so only *via* the assignment of the condition that snow is white, and by appeal to the material equivalence of these two conditions. If this were so, then by insisting on the simplest, most parsimonious, theory of truth for English we would apparently guarantee

6. Davidson is untroubled by this curious consequence. He remarks, "Omniscience can obviously afford more bizarre theories of meaning than ignorance; but then, omniscience has less need of communication." But even God might like to be able to tell whether, in muttering *Snow is white* to Himself, He has said that snow is white or that grass is green.

ourselves a theory which assigned ONLY the condition that snow is white, and hence a theory which could do service as a theory of meaning.

Surprising as it may seem, something along these lines CAN be established. When the sentence *Snow is white* appears as a constituent of a more complex sentence, the contribution that it makes to the truth conditions of the larger sentence is different from the contribution that would have been made by a materially equivalent sentence like *Grass is green*. Consider the sentence *Arctic animals tend to be light in color because snow is white*. And let us allow that this sentence is true. But the sentence *Arctic animals tend to be light in color because grass is green* is certainly not true. Since these sentences have different truth VALUES, they must have different truth CONDITIONS. And since the only difference between them is the exchange of *snow is white* and *grass is green*, the difference in truth conditions must apparently be attributed to these clauses. Thus we have established that these two nonsynonymous sentences, *Snow is white* and *Grass is green*, make different contributions to the truth conditions of larger sentences in which they appear. And this gives us the conclusion we wanted, viz., that these two nonsynonymous sentences must be assigned different truth conditions. As suggested above, some principle of economy could be invoked to insure that whatever truth conditions are needed to distinguish the two sentences when they appear as constituents of larger sentences are also assigned to them when they appear alone as independent sentences.

Assuming that this pattern of argument is applicable to all pairs of nonsynonymous expressions, it would appear to completely undercut worries about having to rely on an unexplicated notion of logical necessity. Considerations of mere descriptive adequacy and simplicity would together ensure the assignment of semantically correct truth conditions to sentences—and would do so in any language at all, just as long as it contained some compound sentence which could play the role of the *because*-construction in our argument above for English. The critical property of such a construction is that its truth value may be changed when a sentence (clause) within it is substituted for by another sentence with the same truth value (or, in general, when some expression within it is substituted for by another with the same extension).

Not all constructions are like this. In a conjunction, for example, the substitution of a sentence for another with the same truth value does preserve truth; if *John likes apples and snow is white* is true, then *John likes apples and grass is green* will also be true. Contexts in which such substitution is not valid are called NONTRUTHFUNCTIONAL or OPAQUE CONTEXTS. As well as the *because* construction discussed above, they include constructions with 'psychological' verbs such as *believe, hope, regret*, etc. For example, given the truth of *John believes that snow is white*, we cannot validly substitute *grass is green* and infer that John believes that grass is green.

Also included in the class of opaque constructions are sentences of the form *Necessarily . . .* and *It is necessary that. . . .* The sentence *It is necessary that snow is white if snow is white* is true, but substitution would produce *It is necessary that snow is white if grass is green*, which is false. Now notice that this is just a different way of stating the observation with which we began this section, viz., that the sentences *Snow is white* and *Grass is green*, though materially equivalent, are not logically equivalent. It was this observation which led to the idea of regarding meanings as necessary truth conditions. The problems involved in explicating necessary truth conditions then led us to the present suggestion, which is that we can retreat to giving mere contingent truth conditions as long as we do so for sentences containing opaque operators like *necessarily*. But it should be clear that this does not really finesse the puzzles about necessity at all. For if we cannot say what necessity is, we cannot give the truth conditions on sentences containing *necessarily*.

Thus we end up much where we began. In order to clarify the nature of meaning we apparently must clarify the nature of necessity, or at least of one of the other opaque concepts such as belief, hope, etc. Later in this section we will question whether necessity, even if it can be defined, really is adequate for the characterization of meaning. And in the next section we will consider other opaque concepts which may succeed where necessity fails. But first it will be useful to take a look at how the formal semantic principles sketched in Section 2.4 would have to be elaborated to provide necessary truth conditions for sentences. For this we may turn to systems of modal logic, i.e. logics for sentences containing operators like *necessarily* and *possibly*.

These semantic systems are based on a formal reconstruction of Leibnitz's construal of necessary truth as truth in all possible worlds. This does not touch the fundamental problems, for it simply shifts the puzzles about necessity onto the concept of possibility. A necessary truth is true in all possible worlds. What is a possible world? Any world in which all necessary truths are true. Nevertheless, the technical achievements of this ('model theoretic') approach to necessity are considerable.

The semantics for the nonmodal logics that we considered in the previous section assigned to a noun phrase the individual to which it refers. In a modal logic, this is insufficient. An example from Quine (1953b) concerns the phrase *the number of planets* which happens to have the same referent as the word *nine* does, viz., the number nine. But the sentence *Necessarily nine is greater than seven* is true, while the sentence *Necessarily the number of planets is greater than seven* is false (since there surely might have been only six planets). Hence *nine* and *the number of planets*, though they have the same referent, must not be assigned the same semantic value, or else the theory will make wrong predictions about truth conditions.

A similar argument can be made against the assignment to predicates of their extensions. Apparently the predicate *has a heart* is co-extensive with the predicate *has kidneys*; it is a matter of fact about the world that creatures that have hearts have kidneys, and vice versa. But these predicates do not make the same contributions to the truth conditions on sentences in which they appear. *Necessarily anything which has a heart has a heart* is true, but *Necessarily anything which has a heart has kidneys* is presumably false (if it is logical necessity that is intended). So it is not good enough for the semantics to assign these two predicates the same value, and hence the values they are assigned cannot be their extensions.

What should be assigned to expressions if not their extensions? Notice that we have so far taken the extension of an expression to be what it applies to in the real world. The extension of the phrase *the number of planets* is nine because there happen to be nine planets in the real world. But if necessary truth is truth in all possible worlds, the values assigned to expressions must indicate not only their extensions in the real world but also their extensions in all other possible worlds. If it is possible that there might have been ten planets, or only eight, seven, etc., then by definition there are possible worlds in which there ARE ten planets, eight planets, etc., i.e., worlds in which the extension of the phrase *the number of planets* is ten, eight, etc. So we must assign as the semantic value of this phrase all of these numbers, each one indexed in some fashion for the set of possible worlds in which it is the extension of the phrase.

Another way of putting this, which comes to the same thing in technical terms but which better reveals the plausibility of regarding these assignments as assignments of MEANING, is to say that an expression is assigned a FUNCTION. In the case of a referring phrase, this will be a function from possible worlds onto individuals; given a characterization of a possible world, the function will pick out that individual which is the extension of the phrase in that world. Informally: if one knows the meaning of a referring phrase, then if one knows what the world is like (i.e., which possible world one is in), then one can tell what the phrase refers to. Meaning and facts about the world interact to determine reference.

These functions which determine extensions have been called INTENSIONS.[7] The intension of a referring phrase, as we have seen, is a function from possible worlds onto individuals. The intension of a sentence, which is an expression whose extension is a truth value, will be a function from possible worlds onto truth values. And the intension of a predicate, which is an expression whose extension is a set of individuals (or a set of ordered pairs of individuals, etc.) will be a function from possible worlds onto such sets.[8]

7. The word "intension" is often used as a synonym for "meaning." However, as it is used here, and as I shall use it throughout this book, it means 'extension in all possible worlds.' On this usage, we can legitimately raise the question of whether intensions and meanings are identical. See below for discussion.

8. Alternatively, the intension of a predicate may be taken to be a function from the intension of a referring phrase onto the intension of a sentence, since a predicate together with a referring

We are now in a position to say something about the truth conditions on a sentence containing a modal operator, such as *Necessarily the number of planets is greater than seven*. First, we want to say that this sentence is true (i.e., true in the real world) just in case the sentence *The number of planets is greater than seven* is true in all possible worlds. In each world, this latter sentence will be true just in case the extension of *the number of planets* in that world is included in the extension of the predicate *is greater than seven* in that world. In other words, the *Necessarily . . .* sentence will be true just in case in each world the extension determined by the intension of the subject phrase is included in the extension determined by the intension of the predicate phrase. (Given that there is a possible world in which there are only six planets, and given that in that possible world, as in all possible worlds, it is false that six is greater than seven, the sentence will in fact be false.)

For more complex sentences, further principles are needed. Intensional logics have been formulated, and are still being developed, which treat quantification, adverbs, complement constructions and so on. Of particular interest is the work of Montague and his associates, since this provides semantic mechanisms which are intended to be applicable to natural languages rather than merely to artificial languages (whose syntax is often both simpler and qualitatively different from that of natural languages). (See Montague, 1974; and Partee, 1975 for a more introductory presentation.)

Linguists with a concern for the description of natural languages sometimes find this work puzzling, because it typically does not offer full specifications of the intensions of particular lexical items, and hence does not in fact characterize the meanings of any sentences at all. It may be stated, for example, that the intensions of some adjectives (the 'nonattributive' ones) are functions from intensions of common nouns to intensions of common nouns. This distinguishes the intensions of adjectives from the intensions of verbs, for example. But it says nothing about the difference between the intension of *happy* and the intension of *sad*, and hence nothing about the difference in meaning between *John is happy* and *John is sad*. To know this we need to know WHICH such function is the intension of *happy* and which is the intension of *sad*. But all that is given is the TYPE of function concerned, and this is the same for both these lexical items and for many more besides.

Thus the emphasis (as in the simpler extensional logics considered earlier) is on the compositional mechanisms which the language employs to construct the meanings of complex constituents out of the meanings of simpler ones. Specifying the meanings of the simplest constituents, the

---

phrase constitute a sentence. The intension of a predicate would then be a function from functions-from-possible-worlds-to-individuals to functions-from-possible-worlds-to-truth-values. See Lewis (1972) for discussion. Still other alternatives are possible, but we will not discuss them here.

primitive vocabulary of the language, is obviously a task of quite a different nature. In extensional systems it is relatively straightforward, but in modal systems there is a fundamental change in the nature of the task. If there is an infinite number, or even a very large number, of distinct possible worlds, it will not be possible or practicable to simply LIST the extension of a phrase in each of these worlds. Rather, it is necessary to give a finite characterization of a function with an infinite domain—for example, a finite characterization of a function from any one of an infinite number of possible worlds onto the happy things in that world. Some approaches to this problem of word meaning will be examined in Section 5.1 and Chapter 6.

We return now to the question of whether the concept of an intension, founded on the concept of necessity as outlined above, is in fact successful as a theoretical reconstruction of the concept of meaning. And though we may agree that intensions are more successful than extensions are, the answer must be that they are not successful enough. For, if our intuitions about meaning are to be trusted, there are differences of meaning not associated with any difference of intension.

The intension of a sentence is a function from possible worlds onto truth values. If functions are individuated by the associations of arguments and values that they determine (by their 'input-output characteristics'), it follows that any two sentences which have the same truth value in each possible world will have the same intension. Now a necessary truth, by definition, has the value True in all possible worlds. Hence all necessary truths have the same truth value in each possible world. Hence all necessary truths have the same intension. Thus the sentences: *Two plus two equals four*; *Three plus three equals six*; *If God exists then God exists*; *Anyone who isn't either French or German isn't French and isn't German*, all have the same intension. But they do not have the same meaning.

It is true that wherever the meanings of expressions are identical, their intensions will turn out to be identical too. But we have just demonstrated that the converse does not hold, and this is where the theory fails. Although the partition of sentences based on identity of intension is finer-grained than that based on identity of extension, it is still too coarse to do justice to the intuitive concept of meaning. In Section 2.4 we determined that meaning, as we think of it informally, cannot be captured in terms of mere truth. In this section we have seen that it also cannot be captured in terms of necessary truth. Apparently what is needed is some yet more restricted notion, which is standardly referred to as ANALYTIC TRUTH or ANALYTICITY. This will be the concern of the next section.

2.6 MEANING AND ANALYTICITY

Analyticity is a more restrictive notion than necessity, which is in turn more restrictive than mere truth. Of the true sentences, only some are necessarily true, and of the necessarily true sentences only some are analytically true (analytic). *Snow is white* is a sentence which is true but not necessarily true and not analytic. *Every man is either five feet tall or not five feet tall* is true, and necessarily true since it is guaranteed by a law of logic, but it is not usually regarded as analytic. *Bachelors are unmarried* is not only true and necessarily so, but is also a standard example of an analytic sentence, that is, a sentence which is true by virtue solely of its meaning.

A similar hierarchy exists for implication. Not all pairs of sentences such that the first materially implies the second are such that the first logically implies (entails) the second, and not all of these are such that the first analytically (or semantically) entails the second. *Snow is white → Grass is green* is an instance of material implication. *Every man is five feet tall → No man is not five feet tall* is an instance of logical implication. And *This man is a bachelor → This man is unmarried* is a standard example of an analytic entailment.

Kant (1781) characterized an analytic sentence as one in which the meaning of the predicate is a part of the meaning of the subject (See Katz, 1966, Chapter 5, and 1972, Chapter 4, for an extension of this definition to a wider class of sentences.) Similarly, a relation of analytic entailment holds between two sentences if the meaning of the entailed sentence is part of the meaning of the entailing sentence. Given this definition of analyticity, the definition of meaning (or at least of synonymy, i.e., sameness of meaning) is quite straightforward: two sentences mean the same just in case each analytically entails the other. (Two subsentential expressions mean the same if they can be substituted for each other, preserving analyticity, in all sentential contexts.)

As has often been observed, most notably by Quine, the trouble with this definition of meaning is that it is circular, and very narrowly so. Analyticity is defined in terms of meaning, and meaning in terms of analyticity. So unless some other, meaning-independent, characterization of analyticity is forthcoming, there can be no legitimate appeal to analyticity to provide an account of meaning. The goal we have been pursuing is the traditional one of reducing meaning to some more basic and better understood entity. But analyticity is too intimately related to meaning to provide such a reduction. In fact, as far as anyone now knows, there is no meaning-independent way of characterizing either analyticity or meaning.

The failure of all the attempts to reduce meaning to something else thus leads to the (at least provisional) conclusion that meaning cannot be reduced to anything else, that it is *sui generis*. Despite Wittgenstein's warnings, there may be no alternative to taking meanings to be entities, abstract entities which have certain properties and stand in certain relations to other abstract entities such as truth, etc. There should, after all, be nothing particularly surprising about this. The reduction of one kind of thing to another can be very revealing, but there is no guarantee that such a reduction will be possible for any particular given kind of thing. However, while there are linguists and philosophers who are prepared simply to accept that meaning is not reducible, and to get on with the job of characterizing its manifestations, there are others who are led by this state of affairs to be sceptical about meaning, to doubt that there IS any such thing as meaning (as distinct from truth conditions, etc.), or at least to doubt that any such thing need be acknowledged in order to say all that is worth saying about language.

Perhaps nothing could convince those who have these doubts that their doubts are misplaced. But there is one line of partial defense against such scepticism that is of interest. It is closely related to an observation of the previous section.

We noted there that we could achieve the effect of assigning necessary truth conditions to a sentence S by assigning truth conditions to the sentence *Necessarily S*. We observed that for opaque contexts like *Necessarily . . .* (in which substitution of coextensive expressions does not always preserve truth), truth conditions can be determined correctly only if what is assigned as the semantic value of an expression is something more discriminating than its extension. Intensions were shown to be adequate to predict truth conditions on sentences with modal operators, but proved to be too weak to discriminate between ALL expressions which differ in meaning. However, other opaque constructions are apparently subject to even more restrictive constraints on valid substitution, and hence demand an even finer discrimination between expressions of the language. And it has been claimed that THESE discriminations do correspond exactly with intuitive differences of meaning.

The opaque constructions in question are those with 'psychological' verbs such as *believe*. These are often referred to as 'verbs of propositional attitude,' and this nomenclature reflects the judgment that the objects of these verbs are propositions, i.e., (roughly) sentence meanings. The claim is thus that for any language containing such verbs, the relatively modest goal of giving a truth definition for the language will actually require an account of meaning for the language. If this is so, it may be concluded that the concept of meaning is not a useless one, and it had better not be an incoherent one.

The reason this is only a partial defense against scepticism is that in principle the sceptic might reply (just as in the case of modal operators) that sentences containing verbs of propositional attitude are meaningless and hence do not HAVE any clear truth conditions. However, this stance is less defensible for propositional attitudes than it is for the modalities. For, as even Quine has admitted, though one can perhaps deny the sensibleness of talk about necessity, it is much less practicable and less plausible to renounce all talk of belief, desires, and so on. Consequently, despite a common assumption to the contrary, the concept of meaning may have a sounder basis than that of necessity.

The class of opaque contexts is very heterogeneous, and some opaque contexts are clearly inadequate to the task of individuating meanings. Contexts with *necessarily*, as we have seen, are too weak. Others are too strong. For example, in a direct quotation context such as *John said "...,"* we cannot validly substitute even *unmarried man* for *bachelor*. From the fact that John said "I am an unmarried man," it does not follow that he said, "I am a bachelor." Identity of FORM is required for substitution in quotation contexts. To avoid the conclusion that no two distinct expressions are ever synonymous, direct quotation contexts must therefore be excluded from the class of contexts in which substitutivity is the criterion for synonymy.

There are those who would narrow this class much further. According to Chomsky (1970b), even some psychological verbs, such as *realize*, must be excluded:

> Thus, is it possible for someone to realize that John is believed to be competent by everyone without realizing that everyone believes John to be competent, or to realize that Bill saw John but not that John was seen by Bill? ... Or, consider such sentences as *everyone agrees that if John realizes that p, then he realizes that—*, where the space is filled either by *p* itself or by an expression *q* distinct from but synonymous with *p*. No doubt the truth value may change, as *q* replaces *p*, indicating that any difference of form of an embedded sentence can, in certain cases at least, play a role in the statement of truth conditions, hence, presumably, the determination of meaning.

What must be determined is whether there are any contexts that are neither too permissive (e.g., *Necessarily ...*), nor too restrictive (e.g., perhaps *Sam realizes that ...*), nor circularly related to meaning (e.g., *It is analytic that ...; ... means that ...*). Katz (1972, Chapter 6) argues that *want* and *believe* create contexts of exactly the right kind. To be precise, Katz's claim is that one expression may substitute for another in such contexts if the meaning of the first is contained in the meaning of the second. Thus it is actually analytic entailment which is defined by reference to opacity; synonymy is then mutual analytic entailment.

It is not immediately obvious that Katz's claim is correct. Could I not believe that John is a bachelor without believing that John is unmarried? It appears that I could if I do not know what *unmarried* means, or if I do know what it means but am simply too stupid to notice that *John is unmarried* follows from *John is a bachelor*. The defense against this objection would be that believing that John is a bachelor just IS believing that he is unmarried (adult, male, etc.), and that therefore, though someone might CLAIM to believe the first but not the second, his claim could not be a true one. Even if this defense is accepted, there is a more sophisticated kind of counterexample to be contended with (due to Mates, 1952; see also the quotation from Chomsky above). It is reasonable to suppose that nobody doubts that whoever believes that John is a bachelor believes that John is a bachelor. But surely it might be false that nobody doubts that whoever believes that John is a bachelor believes that John is unmarried. This is, after all, precisely the doubt that we expressed above. Thus the embedding of opaque contexts within opaque contexts apparently creates contexts in which substitutivity is not licensed even by meaning-inclusion relations. If these contexts are taken as criterial for meaning, we will be led to the quite counterintuitive conclusion that no two expressions ever have the same meaning. But if they need not be taken as criterial, how can we explain why not?

Clearly these issues cannot be resolved in a moment, though until they are, the possibility of defending meaning by appeal to opacity will remain uncertain. We must leave the matter here and turn now from questions of justification to the practical question of how analyticity and meaning can be treated in a formal semantic system. We know the system must assign different values to expressions that are merely logically equivalent and not synonymous. But it is hard to see WHAT different values they could be assigned. Having moved from extensions in the real world to extensions in all possible worlds, there seems to be no further to go in that direction. (Though some have tried; Cresswell, 1973, escalates the model from worlds to heavens.)

Consider two logically equivalent but nonsynonymous sentences, such as *Two plus two equals four* and *Three plus three equals six*. Intuitively what makes these sentences nonsynonymous is the fact that their common intension is arrived at by combination of different intensions for their parts. The functions which are their respective intensions may be identical with respect to the arguments and values (worlds and truth values) that they associate, but these functions have internal structure and differ with respect to it.

Carnap (1947) defined a relation of INTENSIONAL ISOMORPHISM between expressions such that two expressions are intensionally isomorphic just in case both have the same internal structure, and all corresponding parts of the two expressions have the same intension. Carnap suggested that this relation of intensional isomorphism might provide an adequate reconstruction of the intuitive notion of synonymy (that it would make the proper distinctions in belief contexts, etc.). The essence of this suggestion is that meaning is to be captured not by a mere appeal to reference, even reference in all possible worlds, but rather in terms of the compositional properties of the expression by means of which its reference is determined. It is thus a close relation of Frege's theory (see Section 2.4 above) that the meaning of an expression is the manner in which it designates its referent. The sentences *Two plus two equals four* and *Three plus three equals six* both designate the True in all worlds, but because they have different internal composition they get there, so to speak, by different routes.

Applied to the surface sentences of a natural language, the identification of synonymy with intensional isomorphism has some curious consequences. One problem is that there could never be synonymy between a word and a phrase, e.g., between *bachelor* and *unmarried man*, for these expressions are not parallel in structure; one is simple and the other compound. Also, ANY syntactic difference between compound expressions would apparently preclude synonymy between them, e.g., the difference between *my father's father* and *the father of my father*. However, Carnap himself regarded certain syntactic differences between expressions as irrelevant to intensional isomorphism. He wrote (1947, Chapter 1):

> Now it seems advisable to apply the concept of intensional isomorphism in a somewhat wider sense so that it also holds between expressions like '2 + 5' and 'sum(II,V),' because the use in the second expression of a functor preceding the two argument signs instead of one standing between them or of parentheses and a comma may be regarded as an inessential syntactical device.

Obviously the "inessential" syntactic differences must be formally distinguished from essential ones. One way to do this would be to provide a NORMAL FORM for expressions. The expressions of the language under study (the object language) could be translated into a different language (a metalanguage) which has the property that only the essential (i.e., meaning-correlated) syntactic differences in the object language show up as syntactic differences in the normalizing metalanguage. The mathematical expressions *2 + 5* and *sum (II, V)* could be assigned the same translation, and so could the English expressions *my father's father* and *the father of my father*, etc. In general, all and only synonymous expressions would be identically represented in the metalanguage. So if intensions were assigned to expressions AFTER they had been translated into the metalanguage, it would follow, as desired, that all and only synonymous expressions are intensionally isomorphic.

Now, transformational grammars of natural languages often assign identical deep structures to expressions which differ in surface syntactic form. It has been proposed, for example, that the phrases *my father's father* and *the father of my father* have identical deep structures; and similarly for many pairs of sentences including *That it's raining is obvious* and *It is obvious that it's raining*; *John is easy to please* and *It is easy to please John*; *The car hit the truck* and *The truck was hit by the car*. This suggests that the 'language' of deep syntactic structures might be exactly what is needed for the normalization of natural language (surface structure) expressions, i.e., that it is at the level of deep structure that intensional isomorphism corresponds to synonymy. (See Lewis, 1972, for a similar proposal).

Whether or not this is so depends crucially on WHAT level of deep structure one subscribes to, and linguists are by no means agreed about this. The difference between the various competing hypotheses will be treated in some detail in later chapters. But we may note here that there is one current linguistic theory (generative semantics) whose deep structures do identify all and only synonymous expressions. And there are other theories (the standard theory, and its extensions) whose deep structures fall short of this in varying degrees; *my father's father* and *the father of my father* may be assigned the same deep structure, but *bachelor* and *unmarried man* are not, nor are *John opened the door with a key* and *John used a key to open the door*, or *It may rain* and *It is possible that it will rain*, etc. However, these latter theories admit, in addition to a level of deep-structure, a distinct level of SEMANTIC REPRESENTATION at which synonymous expressions do receive identical representations. In other words, all current generative linguistic theories provide some proprietary language of representation in which identity and difference of FORM predicts identity and difference of MEANING.

It should be emphasized that this approach to the formal reconstruction of meaning and meaning relations does not constitute a JUSTIFICATION of the concept of meaning or a reduction of it to other familiar concepts. There WOULD be such a reduction if it turned out that synonymy corresponded to intensional isomorphism at some level of syntactic representation motivated INDEPENDENTLY of semantic considerations. But it is very doubtful that this is the case. The level of semantic representation employed by current linguistic theories is apparently NOT motivated entirely by syntactic observations but is designed precisely to codify intuitive judgments about meaning relations.

So the concept of intensional isomorphism does not explain meaning away, but it does offer some important insights into its nature. Without giving up the relation between meaning and reference which is embodied in the notion of an intension, it accounts for our intuition that meanings are more intricate and more finely individuated than the role of determining extensions strictly calls for. Its emphasis on the internal structure of meanings provides a foundation for the characterization of analytic entailment in terms of meaning inclusion, since for this to make sense, meanings must be the kind of things that can be included in each other. And it also underlines the importance of the recursive semantic rules which linguists and logicians have been occupied in formulating in recent years. For these can be seen as not merely a mechanism for ASSIGNING meanings to sentences but as, in a sense, a PART of those meanings. The semantic representations of generative grammars, which reveal how the meanings of constituents are structured within the meaning of the sentence as a whole, respect this idea that it is crucial to meaning how the truth conditions on a sentence get to be what they are.

Finally, the notion that meaning has a structure often distinct from superficial syntactic structure may suggest an explanation for WHY meaning and analyticity (apparently) bear a special relation to belief and other propositional attitudes. If we can suppose that there is some inner 'language of thought,' we might hypothesize that this is the 'normalizing' language for intensional isomorphism—a language in which all and only synonymous expressions of the natural language have identical translations. Synonymy of linguistic expressions would thus consist in literal indistinguishability with respect to their roles in defining possible objects of belief. The validity of substituting synonyms for synonyms in belief sentences would then reside in the fact that any person in a mental state corresponding to a belief in the proposition expressed by a sentence S_1 is *ipso facto* in the mental state corresponding to a belief in the proposition expressed by a synonymous sentence S_2. The invalidity of substituting a nonsynonymous sentence S_3 (even if it is materially or logically equivalent to S_1 and S_2) would be due to the fact that the proposition expressed by S_3 has a different mental representation, and hence that to believe this proposition is to be in a different mental state. Even if these two distinct mental states tended to co-occur, this would be an empirical fact, and would not support a logical inference from one to the other.

Since some propositional attitudes (e.g., realizing) seem not to toe the line, this tidy picture based on belief can only be a sketch for a much more fully elaborated theory. But some such line of thought does seem to be at least implicit in much current linguistic and psychological research in semantics. (Philosophers tend to be more cautious. But see J. A. Fodor, 1975.) By illuminating the relation between meaning and opacity, this view suggests a way of integrating the truth-and-reference approach to meaning with what is valid about the ideational approach that we dismissed somewhat summarily in Section 2.2. The opacity of human language goes deeper than the contingent fact that English and German and Swahili, etc. all happen to CONTAIN SENTENCES ABOUT beliefs and desires, sentences in which expressions referring to the same object or state of affairs cannot validly be substituted. If these sentences did not occur, the distinction between meaning and reference might be harder to illustrate, but surely it would still be there. For language is used by people to EXPRESS beliefs about objects and states of affairs which they must represent to themselves in some fashion, under some description.

2.7. THE MEANINGS OF NONASSERTIVE SENTENCES

In the last three sections we have been concerned with finding some way of characterizing the propositional contents of those declarative sentences whose standard use is the making of assertions. It was suggested that what should be assigned to such sentences is some (though, as we have observed at great length, not just ANY) specification of the conditions under which the sentence would be true. The truth conditions would characterize what it is that is asserted by the use of the sentence.

Imperative sentences, interrogative sentences, and even some sentences which are declarative in superficial form, are not used for the making of assertions. They are used to give orders, make requests, ask questions, to promise, to warn, to make bets, and so on. And most of these illocutionary acts would seem to have little to do with the concept of truth. It is not at all clear, therefore, that the propositional contents of these sentences can be individuated by reference to truth conditions. In this section we will consider some possible approaches to the semantics of these sentences.

To begin with, let us determine just how far the truth condition approach will take us without any modification at all. At the very least, the individual words in a nondeclarative sentence mean the same as they do in a declarative sentence, and so do subsentential phrases and clauses: the constituents *boots*, *wears his boots*, and *that John wears his boots*, for example, do not shift in meaning between the sentences *Make sure that John wears his boots*, *Do you make sure that John wears his boots?*, *I always make sure that John wears his boots*. So it is only at the highest level of meaning, so to speak, the stage at which the sentence meaning is integrated from the meanings of its parts, that any new semantic principles might be needed for nonassertive sentences.

A bold approach would be to claim that no new principles are needed at all—to claim that these sentences do, despite first impressions to the contrary, have truth values and hence can be assigned truth conditions. An alternative theory would be that though these sentences do not themselves have truth values, their meanings can be characterized as some function of the meanings of related declarative sentences which do. A third possibility would be to extend the truth condition theory analogically, by identifying some property P which stands to nonassertive sentences as truth stands to assertive sentences, so that the illocutionary force potential of a nonassertive sentence can be analyzed in terms of P, and the propositional content in terms of P-conditions.

Let us consider first an elementary version of the second kind of theory, that is, the theory that the meaning of a nonassertive sentence can be characterized as simply the pair of its illocutionary force potential and its propositional content. The former is to be determined on the basis of either the syntactic type of the sentence (e.g., for imperatives and interrogatives) or the presence of an overt 'performative clause' such as *I hereby command . . .* , *I warn you that . . .* , *I bet you a nickel that . . .* and so on. The propositional content is taken to be identical with that of an assertive sentence having the same syntactic structure and lexical items. This sameness of structure would have to be established at some syntactic level more abstract than surface structure, or else there would be no assertive sentence at all corresponding, for example, to a subjectless imperative sentence like *Walk the dog*. But let us bypass the details and simply assume that there is some formal method of establishing classes of sentences with the same propositional content—for example, the class including *Walk the dog, You will walk the dog, Will you walk the dog?, I advise you to walk the dog, I bet you will walk the dog,* etc.

This simple model fails to reveal a number of semantic properties of nonassertive sentences. As it stands, it does not even predict correctly which sentences have a coherent meaning and which do not. A sentence may have a specifiable illocutionary force potential and share its propositional content with some meaningful assertive sentence, and yet not be meaningful itself. For example, the sentence *I command that the green vase broke yesterday* is anomalous, even though it presumably has the force of a command, and shares its propositional content with the acceptable assertive sentence *The green vase broke yesterday.* We thus see that there is an interaction between illocutionary force potential and propositional content.

This interaction also shows up in the definition of synonymy. It is not sufficient to say that two sentences will have the same meaning just in case they have the same illocutionary force potential and the same propositional content, for the sentences *I order you not to touch the applie pie* and *I forbid you to touch the apple pie* mean the same (or very nearly so), and yet they apparently differ both in illocutionary force potential and in propositional content. The relation between them is intuitively quite clear: *forbid* is in some sense the negative of *order*, and the polarity contrast between the two performative verbs cancels out somehow with the polarity contrast between the clauses that follow them.

What this suggests is that some more sophisticated and more intimate relation than mere addition holds between the two 'parts' of the meaning of a nonassertive sentence. And in fact this relation seems to be exactly comparable to the relation that holds between a main clause and a complement clause in an assertive sentence (for example in a sentence which would be used to report the occurrence of the speech act that the nonassertive sentence is used to make). Thus the 'performative' sentence *I command that the green vase broke yesterday* is anomalous in just the same way as the assertive sentence *The teacher commanded that the green vase broke yesterday.* And the synonymy of the performative sentences *I order you not to touch the apple pie* and *I forbid you to touch the apple pie* is matched by the synonymy of the assertive sentences *Mother ordered Molly not to touch the apple pie* and *Mother forbade Molly to touch the apple pie.*

This parallelism establishes that when a verb like *order* appears in a performative clause in a nonassertive sentence it is not just an ARBITRARY indicator of illocutionary force potential, but is a genuine occurrence of the familiar verb *order* which appears in assertive sentences too. The value that the semantic theory assigns to it as its meaning must be the same in both kinds of sentence, and so must the principles which combine its meaning with the meanings of other constituents of the sentence, in particular the clause which appears as its complement. The only difference is that when *order* is used performatively, it signals (in some fashion still to be explained) that an utterance of the sentence constitutes the GIVING of an order rather than the making of an assertion ABOUT an act of ordering.

Having got this far, it is very natural to propose, in the interests of generality, that simple imperative sentences like *Don't touch the apple pie* are assigned their illocutionary force potentials in the same way. This simple imperative sentence is apparently synonymous with the sentence *I order you not to touch the apple pie*; and it has the same semantic properties (e.g., it is anomalous just in case the *I order . . .* sentence is anomalous). It might therefore be viewed as simply an ellipsis of the overtly performative *I order . . .* sentence. This would immediately solve, for simple imperative sentences, the problem of the relation between their illocutionary force potentials and their propositional contents, for this relation would be, once again, just the same as the relation between main clauses and their complement clauses in ordinary assertive sentences.

What remains to be answered in this analysis is the question of what distinguishes the meaning of the performative *I order . . .* sentence (and its imperative ellipsis) from that of an assertive sentence, in particular from that of the assertive sentence which is superficially similar in syntactic form and lexical items. What is the difference in meaning between *I order you not to touch the apple pie* as used to give an order, and *I order you not to touch the apple pie* (or *I am ordering you not to touch the apple pie*) as used to assert that one is issuing (or commonly does issue) such an order? One answer might be (see Lewis, 1972) that there is no difference at all, that all performative sentences really are just assertive sentences though they have the peculiarity that they can simultaneously be used to perform the speech act whose occurrence they are reporting—just as the sentence *In hexameter trochaic am I talking* (though not the sentence *I am talking in trochaic hexameter*) can be used simultaneously to report on, and to perform, an act of talking in trochaic hexameter.

Observe that this theory is of the first type outlined above; it extends the truth condition theory of meaning directly and without modification to nonassertive sentences. If nonassertive sentences can be taken to be assertive sentences, then they will have truth values, and their propositional contents can be characterized by means of truth conditions. Of course, the truth values of such sentences will not be what we are most concerned with in normal conversational contexts, but this does not prove that they have no truth values. (Notice that on this theory, a nonassertive sentence will be true just in case its utterance is 'felicitous.' For example, *I order you not to leave your post* will be true just in case its utterance does constitute a genuine act of ordering. So it is likely to be true more often than not. But it CAN be false, for if the felicity conditions on such an act of ordering are not met—e.g., if the speaker is not in a position of authority over the hearer—then the utterance of the sentence will NOT constitute the giving of an order, and the simultaneous assertion that an order is being given will be a false one.)

This theory will no doubt strike some readers as counterintuitive, and certainly there are puzzles associated with it that would have to be resolved. For example, though we might respond to an infelicitous utterance of the sentence *I order you to finish your hamburger* by saying "You're in no position to do so," it would be distinctly queer to say "That's false." And it would be queerer still to reply to an utterance of the simple imperative *Finish your hamburger* by saying "You're in no position to do so," though the theory claims that this sentence is an ellipsis of an *I order . . .* sentence to which this reply would be appropriate. Indeed, this theory offers no explanation of why the simple imperative (unlike the overtly performative construction) cannot ever be used to REPORT the occurrence of an act of ordering. For these reasons, we may be inclined to take seriously the intuition that there IS, after all, a difference of meaning between a performative sentence and a superficially similar assertive sentence. What could this difference amount to?

A familiar suggestion is that the performative clause analysis should in fact be extended to assertive sentences too. A sentence like *Mice eat cheese* would then be construed as elliptical for the more explicitly assertive sentence *I assert that mice eat cheese*. Ross (1970) has offered syntactic motivation for this analysis of declarative sentences, although his arguments have been challenged (see Anderson, 1970, and Fraser, 1971). Lack of evidence for it as a syntactic (deep structure) analysis would not, however, necessarily invalidate it as a contribution to semantics. If we consider it in this light, the claim is that sentences like *It is raining* and *I assert that it is raining* have the same meaning and illocutionary function, and furthermore that the form of the second of these sentences is more revealing than the first of why that function is what it is. The *I assert . . .* sentence contains an explicit indication of the illocutionary force potential, and is thus the PARADIGM vehicle for the speech act of asserting that it is raining. This claim might be questioned, but let us accept it for the moment and consider what sort of account of the meanings of nonassertive sentences it implies.

The assertives-as-performatives approach attributes a certain semantic structure to sentences, and it thereby makes claims about sameness and difference of meaning. But a full account of sentence meaning must also specify how that structure is to be interpreted, for it is compatible with several very different theories. For example, it might simply be grafted onto a theory like Lewis's, without altering the basic assumption that all sentences are really assertive and have truth conditions. (In that case, not only would *It is raining* be analyzed as *I assert that it is raining*, but *Eat your hamburger* would be analyzed with TWO higher clauses as *I assert that I order you to eat your hamburger*.) But the performative clause analysis of assertive sentences could instead be made the basis of a theory in which no special status is ascribed to assertion *vis-a-vis* other illocutionary acts. Then the analysis of a declarative like *It is raining* would be *I assert that it is raining*, but the analysis of the imperative *Eat your hamburger* would still be simply *I order you to eat your hamburger.* In other words, illocutionary differences would be acknowledged, and would be made explicit by means of the performative verb appearing in the highest clause of the semantic structure assigned to each sentence. Sentences used for giving orders would have *I order*, sentences used for giving advice would have *I advise*, sentences used for making bets would have *I bet*; and, in just the same fashion, sentences used for making assertions would have *I assert*.

This interpretation of the performative clause analysis thus offers a theory of the third type outlined above, i.e., PARALLEL treatments of assertive and nonassertive sentences rather than the reduction of one type of sentence to the other. The same compositional devices would be used to build up sentence meanings of all types, but these meanings would be characterized as TRUTH conditions only for sentences whose performative verb is *assert*. For sentences with performative verbs such as *order*, *advise*, *promise*, the sentence meaning would be characterized in terms of conditions of other kinds, in keeping with their illocutionary force.

For example, since it is of the essence of imperative sentences that (in standard cases) they are used to give orders which are intended to be obeyed, a plausible suggestion is that for imperatives, obedience should fill the role that truth plays in an explication of assertive sentence meanings. The illocutionary force potential of an imperative would be explicated in terms of obedience, and the propositional content of an imperative would be taken to determine obedience conditions. The fundamental idea here is that the propositional content of a pair of related declarative and imperative sentences picks out the same state of affairs in the world, but that the relevance of this state of affairs to the speech act is different in the two cases. For the declarative sentence, it is that state of affairs which must obtain in order for the assertion to be true, and for the imperative, it is that state of affairs which must be brought about by the hearer if the order is to be obeyed.

This approach seems to have much to recommend it. For one thing, it does provide a way of distinguishing truly performative uses of sentences from reportive uses. Consider the sentence *I order you to stop*, which can be used in both ways. When it is used to GIVE an order, its semantic analysis is simply what it appears to be from its surface form, with *I order* as the highest clause. This top clause specifies that the propositional content is to be cast as an obedience condition, and the lower clause specifies this condition to be that you stop. When used to REPORT an act of ordering, the sentence has the analysis *I assert that I order you to stop*. Here the highest clause, *I assert*, specifies that the propositional content is to be cast as a truth condition, and the lower clauses specify this condition to be that I order you to stop. A simple addition to this theory accounts for an observation that we made above, viz., that a simple imperative like *Stop!* cannot be used to report but only to perform an act of ordering. All that is needed is the constraint that at most one clause of the semantic structure, the performative clause itself, can be elided in surface structure. The semantic structure for a REPORTIVE use of *Stop!* would have to contain TWO clauses not present in the surface structure of the simple imperative, and this is not permitted.

At the moment, this proposal is more a program for description than a fully worked out analysis, for of course there are many more kinds of illocution than asserting and ordering. Suitable analogs to truth and obedience must be found for the others. But perhaps we will not have to look too far afield. Bets and predictions appear to be species of assertion and thus analyzable at least partly in terms of truth. Christening, pronouncing man and wife, declaring void, and so on, also concern truth, though they create truths rather than commenting on antecedently given ones. By weakening obedience to compliance we could accommodate requests such as *Would you please drive a little slower?* And it has often been suggested that questions should be analyzed as requests for information, and thus that they too can be assigned compliance conditions. (For a question, compliance would consist in giving the information requested, so its compliance conditions would in effect define the set of its 'possible answers.')

As I have indicated, the mere attribution to sentences of 'invisible' performative clauses does not uniquely constrain a theory of what the meanings of those sentences consist in. The interpretation we have developed here seems to have its merits, but now we must ask to what extent the performative clause analysis actually contributes to them.

Katz (1972, Chapters 4 and 5) has proposed a treatment of a variety of sentence types which assigns truth conditions to declaratives, compliance conditions to imperatives, and so on, but which does not attribute any special status to sentences with overt performative clauses. In particular, it does not assume that an ordinary declarative or imperative sentence receives its interpretation *via* an association with a corresponding sentence containing *I assert* or *I order*. Katz proposes instead that the syntactic structure (and intonation) of declarative, imperative and other types of sentence is interpreted directly.

The syntactic description of English which Katz assumes attributes the characteristic surface structure of an imperative sentence (missing subject, tenseless verb) to the effects of an abstract morpheme *Imp* in the deep syntactic structure. The deep structure of *Go home*, for example, would be *Imp you Pres will go home*. It is this which is to be semantically interpreted. If we ignore the *Imp* for the moment, the result of interpreting the remainder of the deep structure is a set of 'conditions,' as yet undifferentiated with respect to illocutionary force potential. It is the semantic role of the *Imp* to convert these neutral conditions into compliance conditions for the imperative sentence. A related sentence with an overt performative clause in surface (and deep) structure, such as *I order you to go home*, is also assigned compliance conditions, but here the assignment is made on the basis of different lexical and syntactic properties. In this case, though NOT in the case of the simple imperative, it IS the *I order* clause which governs the conversion of conditions.

At this point we run up against a recurrent question in linguistic research: are these theories really distinct or do they make identical claims despite their apparent differences? Katz's theory appears to be less abstract; the theory that attributes a performative clause to every sentence appears to be more general. But both are alike in claiming that a simple imperative sentence is synonymous with an *I order* ... sentence. And (given the particular way we have elected to develop the performative clause theory) both are alike in claiming that the meanings of both sentences are to be expressed as compliance conditions. Their general implications for the nature of sentence meaning are thus the same. Where the theories differ is only in the mechanisms by which the compliance conditions are to be assigned, and the question is what if anything this difference amounts to. If linguistic descriptions are intended to capture a psychological reality, it might appear that any such difference MUST be significant—speakers and hearers must in fact employ one of the proposed mechanisms or the other, or else some third alternative we may not yet have conceived of. In practice, of course, we are very far at present from being able to determine by psychological observation or experiment exactly what processes are involved in producing and understanding sentences of any type. But even the question of principle remains largely obscure, since we lack any detailed and well-motivated account of just what the relation between a formal linguistic description and a theory of language behavior must be. (See Section 3.5 for more general discussion of this problem.)

Until these deep and difficult issues are resolved, it is not easy to adjudicate between theories which overlap as much as these two theories of sentence meaning do. But we can at least attempt to evaluate assumptions they hold in common. And, though widely accepted, they too present certain problems. The root of the trouble is the assumption that an overtly 'performative' sentence like *I order you to whistle* does have a performative use, i.e., that it can be synonymous with the simple imperative *Whistle!* (in addition to being used, unlike the simple imperative, to report the giving of an order to whistle). This assumption may seem too obvious to be challenged, but in at least some cases there are certain basic intuitions which it seems to have difficulty in accounting for.

We say, for example, that the sentence *John loves Mary* entails that John loves someone—if the sentence is true then it must be the case that John loves someone. But if the sentence *I assert that John loves Mary* is (on one reading) simply a more explicit paraphrase of *John loves Mary*, then why do we feel such reluctance about admitting that *I assert that John loves Mary* also entails that John loves someone? Surely the mere assertion that something is so does not (except in very special cases) make it so. A similar point is made by the contrast between the valid argument (a) and the nonargument (b) in (2-4)

(2-4) (a) All men are mortal.   (b) I assert that all men are mortal.
Socrates is a man.   I assert that Socrates is a man.

Socrates is mortal.   I assert that Socrates is mortal.

It is a point of definition that synonymous sentences must have identical entailments. Since the *I assert* . . . sentences appear not to have the same entailments as the corresponding simple declaratives, this suggests that they do not mean the same. It is not usual to talk of the entailments of imperative, interrogative, and other types of nondeclarative sentences (though see Katz 1972, Chapter 5), and so it is more difficult to make an analogous case against the supposed synonymy of these sentence types with their corresponding overt performative constructions, but we may at least consider the possibility that true synonymy is lacking here too.

In pursuing these objections, we must not of course deny that sometimes a person intending to assert that John loves Mary might utter the sentence *I assert that John loves Mary*, nor that someone hearing this utterance might say "That's true" and mean that it is true that John loves Mary. But these are not typical conversational exchanges, and to the extent that they do occur, they might be explained in a pragmatic rather than a strictly semantic fashion. As an analogy, consider the sentence *Can you reach the salt?* It has been pointed out (see Searle, 1975) that an utterance of this sentence is typically construed as a request for the salt, even though, taken strictly, it expresses a question about the hearer's reaching ability. To account for its more typical use, we may assume that the hearer imposes a special interpretation on what is said, prompted by his perception that the speaker would probably like the salt and that he almost certainly has no real interest from any other point of view in whether the hearer can reach it. Asking the question is thus an indirect way of requesting the salt; it CONVEYS the request without actually EXPRESSING it.

In the same fashion, the utterance of *I assert that John loves Mary* may be only an indirect way of asserting that John loves Mary. It may convey this assertion to the hearer even though, strictly speaking, it does not express it. (What it actually expresses is only the assertion that it is being asserted that John loves Mary.) To make this move is thus to deny that simple declaratives and *I assert* . . . sentences have the same meaning, while still allowing for the fact that they are sometimes used with the same communicative function. If this is correct, we must obviously reject any theory which takes the utterance of the *I assert* . . . sentence as the paradigm case of making the assertion. Instead of taking this sentence to display the 'real' form of the simple declarative, we must take the simple declarative to have just the form it appears to have and then explain away, by reference to secondary speech acts, the fact that an utterance of the *I assert* . . . sentence is sometimes construed in the same way. (The assignment of truth conditions to a declarative sentence could not, then, be triggered by the verb *assert*, but would have to be made on the basis of other aspects of syntactic structure along the lines that Katz has suggested.)

This last approach is a very nonstandard one; but it helps to make the point that in this area there are still many more questions than answers. An account of meaning for nonassertive sentences is subject to whatever uncertainties remain with respect to analyticity, intensional structure, and related phenomena which we discussed earlier in connection with assertive sentences. But as we have seen, there is also a considerable divergence of views simply about what the facts are and how they are to be described. The semantics of nonassertive sentences has been a relatively recent concern in both philosophy and linguistics. We may not doubt that eventually these constructions can be fitted into some coherent account of sentence meaning in general, but at present there is no consensus about exactly WHERE they fit.

2.8. PHILOSOPHICAL AND LINGUISTIC APPROACHES TO MEANING

We began this chapter a long way back by asking what meaning is, and then proceeded to say a great deal about what it is not. Even the relatively sophisticated notion that the meaning of a sentence can be expressed as truth conditions (obedience conditions, etc.) had to be tempered by the observation that not every set of conditions under which a sentence is true will uniquely identify its meaning, and that there is apparently no independent way of picking out just those that will. This suggested the conclusion that meanings are just meanings—abstract entities with their own special properties and standing in their own special relations to each other and to a variety of other phenomena including reference, truth, necessity, analyticity, opacity, speech acts. Each of these related concepts is itself in need of clarification. But though the task may be difficult, it doesn't look hopeless; to return to Katz's analogy (see Section 2.1), we seem to be well on the road to doing for meaning what physicists have done and continue to do for physical phenomena like electricity.

None of this, of course, secures the concept of meaning against a determined scepticism, and we must accept that there may be no account of meaning that would do so. Someone could, after all, persist in scepticism about electricity, however well-motivated and detailed a theory we were to provide. He might flatly deny the existence of electrical phenomena, or deny that these phenomena are manifestations of electrical forces, or, in a more sophisticated vein, simply note that we cannot PROVE that they are. And meaning is undeniably in a worse position than electricity, for even the manifestations of meaning are not open to direct sensory experience as are electric shocks, light, heat, and so on. Indeed, meaning is vulnerable in many directions; it is a target for those who distrust any or all of abstract entities, theoretical entities and mental entities. It is also true that whatever insights we now have about meaning have been a long time coming and still leave plenty of room for disagreement.

Scepticism about meaning has not been a characteristic obsession of generative linguists. One legacy of the early work on transformational syntax was that native speakers' intuitions became respectable as a data base, and intuitions about meaning were consulted with none of the embarassment that has led philosophers to explore possible reductions of meaning to something more demonstrable. While acknowledging the problems, the study of semantics within the framework of generative linguistics thus makes the working assumption that there IS something to the notion of meaning, and that an important part of finding out what there is involves the description and generalization of particular semantic phenomena. If pressed, we could retreat to the claim that we are merely doing some preliminary psychology, describing and generalizing certain intuitions that language users find themselves with. But it appears that most linguists would want to take a much stronger position than that.

Thus the point which we have finally reached in this chapter is in many respects where modern linguistic research into meaning began. The meaning of an expression was conceived as distinct from and not reducible to its other properties, and as having an internal structure crucial to the determination of synonymy and other important semantic properties and relations. Among philosophers one might still hear the old refrain that natural languages are too vague and inconsistent for formal semantic treatment. But encouraged by successes in syntax, linguists were convinced that they could pull it off, and they set about doing so with formal mechanisms intended to mesh with those of syntax, and modelled not too distantly upon them.

There were also some deeper differences between the approaches to meaning in the two disciplines, however, and without an understanding of these it may be hard to see how the semantic systems developed by linguists fit in relation to the primarily philosophical issues of the present chapter. Linguistics and the philosophy of language were not, in the early years of generative grammar, so nearly indistinguishable as they are today. And some quite fundamental observations about meaning have only recently begun to influence linguistics.

Perhaps in reaction to deflationary approaches to semantics, which attempted to do without meaning and admit only extensional entities, the relation of meaning to truth and reference was originally ignored by linguists. The goal was to formulate a dictionary and a set of combination rules, integrated into a complete grammar, which would construct semantic representations for sentences. These semantic representations were to reveal the internal structure of meanings, and to serve as a basis for predicting semantic properties and relations in much the fashion that syntactic phrase markers predict syntactic properties and relations. The symbols out of which semantic representations were composed were taken to stand for minimal elements of meaning, and these were identified as 'concepts.' But no attempt was made to put these concepts into any sort of correlation with what they were concepts of. I will now give a brief (and highly selective) history of how truth and reference have begun to take their place in linguistic approaches to meaning.

Initially, the emphasis in linguistic semantics was on capturing synonymy, anomaly (meaninglessness) and ambiguity: sentences were assigned identical semantic representations if synonymous, no semantic representation if anomalous, and n distinct semantic representations if n ways ambiguous. Semantic representations thus stood in a one-to-one correspondence with meanings (see Katz and Fodor, 1963). Gradually, other semantic properties were added to the list. A particularly significant one was meaning inclusion. This was brought in quite early on to explicate analyticity (see Katz, 1964), but it was later extended to account for entailment relations between sentences (Katz, 1972, Chapter 4). Attention came to center more and more on entailment, and (amid intricate debates about the relation between syntax and semantics in natural languages) the realization dawned that a semantic representation is similar in function to the logical form of a sentence (see, for example, J. D. Fodor, 1970; Harman, 1970; McCawley, 1972).

The logical form of a sentence (or perhaps a representation of its logical form) is a structure which determines the logical implications of the sentence. A formula in a system of formal logic is such a structure; application of the inference rules of the system 'generates' the class of sentences which follow from it.[9] If entailment relations can be defined over semantic representations, then these can be likened to logical formulae; and the grammatical mechanisms (sparse in fact, but acknowledged in principle) which determine entailment relations between sentences on the basis of their semantic representations can be likened to logical inference rules. Thus, a grammar for a natural language is seen to be similar to a system of logic, differing primarily in the phonological rules and syntactic transformations that it must contain for empirical adequacy, but not fundamentally in its treatment of meaning.

This by now familiar identification of semantic representation with logical form has to be hedged in various ways. The more familiar, traditional systems of logic deal in material implication rather than in the stronger relation of entailment or the even stronger one, taken seriously in linguistics,

---

9. I ignore here questions about the completeness of the system.

of analytic entailment. So the particular logical forms assigned to sentences by these systems often fail to mark semantic distinctions which a linguistic description is committed to capturing. Also, even the formulae of richer, intensional logics may be unacceptable as linguistic representations because they do not respect established universal constraints on the kinds of formal structures that natural languages utilize. Logic has typically been free of the psychological commitments that have governed the development of generative linguistics.

Nevertheless, this concern with entailment can be seen as the beginning of an integration of reference and truth into linguistic conceptions of meaning. Entailment is a dependency between truth values. A sentence S_1 entails a sentence S_2 if whenever S_1 is true, S_2 must also be true. That is to say, the truth conditions on S_2 are included in those on S_1. A proof-theoretic approach to inference has tended to prevail in linguistics. In other words, entailment is captured by means of inference rules, which derive the semantic representation of one sentence from that of another sentence which entails it. But there is a growing interest in model-theoretic systems, in which truth conditions are assigned to each sentence, and the inclusion relation between truth conditions which comprises entailment is derivative upon these assignments.

If this is to be the goal, linguistics will have to incorporate interpretation rules for its semantic representations of the kind illustrated in Sections 2.5 and 2.6 above (though no doubt considerably more complex in detail). Actual models for natural languages like English are still thin on the ground (though see Keenan, 1972 and the account of 'Montague grammar' in Partee, 1975). But the indications are that we are drawing to the end of the period in which semantic representations form an abstract uninterpreted system which can be connected with reality only by identifying its primitive terms with some universal innate mental entities.

Generative linguistics can perhaps take some of the credit for the rapprochement between the subtleties of 'ordinary language philosophy' and the rigor of formal logic, but there is no doubt that it has benefited in its turn by contact with developments in logic and philosophy. It is encouraging that the two disciplines, each with its own starting points, should have come up with theories compatible enough to permit a fruitful integration. But this integration is still in progress. In the linguistic theories presented in the following chapters, it is more of a promise than a reality. The questions these theories have addressed have been largely internal to linguistics. A semantic component was grafted onto a grammar, previously consisting of syntax and phonology, and there then set in a lengthy period of adjustment to the operation—experiments with the boundary between syntax and semantics, exploration of their formal similarities and differences and of the proper division of labor between them. To these matters we now turn.

3
Semantic Theories in Linguistics

Among the varied observations and proposals about meaning within the framework of generative grammar, three theories can be distinguished that have been developed in some detail. Katz has formulated a theory often referred to as INTERPRETIVE SEMANTICS. More recently, Chomsky and Jackendoff have proposed a rather different but also 'interpretive' theory which has been called the EXTENDED STANDARD THEORY. This is a modification (of a kind we shall discuss shortly) of the STANDARD THEORY, the theory outlined in Chomsky's *Aspects of the Theory of Syntax* (1965), which represents roughly the last major work in generative linguistics before opinions about semantics and its relation to syntax began to diverge. Katz's theory, though it has been developed in a variety of ways since *Aspects*, still accepts the fundamental premises of the standard theory. The first significant breaks from the standard theory were made by Gruber and Fillmore, whose proposals are related (in ways outlined in Section 3.4) to the theory of GENERATIVE SEMANTICS developed by G. Lakoff, McCawley, Postal, Ross, and others. (I will occasionally, for brevity, refer to this theory as GS, and to the Chomsky-Jackendoff theory as EST.)

A point that should be stressed is that the differences between these theories concern syntax as well as semantics. A linguistic theory must specify how syntactic and semantic structures are related, and it is to be expected that different views about the relationship between them will go along with different views about the nature of the structures that are to be related. We shall be concerned with the syntactic aspects of these theories only insofar as they bear on issues in semantics, but at least the broad outlines of the syntactic component of a grammar are relevant. As will be seen in the chapters that follow, many of the recent theoretical disagreements in linguistics have turned on the general organization of a grammar, what components it contains, how they differ, and how they interact with each other. By comparison, differences between the semantic representations that have been proposed are relatively minor.

In this chapter, these different theories of semantics and its place in a grammar will be introduced, with some indication of how they have evolved into their present form. More detailed comparisons of their competing claims will be made in Chapters 4 and 5.

3.1. KATZ'S THEORY

Katz's theory has the longest history. The first published work on the treatment of semantics within a generative grammar was *The Structure of a Semantic Theory* by Katz and J. A. Fodor (1963), and the theory has been considerably refined and extended since. Katz and Fodor first made the two fundamental points that we have already had occasion to stress. The assignment of meaning representations to sentences, like the assignment of syntactic structures, must be effected by recursive rules. And the pairing of a sentence with a meaning is not arbitrary but is mediated by the syntactic structure and lexical content of the sentence. Katz and Fodor assumed the existence of a self-contained syntactic component of a grammar, specifying the syntactic structure and lexical content of each sentence of the language, and they therefore conceived the task as that of (i) giving specifications of the meanings of lexical items and (ii) giving recursive rules operating over syntactic structures for building up meaning specifications for phrases and sentences out of the meaning specifications for lexical items.

The pairings of lexical items with meaning representations together constitute the DICTIONARY for the language, each dictionary entry containing one or more READINGS, where each reading represents one sense of the lexical item. The recursive rules that construct readings for larger expressions out of the readings for their constituents are called PROJECTION RULES. Projection rules project morpheme readings onto phrase and ultimately sentence readings, thereby explaining the ability of native speakers to project their knowledge of the meanings of the finite set of sentences they have encountered onto the infinite set of possible sentences of the language.

The meanings of both lexical items and larger constituents are regarded as concepts, analyzable into simpler atomic concepts which are represented by SEMANTIC MARKERS and DISTINGUISHERS. Semantic markers and distinguishers thus constitute the vocabulary out of which all readings are composed. A distinguisher in the reading for a lexical item was said to be "intended to reflect what is idiosyncratic about the meaning of that item." This has since been revised, and I will reserve discussion of distinguishers until Chapter 5. The semantic markers in the reading for a lexical item are "intended to reflect whatever systematic relations hold between that item and the rest of the vocabulary of the language." Semantic markers and distinguishers are thus close relatives of the semantic components of traditional componential analysis (see Section 5.1).

A dictionary entry was originally characterized as a hierarchically structured complex of grammatical markers, semantic markers, distinguishers, and selection restrictions. The best-known example is the dictionary entry given by Katz and Fodor for the English word *bachelor*.

(3-1)

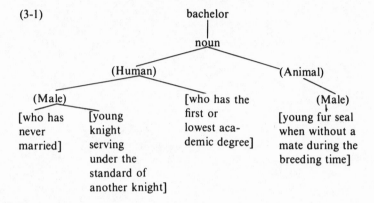

This too has been modified as the theory has developed (see Section 5.1). A dictionary entry is now an unstructured set of readings, and each reading is simply an unordered set of semantic markers, with a possible distinguisher and selection restriction, associated with phonological and syntactic feature specifications. The dictionary entry (3-1) above has been superseded by (3-2) below (overlooking revisions of the actual markers and distinguishers that appear).

(3-2) D, [+N, ...], (Human), (Male), [who has never married]
                    (Human), (Male), [young knight serving. . .]
                    (Human), [who has the first or lowest. . .]
                    (Animal), (Male), [young fur seal when. . .]

(Elements enclosed in parentheses are semantic markers; elements enclosed in square brackets are distinguishers; the unenclosed element in (3-1) is a grammatical marker, since given up in favor of the element [+*N*, . . .] in (3-2), which is a complex symbol containing syntactic feature specifications; the element D is a phonological feature matrix. Selection restrictions are not exemplified in this dictionary entry.)

Semantic markers were once regarded, at least implicitly, as simple unanalyzable units, but for reasons that will be discussed in Section 5.3, complex semantic markers are now allowed. Complex semantic markers contain other semantic markers within them, and also CATEGORIZED VARIABLES which indicate where the readings of other constituents are to be inserted by the projection rules in the course of building up readings for larger constituents. Katz has given one reading from the dictionary entry for the verb *chase*, as in (3-3).

(3-3)

$$(((\text{Activity})(((\text{Physical}))((\text{Movement})((\text{Speed}) \underset{\text{(Fast)}}{} (\text{Following} \underset{<(\text{Object})>}{\overset{[NP,VP,PredP,S]}{X}})))$$

$$((\text{Purpose})((\text{To catch} \underset{<(\text{Object})>}{\overset{[NP,VP,PredP,S]}{X}}))))) \underset{<(\text{Human}) \text{ v } (\text{Animal})>}{\overset{[NP,S]}{X}})$$

The categorized variable $\overset{[NP,S]}{X}$ indicates where the reading for the subject of *chase* is to be inserted. (Note: The subject of a sentence is that *NP* directly dominated by *S*.) The categorized variable $\overset{[NP, VP, Pred P,S]}{X}$ indicates where the reading for the object is to be inserted (the object is that *NP* directly dominated by *VP* which is dominated by *PredP* which is dominated by *S*). The markers in angled brackets underneath these categorized variables specify the selection restrictions on readings inserted into those positions. For example, the selection restriction <(*Human*) v (*Animal*)> beneath the subject variable requires that the reading of the subject phrase should contain either the marker (*Human*) or the marker (*Animal*). (The function of selection restrictions is discussed below.)

Originally, it was assumed that SURFACE syntactic structures would be the input to the projection rules of the semantic component. But Katz and Postal (1964) subsequently argued that it is DEEP syntactic structures which should be semantically interpreted. They argued, case by case, that no syntactic transformation changes the meaning of the structure to which it applies—to be more precise, that the same deep structure is never transformed into two nonsynonymous sentences. Some of the optional transformations proposed in Chomsky's *Syntactic Structures* did affect meaning; the Negation transformation produced negative sentences from the same underlying structures as affirmative sentences, the Question and Imperative transformations derived nondeclarative sentences from the same underlying structures as declarative sentences. But these transformations were reanalyzed by Katz and Postal as obligatory transformations, triggered by the elements *Neg*, *Q* and *Imp* which were posited in deep structures. The presence of these elements served to keep the deep structures of nonsynonymous sentences distinct, so that the semantic differences between the sentences could be read off their deep structures.

Another category of meaning-changing transformations in Chomsky's early theory was GENERALIZED TRANSFORMATIONS. These combined the phrase markers for the various clauses in a complex sentence, which were generated separately by the phrase structure rules. Katz and Postal argued that the only semantic contribution of these transformations was in determining which phrase markers were inserted into which positions in which others, and what their role was (e.g., relative clause, sentential complement, etc.). And they proposed a way of representing this information, too, in deep structures. But this proposal was overtaken by events, for shortly afterwards, Chomsky argued in *Aspects* that the recursiveness of the grammar should reside in the phrase structure component, not in the transformational component, i.e., that the phrase structure rules should generate GENERALIZED PHRASE MARKERS in which the syntactic structures of all clauses of a sentence are already combined. Generalized transformations were then abandoned, and the question of their contribution to sentence meaning no longer arose.

Having established to their satisfaction that no transformation contributed to the meaning of a sentence, so that deep structures COULD serve as the sole input to the semantic projection rules, Katz and Postal argued that deep structures SHOULD be the sole input to these rules. Deep structures contain semantically relevant information about constituency and grammatical relations that is destroyed in the course of deriving surface structures, and they also contain constituents that are deleted by transformations. Deep structures therefore MUST be input to the projection rules. Since, according to Katz and Postal, surface structures and other derived syntactic structures never contain semantically relevant information that is not present in deep structures, simplicity demands that these are NOT input to the projection rules. Thus, a deep structure generated by the phrase structure rules of the grammar is input to two other distinct components of the grammar: the transformational component, whose rules progressively convert it into a surface structure; and the semantic component, whose projection rules progressively flesh out its constituents with readings.

Obviously, application of the projection rules to a deep structure phrase marker must follow the insertion of lexical items, where this includes the insertion of their readings. Originally, there were distinct projection rules for combining (or AMALGAMATING) the readings of different constituent types: one rule for amalgamating the readings of a modifier and its head; one for amalgamating the readings of a noun and a determiner; one for a verb and its object; one for a verb phrase and its subject. This was the way in which differences in syntactic structure were to contribute to the meanings of phrases. But the use of categorized variables has largely taken over this function and now only two projection rules are needed, one to effect the substitution of readings for appropriate categorized variables, the other to simply combine (form the union of) readings which do not contain categorized variables. Katz has collected these two rules into a single one (see Katz,

1972, Chapter 3). The reasons for this change in the theory will be discussed in Section 5.3.

The projection rules apply upwards from the bottom of the syntactic phrase marker to the top, amalgamating readings for lexical items before amalgamating these derived readings into readings for larger and larger constituents. The output of each projection rule is a syntactic phrase marker identical to the input except that a set of derived readings, formed by amalgamation, has been assigned to some node that previously had none. The final result of applying the projection rules is a deep structure phrase marker with readings attached to every node, including the highest *S* node. This is called a SEMANTICALLY INTERPRETED UNDERLYING PHRASE MARKER (which I shall abbreviate as SIUPM).

Exactly how readings are to be associated with nodes in a SIUPM has never been clearly specified. It is probably correct to regard a SIUPM as a multi-dimensional tree structure, with one or more readings attached to each node but in different dimensions from each other and from the syntactic nodes into which the node branches—obviously a reading for a phrase such as *the man* is not a sister constituent to *the* and *man* in the same way that *the* and *man* are sisters to each other. This can be indicated by the use of broken lines, as in (3-4).

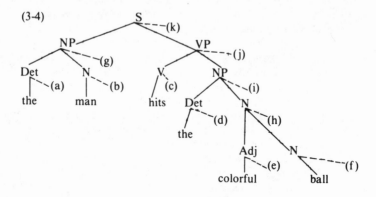

(3-4)

Here I have simplified the real SIUPM by using (a), (b), etc. to abbreviate the sets of readings. The actual sets of readings in this SIUPM include the following.

(3-5) (e)   (i) (Color), [Abounding in contrast or variety of bright colors], < (Physical Object) v (Social Activity) >

        (ii) (Evaluative), [Having distinctive character, vividness or picturesqueness], < (Aesthetic Object) v (Social Activity) >

(f) (i) (Social Activity), (Large), (Assembly), [For the purpose of social dancing]

(ii) (Physical Object), [Having globular shape]

(iii) (Physical Object), [Solid missile for projection by engine of war]

(h) (i) (Social Activity), (Large), (Assembly), (Color), [[Abounding in contrast or variety of bright colors] [For the purpose of social dancing]]

(ii) (Physical Object), (Color), [[Abounding in contrast or variety of bright colors] [Having globular shape]]

(iii) (Physical Object), (Color), [[Abounding in contrast or variety of bright colors] [Solid missile for projection by engine of war]]

(iv) (Social Activity), (Large), (Assembly), (Evaluative), [[Having distinctive character, vividness or picturesqueness] [For the purpose of social dancing]]

This example is adapted from Katz and Fodor (1963). It illustrates another aspect of the theory, which is the blocking of certain amalgamations by the selection restrictions. The set (h) of readings for *colorful ball* contains only four readings. In principle, the projection rule which amalgamates the two readings for *colorful* and the three readings for *ball* to derive readings for *colorful ball* could have produced six derived readings. But two of these derived readings violate the selection restriction which appears within angled brackets in reading (ii) of *colorful*. The selection restriction stipulates that this reading of *colorful* may be combined only with readings containing the marker (*Aesthetic Object*) or the marker (*Social Activity*). The 'dancing' reading of *ball* meets this requirement, but the other two readings do not. (This selection restriction is designed to capture the intuition that a cannon-ball and a child's bouncy rubber ball, for instance, cannot be picturesque in the sense that a graduation ball may be, though they might both be green with purple stripes.) Derived readings which would violate selection restrictions are not constructed. This blocking process captures the phenomenon of the disambiguation of an expression by its linguistic context; two constituents which each have multiple readings may have very few readings in combination. The limiting case of disambiguation is where no derived readings can be formed for a constituent at all (e.g., for *deaf ball* or *waterproof afterimage*). The absence of readings is the theory's reconstruction of the notion of semantic anomaly or (literally) meaninglessness.

The theory also contains definitions of the semantic properties and relations of a sentence and its constituents, definitions which apply to the SIUPM. For example, a constituent is defined as semantically ambiguous if the node dominating it in the SIUPM has more than one reading attached to it; two sentences are defined as full paraphrases of each other if the highest S node in each SIUPM has exactly the same set of readings attached to it. The

SIUPM for a sentence, together with a specification of each of its semantic properties, constitutes the SEMANTIC INTERPRETATION for that sentence.

3.2. GENERATIVE SEMANTICS

The theory of generative semantics evolved in the late 1960s out of a syntactic theory that assigned progressively more abstract deep structures to sentences. The arguments employed were of a kind characteristic of *Syntactic Structures* and subsequent work, particularly arguments based on selection restrictions and grammatical relations. Yet they led to 'deeper' and more semantically explicit deep structures, with correspondingly more work for the syntactic transformations relating deep structures to surface structures, but less work for the interpretive semantic rules relating them to semantic representations.

An early proposal for a relatively abstract syntactic analysis was Ross's (1969) argument that auxiliary verbs are, in deep structure, main verbs taking sentential complements. The deep structure assigned to the sentence (1) would be (3-6).

(1) Rain may be good for the hair.

(3-6)

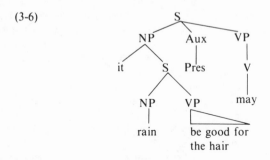

This deep structure is quite unlike the STANDARD theory's deep structure for (1), in which the auxiliary verb *may* appears between the subject and the main verb just as it does in the surface structure. In fact, (3-6) closely resembles the standard theory's deep structure for the synonymous sentence (2), which does contain an explicit complement clause in its surface structure.

(2) It is possible that rain is good for the hair.

On Ross's analysis, though not on the standard theory, the deep structure configurations for these two synonymous sentences are identical, so the interpretive semantic component has less to do in assigning them identical semantic representations. All it need do is note the synonymy of *may* and *be possible*.

The difference in surface structure between (1) and (2) must be accounted for on Ross's analysis. Since the deep structures are identical, the surface difference must be produced by the syntactic transformations. There is of course no sentence such as (3) parallel to (2).

(3) *It may that rain is good for the hair.[1]

Clearly, *may* and *be possible* do not behave exactly alike syntactically. A sentence with *may* must undergo the Subject Raising transformation so that its surface structure subject is the noun phrase which was the subject of its complement clause in deep structure. To capture this difference (and others) between auxiliary verbs and regular main verbs, the auxiliaries are assigned the syntactic feature [+*Aux*], and the Subject Raising rule is made obligatory for verbs with this feature. Thus, the syntactic SIMILARITIES between the two types of element are captured by calling them all verbs (marking them all [+*V*]) and by having them appear in the same deep structure configurations. The syntactic DIFFERENCES between them are produced by syntactic transformations sensitive to the [±*Aux*] feature contrast.

This analysis exhibits two features quite characteristic of the syntactic theory out of which generative semantics developed. One is that the single-clause sentence (1) is derived from a deep structure with two clauses; its auxiliary verb is the main verb of a higher clause in the deep structure. Many other constituents of surface clauses (e.g., adverbs, quantifiers, negation) have also been analyzed as the predicates of higher clauses at the level of deep structure posited by generative semantics.

For example, G. Lakoff (1965) observed that the question (4) and the negative sentence (5) both presuppose that some wife-beating has been occurring, and that they are synonymous, respectively, with the two-clause sentences (6) and (7).

(4) Do you beat your wife enthusiastically?
(5) You don't beat your wife enthusiastically.
(6) Are you enthusiastic in beating your wife?
(7) You are not enthusiastic in beating your wife.

(Note: For many speakers, this is true of only one reading of (4) and (5). These sentences also have another reading which does not presuppose any wife-beating, and Lakoff's analysis is not intended to apply to this reading.) What is questioned and negated in the relevant interpretations of (4) and (5)

---

1. An asterisk before an expression is used to indicate its ungrammaticality.

is thus the adverb only; the scope of the question and the negation is not, as it is in other sentences, the whole sentence or verb phrase.

The standard theory deep structure for sentence (4), for example, would be (3-7).

(3-7)

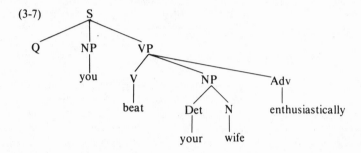

But (3-7) does not explain the special scope restriction, and does not predict the paraphrase relation between the one-clause sentence (4) and the two-clause sentence (6). These facts can be captured by assigning to (4) a two-clause deep structure like (3-8), in which the adverb appears as the verb of the questioned main clause.

(3-8)

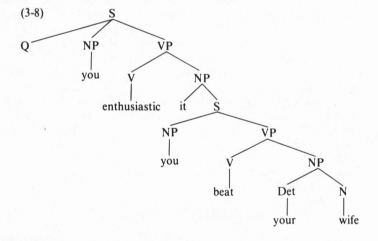

This two-clause deep structure, which is what underlies the two-clause sentence (6), is thus claimed also to underlie the one-clause sentence. To derive the latter, an optional Adverb Lowering transformation is needed that will move the higher verb down as an adverb in the subordinate clause, and delete the remainder of the main clause. The deep structure and transformational derivation of (4) are thus more complex than on the standard theory. But, once again, identity of meaning correlates with identity of deep structure where, on the standard theory, the deep structures would be quite different and interpretive semantic rules would have to capture the meaning relation between (4) and (6).

The other point exemplified in the analysis of auxiliaries as main verbs is the breakdown of traditional category distinctions. This too is characteristic of other generative semantics analyses. Nouns, verbs, adjectives, prepositions, all partially overlap in their syntactic behavior, just as auxiliaries partially overlap with main verbs. Given only traditional (or standard theory) classifications, one and the same syntactic transformation must often apply to items in distinct syntactic classes. Generalization of the transformations can be achieved by combining two or more traditional classes into one broader class, which is then all that the structural analysis of the transformation need mention. All the members of this more general class would then appear in the same structural position in phrase markers. The differences between them would be captured only by assigning them different syntactic features.

Another example of this is G. Lakoff's (1965) proposal that verbs and adjectives should be classified as members of a single category *VERB*, differentiated by the features [+*Adj*] and [−*Adj*]. The motivation for this analysis includes the following. There are synonymous sentences differing only in the category of their predicates, such as (8) and (9).

(8) John considers Mary's feelings.
(9) John is considerate of Mary's feelings.

The grammatical relations between *John* and *considers* and between *John* and *is considerate* are intuitively the same, as are those between *considers* and *Mary's feelings* and *is considerate of* and *Mary's feelings*. And the selection restrictions on the subjects and objects of these predicates are also alike; *Monday*, for example, can be the subject of neither. To capture these similarities, Lakoff proposed assigning pairs of sentences like (8) and (9) deep structures identical except for the features [±*Adj*]. *Considerate* as well as *consider* appears in this phrase marker in a position where, for the standard theory, only true verbs can appear. The copula *be* is not present but is introduced in the course of deriving (9) by a transformation triggered by the feature [+*Adj*]. The deep structure does contain the preposition *of*, and another transformation, triggered by the feature [−*Adj*], deletes *of* in the course of deriving (8). (The preposition is assumed to follow *consider* as well as *considerate* in underlying structures, since it shows up in a nominalization such as *John's consideration of Mary's feelings*.) Thus, the two sentences have virtually the same deep structure, which exhibits some of the properties of each of the two distinct surface sentences. The differences between the two sentences are treated as superficial differences, introduced in the course of the transformational derivation and represented by only a single feature at the deep structure level.

It has since been observed (Bach, 1968) that predicate nominals also share properties with verbs and adjectives. There are synonymous pairs such as (10) and (11), and (12) and (13).

(10) The attempt was a failure.
(11) The attempt failed.
(12) Boris is a brute to Jane.
(13) Boris is brutal to Jane.

Predicate nominals like *a failure* and *a brute* share selection restrictions and grammatical relations with adjectives and verbs: like adjectives, they take a copula; like verbs, they must agree with their subjects; unlike both, they do not prepose around nouns after Relative Clause Reduction. Since the differences can be treated as differences in transformational derivation, all three types of predicate can be assigned the same deep structure category and position. Predicate nominals are represented, in effect, as verbs. On the standard theory, deep structures are much more similar to surface structures; predicate nominals and verbs have quite distinct representations. Their similarities must therefore be captured in the dictionary and semantic component. But Bach's more abstract syntactic analysis already does much of what the standard theory's interpretive semantic component would have to do.

Systematic differences of meaning, as well as identity of meaning, have also been captured transformationally in generative semantics grammars. For example, many adjectives (e.g., *hard*, *thick*) have corresponding, morphologically related inchoative verbs (*harden*, *thicken*).

(14) The metal is hard.
(15) The metal hardened.
(16) The sauce is thick.
(17) The sauce thickened.

In (15), *harden* means 'become hard'; in (17), *thicken* means 'become thick.' G. Lakoff (1965) proposed deriving the inchoative verbs from their corresponding adjectives in the context of *become* (or rather, an abstract pro-verb resembling *become* syntactically and semantically but having no phonological realization). Thus the deep structure for (17) would be (3-9).

(3-9)

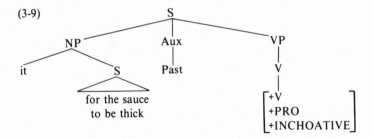

Subject Raising transforms (3-9) into (3-10).

(3-10)

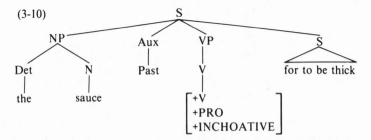

The complementizer *for* and the copula *to be* are deleted, leaving only *thick* under the lower S node. Then an Inchoative transformation applies, substituting *thick* for the abstract inchoative verb to produce a verb with the phonological form of *thick* but also the feature [*+INCHOATIVE*]. (3-10) is thereby transformed into (3-11).

(3-11)

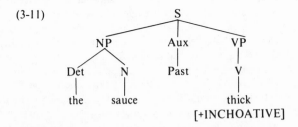

A late 'spelling' rule must then supply the ending *-en* to *thick*.

A similar analysis was also proposed for causative verbs such as *thicken* in the sentence (18).

(18)   The chef thickened the sauce.

Here, the subject of *thicken* is an agent, and that which thickens appears as the direct object. (18) says that the chef caused the sauce to thicken, and it is assigned the deep structure (3-12), which makes this meaning explicit.

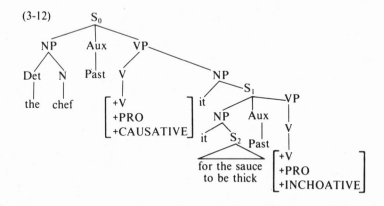

(3-12)

Notice that the clause S_1 in (3-12) is identical with (3-9). This is because the complement of the causative verb is the inchoative sentence (17) (*The sauce thickened*). The derivation proceeds just as for (17), but on the last cycle the newly formed inchoative verb *thicken* is itself raised by a Causative transformation, which substitutes it for the abstract causative pro-verb and thereby derives the causative verb *thicken*. The result is the reduction of the three-clause deep structure (3-12) to the single-clause surface structure (18).

In this fashion, derivational morphology is accommodated within the syntactic component. The relation between *thick* and *thicken* is determined by deep structures and syntactic transformations, not by special morphological rules in the lexicon as in the standard theory. Furthermore, once the necessary transformations have been added to the grammar, similar derivations can be provided for causative and inchoative verbs for which there are NO morphologically related source words. For example, *gain* means 'come to have.' The word *gain* can therefore be omitted from the dictionary of English and derived by the Inchoative transformation—as long as we are prepared to posit an abstract lexical item with the phonological form of *gain* but the meaning and distribution of *have*. Similarly, if *kill* means 'cause to die,' then *kill* can be derived by the Causative transformation from a hypothetical lexical item with the phonological form of *kill* but the meaning and distribution of *die* (which in turn would be derived by the Inchoative transformation from an item meaning 'dead'). The only difference between these derivations and those for verbs like *thicken* is that since these hypothetical verbs do not ever appear UNtransformed in surface structures, the Inchoative and Causative transformations MUST apply to them.

The significance of these analyses is that aspects of the internal semantic analysis of lexical items are captured syntactically. To the standard theory, a word like *kill* is a single, indivisible syntactic unit; the analysis of its meaning into the concepts of causing, becoming and death would be represented only in its dictionary entry. We have already seen that abstract syntactic analyses do part of the job of an interpretive semantic component, in that they assign identical deep structures to many structurally different but synonymous surface structures. Now they can do the rest too, for they can also analyze word meanings into components. Therefore no further semantic interpretation rules are needed at all. The deep structures themselves can do duty as semantic representations.

Notice that in this theory, lexical items (including abstract and hypothetical lexical items) play essentially the same role as semantic markers in Katz's theory. They represent the minimal concepts out of which more complex meanings are composed. The major difference here is that lexical items have phonological properties and are thus language-specific, while Katz's semantic markers are not individuated phonologically and so can be used to represent meaning in all languages. And in fact the next step in the development of generative semantics was a modification of derivations like those above into derivations whose deep structures contain not lexical items but universal semantic elements. This move was made in McCawley (1968a).

A causative sentence such as (19) would now be assigned the deep structure (3-13).

(19) We killed dragons.

(3-13)

The terminal elements in this phrase marker are written in capitals to indicate that they are not language-specific lexical items but are universal semantic primitives.[2] A new transformational derivation goes along with this new deep structure. Transformations are no longer dependent on specific lexical items, as the Causative and Inchoative transformations were. Instead, there are general transformations which have the effect of collecting various semantic primitives together under a single node. In (3-13), when these transformations have collected *CAUSE, BECOME* and *DEAD* into a single constituent, they can be jointly substituted for by the English lexical item *kill*. Notice that unlike lexical insertion in a standard grammar, which inserts lexical items into 'empty' deep structure trees (or substitutes them for dummy terminal symbols), lexical insertion in a generative semantics grammar now substitutes a lexical item for a complex of semantic elements that represent its meaning.

The derivation of sentence (19) (*We killed dragons*) from the deep structure (3-13) proceeds by application of the Subject Raising transformation to raise *DRAGONS* into the clause above. Then a newly introduced 'collection' transformation called Predicate Raising raises *DEAD* and adjoins it to the higher predicate *BECOME*, to form the composite verb *BECOME DEAD*. Thus, the result of this is the derived structure (3-14).

(3-14)

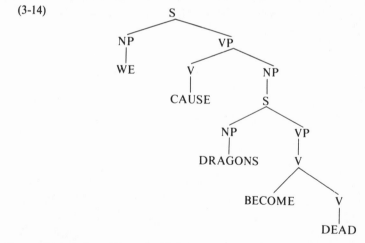

2. For expository purposes, I have simplified the phrase marker (3-13) by using semantic 'primitives' which are probably really not primitive at all, i.e., the concepts they represent probably should be analyzed further into complexes of simpler ones. For example, *DRAGONS* is unlikely to correspond to an atomic concept, and it has been proposed that *DEAD* can be dispensed with in favor of *NOT* together with *ALIVE*. In some cases we may not even know what the proper analysis is, and then the symbols that are used function as temporary placeholders, with the understanding that they will be replaced with more detailed representations as research proceeds. The same is true of the semantic markers in an interpretive semantic theory.

Notice that (3-14) has only two clauses, but one of them contains a complex verb. Subject Raising then raises *DRAGONS* again, into the highest clause, and Predicate Raising raises *BECOME DEAD* and adjoins it to *CAUSE*. This produces the structure (3-15), in which there is only one clause, and the three original verbs have now been combined into a single constituent.

(3-15)

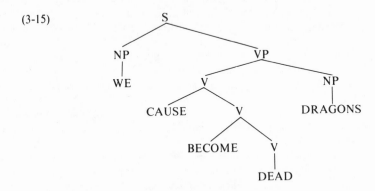

After these collection transformations have applied, lexical items can be substituted for semantic elements, subject to the usual condition on substitution transformations that only single constituents can be substituted for. In (3-15), for example, *kill* can substitute for *CAUSE BECOME DEAD*. But if Predicate Raising had not been applied on the highest cycle (i.e., if the derivation had stopped at the stage of (3-14)), then *kill* could not be substituted, since *CAUSE*, *BECOME* and *DEAD* would not form a single constituent. Rather, the sentence (20) would be derived, in which *die* has substituted for the semantic complex *BECOME DEAD*.

(20) We caused dragons to die.

If Predicate Raising did not apply on either cycle, the structure at the point of lexical insertion would be (3-13), and each verb would have to be substituted for independently, giving the sentence (21).

(21) We caused dragons to become dead.

Three sentences, (19), (20), and (21), are thus derivable from the same underlying structure (3-13), depending on what options are taken in the transformational component. The synonymy of these sentences is thus predicted without recourse to semantic projection rules.

Predicate Raising is a very general rule and it sometimes results in a semantic complex which does not correspond to any lexical item in the language. For example, with *ANGRY* in place of *DEAD* in (3-13), Predicate Raising of *ANGRY* would give *BECOME ANGRY*, and since there is no verb in English with this meaning, the structure could not undergo lexicalization into an English sentence; it would have to be discarded. Notice, however, that *BECOME ANGRY* would be a necessary intermediate stage in the derivation of *CAUSE BECOME ANGRY* which would underlie the causative verb *to anger*. Hence *BECOME ANGRY* must not be discarded at the point of Predicate Raising. Rather, Predicate Raising must be allowed to apply freely, and unlexicalizable products of it subsequently filtered out. The earlier approach employing the Inchoative and Causative transformations had to filter out improper derivations by marking each lexical item for the various transformations it could or must undergo. But the present approach can simply use the dictionary of the language to impose the necessary restrictions—if the language contains no lexical item corresponding to a bundle of semantic elements in a phrase marker (e.g., *BECOME ANGRY*), then the derivation will necessarily block at the point of lexical substitution, for there will be nothing to substitute. In this way the dictionary provides an automatic filter on derivations.

Once syntactic structures are allowed to contain universal semantic elements as their terminal symbols, the syntactic deep structures of sentences can serve as their semantic representations. The interpretive semantic component can be dispensed with entirely—hence the name "generative semantics." The derivation of a surface structure begins with the generation of a semantic representation which is simultaneously a syntactic deep structure, and this is then mapped by the successive application of syntactic transformations onto a surface structure. There is no LEVEL of structure, like the standard level of deep structure, which mediates the correlation of semantic representations with surface structures. The rules which operate on structures containing semantic elements are claimed to have exactly the same general formal properties as the more familiar syntactic transformations which apply at later stages of derivations. Indeed, many of the standard cyclic transformations such as Passive, Equi-NP Deletion, Subject Raising, and so on must apply BEFORE lexical substitution, i.e., must apply to phrase markers containing semantic elements rather than lexical items. (This is because these rules are needed as 'collection transformations' to group semantic elements together ready for lexicalization.) The point of lexical substitution might have been taken to define a significant linguistic level intermediate between the semantic and surface levels, but in fact it has been argued that lexical insertion is 'staggered,' i.e., that not all lexical items are inserted at the same stage of a derivation. Some lexical items may be substituted before the application of a certain transformation and some lexical items after it. (The terms 'prelexical transformation' and 'postlexical transformation,' though they are often used informally, are therefore not strictly defined.)

The theory of generative semantics is the offspring of collaboration between a number of linguists. What I have presented here is a composite.

The central principles are generally accepted, but because the theory is continuously evolving, the reader will find some variation in the deep structures and rules proposed in generative semantics publications at different dates and by different authors.

3.3. THE EXTENDED STANDARD THEORY

The pushing back of the level of deep syntactic structure until it becomes indistinguishable from the semantic level has been resisted. Chomsky has argued that constructions which are assigned identical underlying structures in generative semantics grammars exhibit significant syntactic differences which cannot naturally be captured by a difference of transformational derivation but only by a difference of deep structure. Since this may be true of synonymous sentences, the level of deep structure must be distinct from the level of semantic representation, and the grammar must include an interpretive semantic component.

The first and most detailed argument of this kind is contained in *Remarks on Nominalization* (1970b), where Chomsky disputed the common claim that a 'derived nominal' such as (22) should be derived transformationally from the sentential deep structure (23).

(22) John's eagerness to please
(23) John is eager to please.

Despite the similarity of meaning and, to some extent, of structure between these two expressions, Chomsky argued that they are not transformationally related. His objections do not preclude ALL transformational derivations; indeed, many of his arguments turn on a contrast between derived nominals and 'gerundive nominals' such as (24), which, it is claimed, CAN be transformationally generated.

(24) John's being eager to please

A gerundive nominal does exhibit sentential structure. For example, it takes adverbs, as in (25). By contrast, a derived nominal such as (26) takes only adjectives, as ordinary noun phrases do.

(25) John's obviously being eager to please
(26) John's obvious eagerness to please (*John's obviously eagerness to please)

A derived nominal also resembles other noun phrases in taking a determiner, in requiring a preposition before a modifying noun phrase, and in pluralizing.

(27) the proofs of the theorem (*the proofs the theorem)

But a gerundive nominal, like a sentence, has a subject rather than a determiner, does not take a preposition (unless there happens to be one associated with the verb in sentential contexts), and cannot pluralize.

(28) *the proving the theorem (cf., John's proving the theorem)
(29) *John's cleverly proving of the theorem (cf., John's cleverly proving the theorem)
(30) *John's provings the theorem

These differences between derived nominals and sentences COULD perhaps be handled by a transformational derivation if sufficient constraints were imposed on the rules (though it is hard to see what sentence could serve as the underlying form for a plural nominal like (27)). But this treatment, even if technically possible, would apparently miss the generalization that all the DIFFERENCES between derived nominals and sentences are SIMILARITIES between derived nominals and ordinary noun phrases. This generalization is captured by postulating, as Chomsky does, the direct generation of derived nominals AS noun phrases in deep structures.

The transformational treatment is typical of generative semantics grammars, because in the absence of interpretive semantic rules, the semantic similarities between derived nominals and sentences must be captured by assigning them similar deep structures. However, the consequent postulation of a Nominalizing transformation for derived nominals makes it difficult to explain the fact that derived nominals (unlike gerundive nominals) correspond only to DEEP structure sentential structures. There is, for example, no derived nominal (31) corresponding to the transformationally DERIVED sentential configuration (32).

(31) *John's easiness to please
(32) John is easy to please.

Sentence (32) is derived from a deep structure of the form (33) by the Object Raising or Tough Movement transformation.

(33) To please John is easy.

The fact that (32) has no corresponding derived nominal can be explained on Chomsky's hypothesis that derived nominals are simply ordinary noun phrases whose head noun happens to bear a LEXICAL relation to some verb or adjective in the language. For at the lexical level, the adjective *easy* is not permitted to precede an infinitival complement. (The fact that it does so at the surface level in (32) is due to the operation of transformations.) Hence if the lexical properties of the nominal *easiness* parallel those of the adjective *easy*, then this nominal obviously cannot appear in the context (31) before an infinitival complement.

For these reasons, Chomsky rejected the abstract syntactic analysis on which derived nominals have sentential deep structures, and proposed that they be generated directly as nominals. They are like sentences (and gerundive nominals) in some respects, but unlike them in others. Contrary to the generative semantics approach, Chomsky uses the syntactic deep structure to capture the differences, and proposes capturing the similarities in the lexicon by assigning a single lexical entry to both *easy* and *easiness*, *eager* and *eagerness*, *prove* and *proof*, etc. (See Section 5.2 for further discussion.) This is what has been called the 'lexicalist' analysis of derived nominals, and it is characteristic of the extended standard theory.

In insisting on a level of deep syntactic structure distinct from the semantic level, and on the need for interpretive semantic rules, the extended standard theory is in agreement with Katz's theory. The fundamental difference between the two concerns the structures that are input to these semantic rules. In Section 3.1 we observed that Katz has claimed that only deep syntactic structures need be input to the semantic component, for these contain all the information relevant to the operation of the semantic projection rules. But Chomsky (1970a) has since argued that phonologically specified surface structures must be semantically interpreted in addition to deep structures. And Jackendoff (1972) has argued that end-of-cycle structures must be semantically interpreted (i.e., that some interpretation rules apply within the transformational cycle, to the structure which exists after all the syntactic transformations have applied on that cycle, and before any apply on the next).

In support of surface structure interpretation, Chomsky observed that the focus and presupposition of a sentence are regularly correlated with its stress and intonation pattern, and must be characterized in terms of surface structure constituents. Let us consider the sentence (34), with main stress on the word *shirt*.

(34) Was he warned to look out for an ex-convict with a red SHIRT?

This sentence has several possible interpretations, which differ with respect to which part of the sentence is questioned (its focus), and which part is taken for granted (presupposed) in the asking of the question. On one interpretation, (34) presupposes that he was warned to look out for something, and asks whether that something was an ex-convict with a red shirt. Now THIS interpretation COULD perhaps be handled by a grammar in which only deep structures are semantically interpreted. For (34) on this interpretation could be assigned a deep structure of the form (35), and the deep structure division of this sentence into noun phrase and verb phrase would then correspond exactly with the semantic division into presupposition and focus.

(35) *Q* What he was warned to look out for was an ex-convict with a red shirt.

However, not all of the possible interpretations of (34) lend themselves so readily to a deep structure analysis. For example, there is an interpretation on which (34) presupposes that he was warned to look out for an ex-convict with something red, and asks whether that something was a shirt. Here the deep structure approach fails, for there is no well-formed deep structure of the form (36) from which (34) on this interpretation could be derived.

(36) *Q* What he was warned to look out for an ex-convict with red was a shirt.

A deep structure account of focus and presupposition will run into trouble in all cases where the focus is a surface structure constituent which does not correspond to any single deep structure constituent. For example, on one interpretation of (37) the focus is *certain to win*. But the deep structure of (37) is (38), in which *certain* and *win* are not even in the same clause.

(37) Is John believed to be certain to win?
(38) *Q NP* believes [[for John to win] to be certain]

And there appears to be no general way of predicting, at this level of derivation, that the focus includes just *certain* and *win* but not the other constituents of the sentence. Furthermore, this deep structure might have been transformed not into (37) but into the surface structure (39), which has no interpretation with focus on just *certain* and *win*.

(39) Is it believed to be certain that John will win?

If sentences with the same deep structure but different surface structures can have different foci and presuppositions, then it clearly cannot be the deep structure that the interpretation rules apply to. The position of the main stress in a sentence contributes to determining its possible foci; on the assumption that stress is assigned at the surface structure level, surface structures must therefore be the input to the interpretation rules.

Jackendoff (1972, Chapter 4) has argued for an interpretive approach to pronominalization, as opposed to the commonly assumed transformational approach; and he has observed that the interpretive rules must apply to end-of-cycle structures. The transformational approach derives the sentence (40) (on one interpretation) from the deep structure (41), by reduction of the second *John*$_i$ (under identity, including referential indices, with the first *John*$_i$).

    (40) John wanted Sam to congratulate him.
    (41) John $_i$ wanted [Sam$_j$ congratulate John$_i$]

But Jackendoff argues for the deep structure (42), which already contains the pronoun, and he postulates an interpretive rule which will mark the pronoun *him* as coreferential (on one interpretation) with *John*.

    (42) John wanted [Sam congratulate him]

This approach avoids what is known as the Bach-Peters paradox—the fact that on the transformational treatment, a sentence like (43) would need the infinite deep structure (44).

    (43) The man who deserves it will get the prize he wants.
    (44) The man [who deserves the prize [which the man [who. . . .] wants]] will get the prize [which the man [who deserves the prize [which. . . .] wants]].

It also extends naturally to coreference relations with 'pronominal epithets' such as *the poor thing* in (45), which could not be derived by the transformational reduction of a repeated noun phrase.

    (45) We took the bird in but the poor thing died that afternoon.

The interpretive theory of pronouns can also deal naturally with NON-coreference relations, as between *John* and *someone else* in (46).

    (46) John wanted Mary to marry someone else.

And once the Pronominalization transformation is given up in favor of an interpretive rule, the arguments that the transformation must be cyclic (see Ross, 1967) become arguments that the interpretive rule must apply within the transformational cycle.

    Another argument for derived structure interpretation rules concerns the scope of quantifiers and negation. From *Syntactic Structures* on, there have been disagreements about the semantic effects of reordering transformations on sentences containing quantifiers. Chomsky (1957) said that the two sentences (47) and (48) differ in meaning, with (48) entailing that everyone knows the SAME two languages.

(47) Everyone in the room knows two languages.
(48) Two languages are known by everyone in the room.

Since these two sentences are assumed to be related by the Passive transformation, it would follow that the Passive transformation changes meaning. Another way of putting this is that if (47) and (48) have the same deep structure but different meanings, it cannot be true that deep structures fully determine the meanings of sentences.

Katz and Postal (1964), in arguing that deep structures do fully determine meaning, claimed that these two sentences ARE synonymous, that they are both ambiguous, and that the only effect of the surface structure is to determine which interpretation is the preferred or more natural one. This, like the preference for one rather than another interpretation of an ambiguous word, is something that the grammar might reasonably not be required to account for. The debate is complicated by the fact that the intuitions of some speakers, for some sentences, follow Chomsky's, while others follow Katz and Postal's.

More recently, other examples have been given which are claimed to be truly unambiguous. Jackendoff (1972, Chapter 8) claims that the sentence (49) is unambiguous; it says that many of the arrows have the property of not having hit the target.

(49) Many of the arrows didn't hit the target.

But, according to Jackendoff, (49) has no synonymous passive. The passive sentence which is most directly related to it syntactically is (50).

(50) The target wasn't hit by many of the arrows.

But (50) is claimed to have the different interpretation that not many of the arrows have the property of having hit the target. If this is so (and it is debatable), the only alternative to allowing the Passive transformation to change meaning is to prevent it deriving (50) from (49) by adding contextual restrictions concerning the presence and position of quantifiers. But this would complicate the rule considerably. Jackendoff therefore argues that transformations do NOT necessarily preserve meaning and that the scope relations between negation and quantifiers in a sentence must be determined AFTER the Passive transformation has applied.

The extended standard theory thus directly contradicts the Katz and Postal principle that transformations do not affect meaning and that only deep structures need be semantically interpreted. However, Chomsky and Jackendoff have not abandoned this principle entirely. Rather, they maintain that it is true only of grammatical relations; the grammatical relations relevant to meaning are those represented at the deep structure level. It is phenomena such as focus and presupposition, coreference, and the scope of logical elements (which perhaps seem, in a way yet to be made precise, to form a natural class) that are to be determined by the interpretation of derived structures.

Katz has, tentatively, resisted this revision of the standard theory. He claims (1972, Chapter 8) that focus and presupposition, for example, are RHETORICAL properties of sentences rather than true semantic properties. The fact that they are determined by derived structures therefore does not invalidate the Katz and Postal principle since this is intended to apply only to meaning in the strict sense. For the scope relations between logical elements such as quantifiers and negation. Katz takes the opposite tack. He admits that these are truly semantic properties, but challenges the data by claiming that scope relations are NOT changed by the application of transformational rules.

Generative semantics, on the other hand, has accepted many of the observations on which the extended standard theory is based. G. Lakoff (1971) has agreed that the semantic representations of sentences must include specifications of focus and presupposition. These, and specifications of some other properties too, are not an integral part of underlying phrase markers but are merely associated with them, so that a GS semantic representation has the form $(P_1, PR, Top, F, \ldots)$ where PR is a conjunction of presuppositions, Top is the topic of the sentence, and F is its focus. P_1 is the underlying phrase marker for the sentence; clearly it can no longer be identified with the semantic representation, though it is still a major part of it.

Generative semantics is also in agreement with the standard theory about the relevance to meaning of transformationally derived phrase markers. A generative semantics grammar has no interpretive semantic rules, and its meaning representations consist primarily of deep structure phrase markers. How, then, can the semantic effect of the transformational component be accounted for? Arguments like Jackendoff's in connection with quantifier scope and the Passive transformation suggest that it can't be. These arguments take the general form of demonstrations that transformations which would derive sentences from deep structures uniquely specifying their meanings are either impossible or at least prohibitively complicated. It is true that Katz and Postal managed to establish meaning-preserving derivations, by postulating the deep structure constituents *Neg*, *Q*, and *Imp* (see Section 3.1), which simultaneously carried meaning information and governed the application of the transformations associated with those meanings. But those analyses dealt with only a handful of transformations. To preserve pronominalization and quantifier scope relations throughout the transformational derivation would appear to require constraints on a great many different movement and deletion rules, which interact with each other in complex ways.

The generative semantics solution to this problem takes the form of GLOBAL CONSTRAINTS on transformational derivations. A global constraint or global rule is one which (unlike standard syntactic transformations) may refer to two or more different and NONADJACENT structures in a derivation. G. Lakoff (1971) has proposed global derivational constraints which prevent transformations from applying to produce a derived structure whose interpretation would diverge from the meaning represented by the semantic representation which initiates the derivation. The constraints compare derived syntactic structures (possibly end-of-cycle structures) with semantic representations. These are required to bear some designated relation to each other, and the application of any transformation that would destroy this relation is disallowed. Since they correlate meaning representations with derived syntactic structures, these global constraints achieve the same effect as interpretive rules which apply to derived syntactic structures. They do not take the same form as interpretive rules, but whether they are a genuine alternative or are only 'mere notational variants' of interpretive rules is unclear at present. (See Sections 3.5 and 4.1 for further discussion.) The important point for our present purposes is that the postulation of some quite simple and general global constraints, which will govern the whole transformational derivation, makes it unnecessary to add contextual restrictions to each individual transformation in order to capture its effect on semantic scope relations.

In this preliminary comparison of the three theories, we should also note that the extended standard theory's conception of semantic representations is rather different from that of Katz's theory or generative semantics. Katz's semantic representations are complexes of semantic markers attached to the nodes of deep structure phrase markers. GS semantic representations are syntactic phrase markers with semantic elements as their terminal symbols (together with specifications of focus, etc., as indicated above). But on the extended standard theory, more than one phrase marker in the syntactic derivation of a sentence must be semantically interpreted, since some semantic information is contained in deep structures and some in derived structures. Therefore, either the semantic information derived from these different phrase markers must be integrated somehow into a single semantic representation, or else the semantic representation of a sentence must consist of a number of separate parts.

Jackendoff (1972) has opted for the latter alternative. He proposes that the semantic representation for a sentence consists of at least four distinct elements: a representation of FUNCTIONAL STRUCTURE (roughly, what are the subjects and objects of which predicates); a TABLE OF COREFERENCE indicating which noun phrases are interpreted as referring to the same things; a representation of FOCUS AND PRESUPPOSITION; and a representation of MODAL STRUCTURE (roughly, the scope relations between elements such as quantifiers, negation, modal verbs). (See Section 5.5 for more details.)

In very recent work, Chomsky (1975, Chapter 3) has argued for the other alternative, i.e., integrated semantic representations, as in the other theories. But this is a part of the very radical claim that surface structures and ONLY surface structures are to be semantically interpreted. This claim would be quite implausible if made about standard surface structures for Katz and Postal were clearly correct in their observation that semantically relevant information about grammatical relations is missing from surface structures because constituents have been reordered or deleted by the transformations. But the surface structures that Chomsky assumes are supplemented with 'traces,' which mark sites from which constituents have been moved by transformations. The traces in effect encode information about deep structure configurations into surface structures. Semantically relevant deep grammatical relations are thus represented simultaneously with the surface configurations of constituents which determine scope relations (see Chapter 6 for further discussion).

Finally, it should be observed that all three of the theories outlined so far differ in their conception of deep structure. There is an obvious difference between standard theory deep structures and the more abstract GS deep structures which do double duty as semantic representations. The extended standard theory has moved away from the standard theory in the opposite direction. Its deep structures are less abstract even than those of the standard theory, i.e., they differ less from surface structures. This is because, as we have seen, some traditional transformations such as Pronominalization have been dispensed with in the extended standard theory, and replaced by semantic interpretation rules. Syntactic derivations are correspondingly shorter, and the deep structures that initiate them are shallower. These variations in the depth of deep structures on the three theories amount to different views about the proper division of labor between syntactic and semantic rules in correlating the meanings and forms of sentences.

3.4 FILLMORE AND GRUBER

Fillmore's theory of case relations may be more familiar to many readers than the other semantic theories presented so far. It has been employed as a descriptive framework by field linguists, and has been applied in the study of language acquisition (see Brown, 1973). But it is no longer receiving as much attention from theoretical linguists as it was a few years ago. The reason, perhaps, is this: the theory defines a level of deep structure more abstract and more 'semantic' than the standard deep structure level, and correspondingly employs fewer interpretive semantic rules. Those who might be expected to be sympathetic to this position, i.e., generative semanticists, have in fact overtaken it. GS has a deep structure level IDENTICAL to the semantic level, and has correspondingly NO interpretive semantic rules at all.

Fillmore (1968) proposed that the deep structure of any sentence consists of a MODALITY constituent (roughly, but only roughly, equivalent to the *Aux* constituent of standard grammars) and a PROPOSITION. The proposition consists of a verb followed by a sequence of one or more case categories, each of which is developed as a case marker (preposition, postposition, or case affix), and a noun phrase. For example, the sentence (51) would be assigned the deep structure (3-16).

(51) John opened the door with a key.

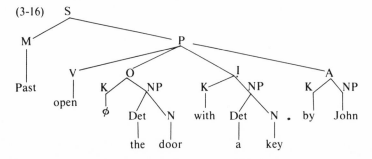

Note: M = Modality, P = Proposition, O = Objective case, I = Instrumental case, A = Agentive case, K = Case marker.

One of the noun phrases in the proposition will be raised into subject position by a transformation. For sentence (51), it is the agentive phrase *by John* that is raised, and it consequently loses its preposition.

The fact that no special distinction is drawn in deep structures between the subject of a sentence and its other noun phrases allows the similarity between sentences such as (51) and (52)–(54) to be captured at the deep structure level.

(52) The key opened the door.
(53) The door opened with a key.
(54) The door opened.

Sentences (52) and (53) will have deep structures identical to (3-16) except that they contain no agentive constituent. The deep structure of (54) will be like (3-16) but without either the agentive constituent or the instrumental constituent. The difference between the deep structures is thus solely a matter of how many and which of the case categories that can appear with *open* do appear with it. The lexical entry for *open* can specify simply that it obligatorily takes an object, and optionally takes an agent and an instrument. This contrasts with a standard grammar, which would assign (51), (52), and (53) quite different deep structures because they have different subjects. (It would also need to specify somehow that *open* can take an instrumental *with*-phrase only if its subject is not interpreted as an instrumental. This follows automatically from Fillmore's analysis.)

The fact that even a direct object can have a case marker in deep structure means that a pair of sentences as in (55) can be assigned the same deep structure, containing both *for the trouble* and *on John*.

(55) (a) We blamed the trouble on John.
     (b) We blamed John for the trouble.

A transformation will optionally rearrange the order of these two phrases, and whichever ends up next to the verb will lose its preposition. Again, the standard theory would assign (55) (a) and (b) different deep structures, because they have different direct objects, and the relation between them could not be captured in the syntactic component.

The Dative transformation, which relates sentences such as those in (56), also falls into place as just one among a number of rules which provide alternative orderings of the case categories.

(56) (a) I gave the books to my brother.
     (b) I gave my brother the books.

Another such phenomenon is the alternation with *with* phrases as in (57)–(59).

(57) (a) John sprayed paint on the wall.
     (b) John sprayed the wall with paint.
(58) (a) They loaded hay on the wagon.
     (b) They loaded the wagon with hay.
(59) (a) Bees are swarming in the garden.
     (b) The garden is swarming with bees.

The Passive transformation can also be incorporated into the rule that selects and positions the subject. Normally (i.e., in active sentences), if the proposition constituent contains an agent phrase this must be selected as the subject. But other phrases can be selected instead as long as this is 'registered' by insertion of the passive auxiliary *be* + *EN*.

Fillmore's theory provides a way of relating causative verbs with their noncausative counterparts. The verb *open* in (51) is causative, and the verb *open* in (54) is a noncausative inchoative, but Fillmore takes them to be one and the same verb differentiated only by their different case frames. In particular, he assigns them the same semantic representation. The difference in meaning between the two sentences is ascribed not to the verb but to the presence or absence of an agent phrase. Morphologically unrelated causative and inchoative verbs such as *kill* and *die* can be treated in a similar way. They will be specified as synonymous, but where *kill* obligatorily takes an agent, *die* obligatorily does not. Pairs of verbs related as converses, such as *like* and *please* in the sentences (60) and (61), can also be regarded as synonyms, differing not even in case frames, but only with respect to which case must be selected as the subject.

> (60) The audience liked the overture.
> (61) The overture pleased the audience.

Fillmore's treatment of converse verbs is very like the generative semantics treatment, which uses a prelexical Flip or Psych-Movement transformation to derive a sentence like (61) from an underlying structure resembling (60). (See Postal, 1970, and the example in Section 4.4). The sentence-initial position of verbs and the nondifferentiation of subjects in underlying structures has also become a feature of generative semantics, though for somewhat different reasons (see McCawley, 1970). The similarities between the two theories are clear. But there are also significant differences, which the treatment of causatives reveals.

Fillmore assumed that the causative element in the meaning of *kill* would be introduced by interpretation of the agent phrase. Generative semantics, on the other hand, has drawn out the relation between agent and causation quite explicitly in underlying structures by representing the agent phrase as the subject of a semantic predicate *CAUSE* (see Section 3.2). In other words, one of Fillmore's case categories has been identified in GS grammars with a specified argument (the 'subject') of a relational semantic element. The SYNTACTIC relation between a noun phrase and a lexical verb is traced back to a deeper relation between SEMANTIC elements. Another example of this is Lakoff's (1968) proposal that instrumental phrases appear in underlying structures as the object of the verb *use* (or the semantic predicate *USE*). The sentence (51) (*John opened the door with a key*) would be derived from a structure of the form (62).

> (62) John used a key for [John open the door]

(The complement clause *John open the door* in (62) would of course itself be further analyzed since it contains a causative verb.) Here, too, a Fillmore case category has been identified with one of the arguments of a semantic predicate which represents a component of the meaning of the lexical verb.

These observations connect with a familiar objection to Fillmore's theory, which is that the set of case categories needed for the full description of natural languages, though it may be finite, is probably not small. Fillmore has identified six categories: agentive, instrumental, dative, factitive, locative and objective, the last of which is a rag-bag category that almost certainly must be further subdivided. Fillmore himself judges that even more categories will be needed. (Among those that have been suggested are goal, beneficiary, theme.) The large number of distinct case categories can be naturally handled, and indeed can be explained, by regarding Fillmore's underlying level of representation not as a genuine linguistic level but merely as an incomplete formulation of the semantic level. In Fillmore's underlying structures, lexical items appear as unanalyzed units. Only at the semantic level is a verb, for instance, analyzed into its semantic components. But it may be more revealing to regard the noun phrases which are associated in a variety of case relations with the LEXICAL verb as the arguments of the primitive SEMANTIC predicates into which it is analyzed. These semantic predicates typically have very few arguments, perhaps three at the most, but there are a lot of them and hence there will be a lot of distinguishable 'case categories.' (Those which Fillmore has identified appear to be those associated with semantic components that are particularly frequent or prominent, such as *CAUSE, USE, BECOME, AT*.)

This more frankly semantic approach to case minimizes the amount of arbitrary listing in the description of languages. It would no longer be necessary to list for each lexical verb of a language what case categories it can co-occur with, for this would be predictable from its internal semantic analysis, which must be given by the grammar anyway. Of course, the number and kind of arguments associated with each semantic predicate must be listed, but this too would have to be included anyway in the grammar (or, if universal, in the linguistic theory). As a contribution to semantics, therefore, it seems best to regard Fillmore's analyses as merely stepping stones on the way to a more complete specification of the meanings of verbs. Whether there are any SYNTACTIC properties of case categories that Fillmore's theory predicts but which are missed by the semantic approach is another question, and one that is not strictly the concern of this book. But we can at least presume that generative semantics is satisfied that no syntactic generalizations are lost by giving up the case structure representations in favor of more abstract semantic representations.

Turning to the response of the standard and extended standard theories to Fillmore's proposals, we find that both Katz and Jackendoff have quite explicitly identified case relations in terms of semantic elements. Katz (1972, Chapter 3) writes:

> Suppose we adopt the traditional notions of agent and recipient as, respectively, the instigator and performer of the action expressed in the verb and the receiver of this action. We might formalize the notions, roughly, as follows. A reading R denotes the agent if R substitutes for

the categorized variable subscripted i in a reading of a predicate of the form (3.85), and a reading R denotes the recipient if R substitutes for the categorized variable subscripted j, where $i \neq j$:

$$(3.85) \; (((\text{Activity}), (\quad), \ldots, (\ldots X_{<j>} \ldots), \ldots, (\quad)) \; X_{<i>} \;)$$

Katz's identification of the recipient is somewhat vague, and it may have to be tightened to distinguish this case category from others. But at least his formula (3.85) clearly defines the agent as the 'subject' of the semantic primitive (Activity). In a similar vein, Jackendoff (1972, Chapter 2) writes:

> The thematic relations can be defined in terms of . . . semantic subfunctions. Agent is the argument of CAUSE that is an individual; Source and Goal are the initial and final state arguments of CHANGE. Location will be defined in terms of a further semantic function BE that takes an individual (the Theme) and a state (the Location).

If a full semantic description does make Fillmore's case representations redundant, we would not expect the standard theory to adopt them. But there is also a positive reason for the standard theory to reject Fillmore's proposals. As Fillmore (1968) noted himself, his transformations are not meaning-preserving. The (a) and (b) sentences in (57)–(59) above do not mean exactly the same. For example, (57b) is usually taken to imply that John covered all (more or less) of the wall with paint, but (57a) is consistent with his having sprayed only a small patch. Fillmore commented: ". . .I am inclined to tolerate the reintroduction into grammatical theory of transformations with semantic import (of this highly restricted kind)." It is, however, a fundamental principle of the (nonextended) standard theory that transformations do not change meaning.

To the extended standard theory, on the other hand, which permits the semantic interpretation of derived syntactic structures, this property of Fillmore's rules would be no bar. However, Chomsky (1972a) has rejected case theory on other grounds. He has observed that the level at which interpretive rules should apply to pick up the semantic difference between sentences like (57) (a) and (b) is precisely the standard deep structure level. This is because the interpretations of the noun phrases in these sentences ARE preserved under STANDARD syntactic transformations such as Passive and Subject Raising.

(63) (a) Paint was sprayed on the wall by John. [perhaps only part of the wall, cf. (57a)]
   (b) The wall was sprayed with paint by John. [all of the wall, cf. (57b)]

(64) (a) Bees are certain to be swarming in the garden. [perhaps only part of the garden, cf. (59a)]
    (b) The garden is certain to be swarming with bees. [all of the garden, cf. (59b)]

Once these transformations have applied, identification of the noun phrases that have this semantic feature of 'completeness' would be difficult, because they can appear in a variety of positions in the derived phrase marker. To be most economical and general, the interpretation rule which assigns the 'completeness' feature must therefore apply BEFORE these transformations. But the meaning difference between sentence pairs like (57) (a) and (b) shows that this interpretive rule must apply AFTER Fillmore's subject-forming rule. In other words, it applies at the standard deep structure level.

This argument shows that acceptance of Fillmore's level of case representation does not allow one to dispense with the standard deep structure level. At best, BOTH levels would have to be admitted. Chomsky does not prove that adopting both levels would be incorrect, but he argues that a grammar which generated Fillmore's case structures and related them by meaning-changing rules to standard deep structures would be merely a notational variant of a grammar which directly generates standard deep structures and uses interpretive semantic rules to map them onto case structures.

Gruber's theory is roughly contemporaneous with Fillmore's and is similar to it in a number of fundamental respects. Gruber (1965, 1967) also proposed a level of representation 'shallower' than the semantic level but 'deeper' than the standard deep structure level. And he also used this level to relate sentences with converse verbs, sentences like (51), (52)–(54), and so on. I have concentrated on Fillmore's version of these proposals because his work is more readily available and more widely read than Gruber's. But the two theories are by no means identical, and one significant aspect of Gruber's should be emphasized.

Gruber called his proposed level of representation the PRELEXICAL LEVEL. As this indicates, the terminal elements of tree structures at this level are not lexical items but are, in effect, semantic primitives. Fillmore's underlying structures for sentences like (60) and (61) contain the two distinct lexical items *like* and *please* and his Subjectivalization transformation is sensitive to the difference between them. Which noun phrase is raised into subject position depends on which verb is present. By contrast, Gruber's prelexical representations of these sentences would be identical, and contain only semantic primitives common to both verbs. Transformations can apply to these prelexical representations BEFORE lexical items are inserted. Lexical items carry contextual specifications which govern the types of structure into which they can be inserted. Thus instead of deciding which transformations to apply on the basis of a previous choice of lexical item (which is Fillmore's approach), Gruber decides which lexical items to insert on the basis of which prelexical transformations have applied.

This is obviously closely akin to the prelexical transformations and post-transformational lexical insertion which are fundamental to generative semantics. Gruber's prelexical structures, at least in early versions of the theory, were less abstract and semantically explicit than GS underlying structures; like Fillmore, Gruber assumed that some interpretive semantic rules would still be needed. Also, Gruber does not require, as generative semantics does, that a lexical item can substitute only for a single constituent of the prelexical structure. His derivations therefore differ in details from GS derivations. But though these differences may turn out to be significant, the similarities also stand out. To a large extent, Gruber's theory has been absorbed by generative semantics.

Also, Gruber's system of THEMATIC RELATIONS (which are what correspond to the case relations of Fillmore's theory) have been adopted by Jackendoff as part of the semantic representation system of an extended standard theory grammar. However, Jackendoff does not accept the organizational principles of Gruber's theory; he rejects the prelexical level, and derives the thematic relations from standard deep structures by means of interpretive rules. (See Jackendoff, 1972, Chapter 2, which also contains a comparison of Gruber's theory with Fillmore's.)

I shall not discuss either Fillmore's theory or Gruber's any further in this book.

3.5. METHODOLOGICAL ISSUES

In this section I have thrown together a variety of methodological questions which rear their heads periodically in linguistics and particularly in semantics. I do not expect this discussion to keep their heads down for good, but it should at least reveal their features. To understand much of what goes on in semantic research, it is necessary to appreciate the difficulty of determining what kinds of argumentation are legitimate, and what empirical consequences a particular semantic theory will have.

I begin with the fact that it has been generally (though perhaps not universally) recognized that some of the arguments appealed to in the development of current linguistic theories do not establish what they were taken to establish. This doesn't mean that the conclusions drawn from these arguments must be false. After all, a linguistic theory inspired by a turnip field might conceivably turn out to be true, and the arguments at issue here are by no means as irrelevant as turnip fields. However it does mean that other arguments in support of these theories are needed. And we may gain some insight into what would count as a GOOD argument by diagnosing where the old ones went wrong.

The arguments in question concern the relation between syntax and semantics. As we saw in Section 3.3, the locus and even the existence of a linguistic level that mediates between the surface level and the semantic level is a major point of dispute between current semantic theories. In *Syntactic Structures*, Chomsky supported the claim that sentences with distinct surface structures should be derived from the same deep structure by pointing to the fact that these sentences have identical selection restrictions. For example, all and only the acceptable subjects of an active verb are acceptable as the agents of that verb in the passive, and all and only the acceptable objects of the verb in the active are acceptable subjects in the passive. (Consider the examples: *John admires sincerity*; *Sincerity is admired by John*; **Sincerity admires John*; **John is admired by sincerity*.) To set up distinct sets of selection restrictions, one for active sentences and one for passives, would miss the fact that one set is simply the inverse of the other. It would be more economical to derive active and passive sentences from the same deep structure, and impose a single set of selection restrictions on their common deep structure.

In *Aspects*, Chomsky further developed his theory of lexical insertion and the way in which it is governed by selection restrictions. A fundamental assumption was that lexical items which violate selection restrictions may not be inserted into deep structure phrase markers. Thus illicit combinations of words are never generated. Meanwhile, in *The Structure of a Semantic Theory*, Katz and Fodor had introduced selection restrictions in the semantic component. As outlined in Section 3.1, these restrictions governed the semantic projection rules and blocked the amalgamation of incompatible readings. Notice that this presupposes that deep structure phrase markers containing incompatible lexical items HAVE been generated.

Some of Chomsky's selection restrictions, imposed on syntactic structures, were identical with selection restrictions which, in Katz's theory, would be part of the semantic component. Thus the treatment of selection at this stage was schizophrenic. There were two distinct formal mechanisms, but it was not clear that there were two distinct phenomena to correspond to them or, if so, which examples fell into which category. Is the sentence (65) semantically anomalous or syntactically ill-formed?

(65) Colorless green ideas sleep furiously.

In 1957 Chomsky said the former; but his 1965 theory appears to imply the latter.

McCawley (1968b) took up the issue, and argued that all selection restrictions are semantic. He pointed out that whether or not a noun phrase is an acceptable subject for a predicate depends on an interaction of all the constituents of the noun phrase, not just upon some isolated and arbitrary feature of the head noun. For instance, if the sentence (66) is unacceptable because *corpse* does not qualify as a subject for *admire*, then so is the sentence (67).

(66) This corpse admires sincerity.
(67) This dead man admires sincerity.

But in (67), the unacceptability cannot be due to the noun *man* but must be ascribed to the properties of the adjective *dead*. For *man* certainly can appear in the subject of *admire*.

(68) This tall man admires sincerity.

To rule out (67) syntactically, it would be necessary to assign some syntactic feature to *dead*, and to complicate the selection restriction on *admire* by making it sensitive to the features of modifiers as well as of head nouns. But to do that would be to miss the real point, for these additions to the syntactic selection mechanisms would exactly duplicate the machinery of the semantic component. A sentence like (69) is just as unacceptable, and for the same reasons, as (66) and (67).

(69) This man that I proved that John was mistaken in believing to be alive admires sincerity.

But the fact that the subject phrase of (69) refers to a dead man is determined by the meanings of *prove*, *mistaken*, *believe* and *alive* and by the way in which these words are combined. It is determined, in other words, by the SEMANTIC content of the whole noun phrase. Furthermore, the fact that *admire* carries this selection restriction seems to be a fact about its meaning; *admire* surely could not mean what it does if it could accept without anomaly subject noun phrases referring to inanimate objects.

We should note that there is disagreement about how generally McCawley's conclusion holds. Katz (1972, Chapter 8) has argued that there do exist nonsemantic selection restrictions. He claims, for example, that *footwear* means the same as *articles of wearing apparel for the feet*, although the former selects the determiner *much* but not *many* or *three*, while the latter selects *many* and *three* but not *much*. Also, *addled* has been said to mean the same as *spoiled* or *rotten* but, unlike these latter words, to be restricted in application to eggs and brains; if so, its selection properties are not determined by its meaning.

Nevertheless, an enormous number of the observed selection restrictions, including many previously taken to be syntactic, are not arbitrary, are not language-specific, and are not idiosyncratic to particular lexical items.

Their source is quite obviously the meaning of the word—ANY word with that meaning would have the same restrictions on its distribution in intelligible sentences. These selection restrictions therefore must be regarded as semantic constraints, stemming from the meanings of the constituents that carry them and sensitive to the meanings of the constituents that they co-occur with. Some very general conclusions have, however, been drawn at various times from the assumption that selection restrictions are SYNTACTIC constraints, and these conclusions have in some cases not since been relinquished.

Katz and Postal, in arguing that deep structures contain all the information relevant to meaning (see Section 3.1), dispensed with apparent counter-examples by hypothesizing abstract constituents *Neg*, *Imp*, and *Q* to appear in deep structure and carry semantic information about sentence type. Now unless there is INDEPENDENT evidence for the presence of these elements in deep structures, Katz and Postal's observations only make the not very surprising point that deep structures COULD (at least in these cases) be packed with sufficient information to determine meaning. It would not follow that deep structures SHOULD be provided with this information i.e., that in an OPTIMAL grammar for a language only deep structures would be semantically interpreted. Katz and Postal did provide supporting arguments for their analysis, and characterized them as "independent syntactic arguments." But these arguments were based largely on selection restrictions.

It was observed, for example, that certain adverbs do not appear in interrogative sentences, though they do appear in declaratives. Thus, the interrogative (70) is unacceptable, while the declarative (71) is acceptable.

(70)   *Probably is he a doctor?
(71)   Probably he is a doctor.

If selection restrictions are syntactic, and constrain deep syntactic structures, then there will have to be some deep structure difference between interrogatives and declaratives to predict this selectional difference. So the presence of *Q* or something like it is apparently justified on syntactic grounds. But if instead the principles governing the selection of these adverbs are semantic, then no conclusion about the nature of syntactic deep structures follows. Instead of interpreting *Q* in deep structure, the semantic rules might (for all these observations show) interpret the inversion of subject and auxiliary in the surface structures of questions and then use this semantic information to determine the acceptability of adverbs. To summarize: positive motivation for the claim that deep structures fully determine meaning requires positive motivation for the existence of *Q*, or some similar marker of interrogation, in deep structures. But the only positive arguments that have been offered depend on the apparently false assumption that selection restrictions must be imposed in the SYNTACTIC component.

Thus, quite apart from specific counterexamples to the Katz and Postal principle (see Section 3.3), the examples which are compatible with it are only that; they do not constitute positive support for it. Transformational theory may be powerful enough at present to permit the construction of grammars that do conform to this principle, but it is well known that transformational theory is TOO powerful at present. Generative linguistics has moved past the stage where the major problem was to develop descriptive devices rich enough to characterize all the phenomena that do occur in human languages. The pressing task now is to restrict these devices in such a way that they offer some explanation of why, in a system as rich as natural language, many easily conceivable phenomena do NOT occur. Proposed enrichments of the theory must therefore be taken very seriously and argued for on much stronger grounds than the abstract morphemes postulated by Katz and Postal.

The arguments for generative semantics deep structures also rely heavily (as noted in Section 3.2) on selection restrictions, grammatical relations, and the principle that transformations may not contribute to the meanings of sentences. For example, the arguments for the Causative and Inchoative transformations (and for the prelexical Predicate Raising rule which has superseded them), are presumably based on the goal of economizing in the statement of selection restrictions. If *redden*, for example, is derived from *red*, then the grammar need not contain separate statements to the effect that the sky can be red but ideas cannot, that the sky can redden but ideas cannot, that the sunset can redden the sky but nothing can redden ideas. But if selection restrictions such as these are SEMANTIC, the argument for the SYNTACTIC derivation of *redden* from *red* does not go through. The observations would be accounted for equally well by a grammar that did not relate these items syntactically but merely assigned them overlapping semantic representations.

Another example is G. Lakoff's (1966) argument for analyzing negation as a higher predicate. Even if we posit a *Neg* constituent in deep structures, as Katz and Postal did, the traditional transformations for positioning this *Neg* (as in Klima, 1964) are not meaning-preserving. The sentences (72) and (73) have different meanings but would be derived from the same deep structure (74).

(72) Someone cannot lift 200 lbs.
(73) No one can lift 200 lbs.
(74) *Neg* someone can lift 200 lbs.

The difference between the two sentences would emerge only in the transformational derivation, where the *Neg* is either positioned within the *Aux* or is blended with the pronominal subject. Without questioning whether a grammar which thus violates the Katz and Postal principle really should be rejected, Lakoff concluded that the Klima analysis must be wrong, and that (72) and (73) must be assigned distinct deep structures. These would have the *Neg* in different positions, in order to indicate its different semantic scope. We obviously should not be surprised that deep structures motivated in this fashion turned out to be indistinguishable from semantic structures.

Arguments for deep syntactic structures have also been based on grammatical relations. One of Lakoff's arguments for assigning adjectives to the same deep structure category as verbs (see Section 3.2) takes this form. Two sentences with different surface structures are claimed to exhibit the same grammatical relation between their various constituents, and this similarity is captured by assigning them the same deep structure. The critical question here is what is to count as a grammatical relation—a 'real' grammatical relation as opposed to a merely superficial one. Katz (1972, Chapter 3) has suggested that the true grammatical relations are those relations relevant to the determination of meaning. Chomsky (1965, Chapter 2) has suggested that there is a true grammatical relation between two constituents just in case a selection restriction holds between them. So it appears that arguments based on grammatical relations are arguments based either directly on meaning, or on selection restrictions which correlate with meaning.

The general point is simply this. To the extent that the arguments given for proposed deep structures are based on meaning properties and relations, these arguments are inconclusive. They may lead to conclusions about the semantic representations of sentences but not to conclusions about their deep syntactic structures. They cannot establish the existence or non-existence of a level of deep syntactic structure distinct from the level of semantic representation. Nor, if there is such a level, can they tell us anything about the nature of its structural representations. Hence they obviously cannot tell us anything about the RELATION between this level, if it exists, and the semantic level. This is an important point. The observation that selection restrictions are semantic may appear to support the GS position that deep syntactic structures are simultaneously semantic structures. But of course, this follows only if we retain the old assumption that selection restrictions apply at the deep structure level. G. Lakoff (1968) has proposed that we should, since to do so is to embrace the strong hypothesis that the representations of sentences which are needed to capture certain semantic relations, and the representations to which syntactic transformations apply, are one and the same. Extended standard theorists have opted (though without much fanfare) for the other alternative; they tend to eschew selection restriction arguments for deep syntactic structures, and to appeal only to arguments which turn on the SHAPES of sentences rather than on their meanings. This retrenchment is one of the reasons why extended standard theory grammars contain, as we observed in Section 3.3, fewer transformations and correspondingly 'shallower' deep structures than the original standard theory or generative semantics grammars. This approach too can claim to lead in the direction of a stronger theory, though its strengths are different from those claimed for generative semantics. The syntactic transformations of an extended standard theory grammar are fewer and more homogeneous, with the result that stronger universal constraints on possible syntactic transformations can be formulated.

What do we do in cases like this where theoretical desiderata pull in opposite directions? One thing is clear: the relation between semantic and syntactic structures is an empirical question and it must not be established by methodological fiat. Ideally, we would determine independently the necessary properties of syntactic and semantic structures, and then consider how they are similar, how they differ, and what kinds of mechanisms (if any) are necessary to correlate them. This is what Katz and Postal intended to do, though, as we have seen, it is doubtful that they succeeded. When their proposal was made we knew less about both syntax and semantics than we do today. It is legitimate to bring the uncertainties in both areas to bear on each other and to develop the best integrated theory consistent with what is known about both. But as some of the uncertainties are resolved we must continually reconsider the nature of the integration.

These morals are far easier to state than to abide by. Form and meaning are not neatly titrated out for us in a natural language. What we observe is certain restrictions on the distribution of words and phrases in the sentences of the language. Some combinations are acceptable and some are not. In many cases, there is a semantic explanation for the distributional facts. In others, it is not clear whether there is or not. For example, in English, verbs which take the progressive auxiliary *be +ING* typically refer to actions or changes of state, while those which do not take the progressive refer to continuing states. (The standard examples are *learn* (nonstative) and *know* (stative), e.g., *John is learning how to skate* vs. **John is knowing how to skate.*) Does the progressive auxiliary have a meaning which is coherent only with nonstative verbs? If so, the best grammar is presumably one which contains no syntactic co-occurrence restriction, for the meanings of these verbs must in any case be described by the grammar and the restriction would simply follow from the meanings.

In other cases, the meanings of expressions seem to be insufficient to explain their distribution. It is no puzzle that we can say *I lifted it with the tweezers* and not **I read it with the tweezers.* But since we can say *I saw it with my own eyes*, why can't we say **I realized it with my own brain/mind*? A less frivolous example is that most English speakers accept the sentences *I believe him to be dishonest, I know/imagine/consider him to be dishonest*, but not the sentence **I think him to be dishonest.* The exclusion of *think* from this construction seems to be quite arbitrary, for other verbs of the same general semantic type do appear in this context. And there is nothing semantically anomalous about the proposition that would (by analogy) be expressed by *I think him to be dishonent*—it is just that it can't be said that way. This example thus seems to demand some arbitrary syntactic or lexical feature assigned to the verb *think*. Even here, however, there are more and less semantically based descriptions of the facts to choose between. At one extreme, the words that can appear in the syntactic construction in question are simply assigned arbitrary specifications to that effect in the dictionary, ignoring the partial overlap with semantic class. At the other extreme, membership in the semantic class is made a sufficient condition for appearance in the construction, though certain words must then be assigned arbitrary lexical specifications which overrule the general semantic principle. (For a discussion of lexical exceptions to rules see G. Lakoff, 1965.)

These particular examples are relatively trivial, but they are not unrepresentative of a very general problem—the linguistic facts all too often seem to underdetermine the correct description. Yet decisions at this level can add up to produce profoundly different outlooks on the nature of human language. One picture is that what we call "syntax" and "semantics" are simply opposite edges of a single unified system; syntactic patterns in a language truly reflect underlying semantic structure—except for occasional lapses. Another is that syntax and semantics are fundamentally distinct systems, held together by largely arbitrary connections. Possibly they even have distinct evolutionary sources; syntactic structures would then obey their own logic even though they have been pressed into service for the expression of ideas. Some of the specific issues that semantic theories have been concerned with may seem rather far removed from these vague and sweeping generalizations, but the goal of linguistics is after all a theory of the organization of natural languages, and it is important to see how general theoretical claims rest on descriptions of particular low-level facts.

How do we set about deciding on CORRECT descriptions? It sounds straightforward enough, but it raises problems which we have already been faced with in this book and will have to face again. If linguistics is an empirical science, linguistic claims should be testable against empirical data. The existence of competing scientific theories can be healthy and productive, even if it sometimes takes years or centuries for the data that decide between them to become accessible. But linguistics seems to be particularly prone to uncertainty about what empirical facts, even in principle, would support or disconfirm its competing theories. This could suggest that linguistics is not, after all, a real science. It is also compatible with linguistics being a science but a very difficult one. But why should it be so difficult?

Many linguists agree with Chomsky that linguistics is a branch of cognitive psychology, but its methods are not those of the psychology laboratory. The immediate object of study is not people but the language they use—the domain of objects (sentences) which they produce and understand. The justification for calling this psychology is that the properties of objects which an organism can manipulate have implications for the properties of the organism which can manipulate them. When Chomsky demonstrated the inadequacy of phrase structure grammars, he did not look inside speakers' heads or measure reaction times in the lab. He merely observed the existence of dependencies between parts of a sentence, dependencies which speakers abide by but which are beyond the bounds of any phrase structure grammar to capture. This indirectly revealed something about the kinds of mental operation that people must be capable of.

Putting a psychological interpretation on a linguistic theory increases the range of empirical facts about which claims are made, and thus gives substance to the question of whether or not it is a true theory. If languages are regarded as merely abstract entities, then the grammars that the theory makes available need only determine, somehow, which are the well-formed sentences and what their semantic and phonetic properties are. Any two theories which meet this requirement will be equally good. But if the fact that language is used by people is taken seriously, and if the linguistic theory is intended as a contribution to an account of the psychological mechanisms underlying a person's knowledge of his language, then the representations and rules which grammars employ are open to empirical test too.

Let us accept, then, that linguistic theories are theories of linguistic competence. (Though the notion has not been defined to everyone's satisfaction, a person's linguistic COMPETENCE is supposed to be the body of knowledge that he has about his language, which is drawn on in production, perception and other linguistic skills. It is to be distinguished from linguistic PERFORMANCE, which is a matter of the psychological mechanisms that are involved in accessing and using this knowledge on particular occasions.) This characterization of linguistics may have the advantage of drawing psychologists to our aid. But it does not much change the general problem. We are still engaged in reconstructing an extremely complex mental reality from very peripheral manifestations—a whole dinosaur from the odd shinbone. It is no wonder if theories about this mental reality connect with the available data only in very indirect ways, and that linguists must exercise considerable ingenuity in forging these connections.

A persistent problem has been that of deciding when two linguistic theories really differ in empirical consequences, and when they merely use different terminology to make the same claims about the subject matter, in which case they are 'mere notational variants' of each other. There is, very often, some unclarity about which aspects of a linguistic theory are INTENDED to carry empirical content and which are merely the medium in which the empirical claims are expressed. There is also the question of how to interpret formal grammars as models of linguistic competence. Suppose, for example, that one grammar of English uses a syntactic feature [+ *Adj*] to mark a lexical category, where another grammar uses the node label *Adj*. We can at least imagine making direct psychological observations that would confirm the psychological reality of the lexical category. But what psychological facts would be relevant to the decision between feature and node label? What does one grammar claim about linguistic competence that the other does not?

A clear illustration of notational variance is the difference between two systems of formal logic: one in which predicate terms are written before their associated arguments (e.g., *Rab*); and one in which predicates appear between their arguments (e.g., *aRb*). This difference in formalism has no effect on the class of propositions that can be expressed in the two systems or on the theorems that can be proved. The formulae of one are uniquely and mechanically translatable into those of the other. Moreover, psychological reality is typically not claimed for these logical systems. There can therefore be no question about which one of them is true and which false. They seem to be a paradigm case of equivalent systems.

If these two systems were proposed as theories of linguistic competence, however, it seems practically certain that they would embody incompatible assertions. At least one of them would have to be false. In fact, McCawley (1970) has argued that in the underlying structures of English, the verb does not follow the subject as it does in surface structures, but is the first element in its clause. Insofar as the representations assigned to sentences by a grammar constitute hypotheses about mental representations, this grammar presumably does differ in content as well as notation from the more traditional theory that subject phrases precede verbs at all derivational stages in English. That is to say, it is hard to see how competence could possibly be structured so that the question "verb first or verb second?" did not sensibly apply to it. (Unless, of course, the right answer is that deep structure constituents are not ordered at all. Then both theories would be false, but they would still be different.)

McCawley's arguments for his claim are typical linguistic arguments. They turn on the observation that a number of transformational rules can be simplified if verbs are clause-initial in underlying structures. Whether arguments of this kind can be conclusive is a deep problem. It is not self-evident that every simplification that a linguist can make in the description of a language is actually taken advantage of by the native speaker. (Though if the linguistic generalizations captured by grammars are NOT attributable to the psychology of language users, it is a puzzle why they exist.) In general, it is unclear whether linguistic data alone will be sufficient to select a unique 'psychologically real' grammar for English or any other natural language, or whether experimental methods must be resorted to.[3]

All this is intended by way of a partial diagnosis of the sources of the difficulties that abound in adjudicating between competing linguistic theories. We may all agree that when two theories make exactly the same

3. I intend the word "experimental" only very loosely here. Facts which might, under a suitable interpretation, narrow the theoretical options may derive from such areas as language change and language acquisition. Linguists sometimes advert to the former but only rarely to the latter. The practice of responding to some sources of data and ignoring others raises further questions of principle which are not often discussed.

empirical predictions they are notational variants, and hence can be judged only with respect to elegance, comprehensibility, etc. But except in cases of gross disagreement about the meaning of a sentence or its grammaticality, we often do not know which theories make the same empirical predictions. This has particular bearing on the relation between syntax and semantics. Linguistic descriptions are anchored at some points by relatively direct empirical observations. The combinations of words that people utter are observable. The meanings of these utterances are also, in their own fashion, open to inspection. But the derivations that mediate between the two must be inferred, and typically by a long chain of inference whose steps cannot be directly tested. It is therefore not surprising that the major disagreements in linguistics, and the ones that are hardest to settle, concern the middle stages of derivations—which is where syntax and semantics meet.

One final comment on evaluation. Current semantic theories are not, and are not intended to be, complete and final. They do not make claims about every single semantic phenomenon, and many of the claims they do make could be modified or abandoned if need be without loss of the (apparently) distinctive characteristics of the theory. This has occurred frequently. The theories we are concerned with have not been developed in isolation from each other; as observations are made by proponents of one theory, they have been (if not rejected) incorporated into the others. As just one example, when Chomsky drew attention to focus and presupposition (see Section 3.3), representations of these properties were introduced into the semantic representations of generative semantics. This required revision of the GS claim that semantic representations are of exactly the same form as syntactic phrase markers. And, together with other observations about the correlation of meaning with derived syntactic structures, it necessitated the introduction of global rules into GS grammars. It did NOT lead to the collapse of the theory of generative semantics.

We cannot rule out the possibility that some theory will prove completely helpless in the face of the data, but it is not realistic to think of this as the paradigm. Progress is likely to consist not in the outright falsification of all but one of the competing theories, but rather in their gradual convergence. The only sign that a theory is fundamentally wrong may be that it becomes more and more baroque as it attempts to accommodate new empirical observations—observations which fall naturally under the existing principles of other theories. As adjustments to the data are made, the differences between theories could, at least in principle, melt away to the point where only notational differences remain. This prospect means that an understanding of what constitutes a mere notational difference will become even more important. It also means that when comparing current theories we must bear several questions in mind. In what respects do they genuinely differ? Where they differ, which is correct? How could an incorrect one be emended? And then, as repairs are made, the question of whether there is a genuine difference will arise all over again.

4
The Mapping between Syntactic and Semantic Structures

In the last chapter, current semantic theories were outlined. In this chapter and the next one, they will be compared and contrasted with respect to the types of derivation they postulate, and the semantic representations they assign to sentences.

Sentences have syntactic structures, and they have meanings, and the two are obviously related by general principles. As we have already noted, current linguistic theories differ more in their conception of these principles than in their views about what meaning is and how it should be represented. We can pretend, for the purposes of this chapter, that all linguists agree on the surface structures and semantic representations of all sentences. What remains is a host of questions about the number of intermediate structures in derivations, the properties of those structures, and the properties of the rules that interrelate them.

4.1. DIRECTION OF DERIVATION

The notion of the DIRECTION of a derivation has been a source of confusion and dispute from the very early days of transformational linguistics. The theory was then often misinterpreted as a theory of speech production, because the rules of a transformational grammar first define the deep structure of a sentence, then define its surface structure, and finally specify how it is to be pronounced. But Chomsky made it perfectly clear (e.g., in Chomsky, 1965, Chapter 1) that the rules of a grammar are not intended as reconstructions of psychological computational processes occurring in the mind or brain of the language user as he speaks (or understands) sentences. Rather, they encapsulate, in a form neutral between speech production and speech perception, a body of information that the language user must access and employ in some fashion when he speaks or hears his language.

Developing a model of just HOW the grammar is made use of in these two rather different tasks of speech and comprehension is a major concern of psycholinguistics. To suppose that the rules, in the order specified by the grammar, are directly employed as a 'recipe' for constructing and interpreting sentences leads to absurdity. A person obviously does not make the decision to utter a noun phrase before the decision about what lexical items it will contain, i.e., what it will be used to talk about. Equally obviously, in understanding a sentence, one does not construct a deep structure before attending to any aspects of surface structure. Both inverting the grammar in order to reverse the direction of its derivations, and inverting the apparent direction of the psychological processes by positing analysis-by-synthesis routines, have been tried without much success in accounting for the known facts about the psychological operations involved in language use. To some linguists and psychologists, this has thrown doubt on the premise, *viz.*, that the kind of grammar developed in response to linguistic observations maps a component of the psychological mechanisms for language use. Others assume that a grammar MUST be psychologically real in this sense, for otherwise the existence of the linguistic generalizations it captures would be inexplicable, and so they seek a different and more subtle relation between linguistic rules and psychological processes (See J. A. Fodor, Bever and Garrett, 1974, Chapter 6). These are important and intriguing questions, but we must set them aside and concentrate instead on the motivation and significance of directionality in the grammar itself, regardless of the procedures by which a grammar may be implemented in language performance.

Though the early misconceptions about the intended role of a grammar have become less common, the question of directionality has arisen again with the development of generative semantics as an alternative to an interpretive semantic theory. The initial structure of a generative semantics derivation is the semantic structure of the sentence, and this is progressively transformed into a surface structure. On the standard theory, the initial structure is a syntactic deep structure which is similarly transformed into a surface structure but which is correlated with a semantic structure by interpretive rules, rules which take the syntactic structure as input and derive the semantic structure from it. If we ignore for the moment the possibility of semantic rules interpreting DERIVED syntactic structures, we have the simple picture (4-1), in which the arrows relating syntactic and semantic structures point in opposite directions.

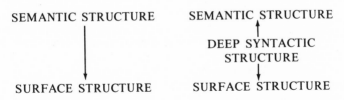

(4-1) Generative semantics.   Standard theory.

This difference between generative semantics and the standard theory is a striking one, and it is tempting to try to choose between the two theories on the basis of it, to the exclusion of other differences between them. I emphasize, therefore, that as these theories now stand, generative and interpretive semantics differ over the nature of semantic representations, over the properties of the rules that relate them to syntactic structures, over the existence of a significant linguistic level intermediate between the semantic and surface structure levels, and over a whole host of more specific issues.

Some of these differences are, however, connected with the difference in direction of derivation. We might suppose that we could isolate the issue of directionality by comparing two (imaginary) grammars, G_1 and G_2, which are identical except that the rules of G_1 are the inverses of the rules of G_2 (i.e., the input to each rule of G_1 is the output of the corresponding rule of G_2, and vice versa), and the order of application of the rules in G_1 is the inverse of the order of application of the corresponding rules in G_2. The set of structural representations constituting the derivation of a given sentence would be identical for both grammars, but these structures would be generated in reverse order. But now notice that where G_1 has a deletion rule, the corresponding rule in G_2 will be an insertion rule; where G_1 has a rule moving a constituent to the left, the corresponding rule of G_2 will move that constituent to the right. This is illustrated in (4-2).

(4-2)	G_1	Derivation	G_2
	step 1: d is moved to	abcd	step 2: d is moved to
	left of bc	adbc	right of bc
	step 2: a deletes	dbc	step 1: a is inserted
	before d		before d

The difference in direction of derivation is inevitably accompanied by a difference in the operations that particular rules perform.

In Section 4.2, we will consider the possibility of constraining the rules of a grammar so that they can perform certain types of operations but not others. We might then be able to decide between the grammars G_1 and G_2 on this basis. But let us temporarily abstract from this issue by supposing that the rules of G_1 and G_2 all conform to the definition of a possible rule of grammar. Could there, nevertheless, be some reason for preferring either G_1 or G_2? The consensus of opinion, even among those who agree about almost nothing else, appears to be that there would be no significant difference between the two grammars—as long as the old confusion of grammars with psychological models of speech production and perception is avoided. (See Chomsky, 1970b, G. Lakoff, 1971, Postal, 1972; and Zwicky, 1972, for a contrary opinion.) Nevertheless, it seems difficult to reconcile this position with the fact that the standard direction of the mapping between deep and surface syntactic structures, and of the mapping between morphophonemic and phonetic representations, have never been challenged. Surely there is some reason behind the directions of syntactic and phonological derivations. And if so, similar considerations might determine a proper direction for the mapping between syntactic and semantic representations.

The standard syntactic derivation of the sentence (1) below contains, among others, the structures (2) and (3).

(1) Who do you expect to murder Jemima?
(2) *Q* You *Pres* expect ₛ[*WH+pro* murder Jemima]
(3) *Q WH+pro* you *Pres* expect ₛ[murder Jemima]

The structure (3) is derived from (2) by the *WH*-Fronting transformation. If the direction of derivation is not significant, then there ought to be no preference for the standard derivation over an inverse derivation in which the usual transformations, with their structural descriptions interchanged with their structural changes, apply in the opposite order to derive deep structures from surface structures. The expression (2) would then be derived from (3) by a '*WH*-Backing' transformation. But is *WH*-Backing really as good as *WH*-Fronting?

In questions, *WH*-Fronting moves a noun phrase containing *WH* into sentence-initial position. In deriving (3) from (2) above, it moves the subject of *murder*; in deriving the sentence (4) below, it moves the direct object of *murder*.

(4) Who do you expect to murder?

The *WH*-Fronting rule 'knows' which noun phrase to move (the one containing *WH*), and it 'knows' where to move it (since sentence-initial position can be defined). But *WH*-Backing would have to move a sentence-initial noun phrase containing *WH* back into its proper position in the sentence—into subject position in the complement clause in (2), and into direct object position in the complement clause in (4). *WH*-Backing knows which noun phrase to move, but how could it know where to move it? What indicates that there is an appropriate gap for the interrogative pronoun to move into at the end of (4) but not at the end of (3)? A gap, after all, is just a nothing. Two words are adjacent that otherwise would not have been.

The information that determines where there is a gap, and which gap has to be filled by the *WH*-Backing transformation, is information about the deep structures of these sentences, and about other transformations that do and do not apply in their derivations. It includes the following facts and inferences.

(4-3) (a) *murder* must have a subject in deep structures. [*murder* has no subject in either (3) or (4); hence there is a gap before *murder* in both examples.]

(b) *murder* must have one and only one direct object (i.e. noun phrase without preposition) in deep structures. [*murder* has a direct object in (3) but not in (4); hence there is a gap after *murder* in (4), but not in (3).]

(c) *expect* must have a subject in deep structures but does not take an object in addition to a complement clause. [*expect* has a subject in both (3) and (4); hence there is no gap before *expect* in either example. Since *expect* does not take an object, there is no gap after *expect* in the main clause in either example. Therefore, the only gaps are before *murder* in (3), and before and after *murder* in (4).]

(d) The transformation which is the inverse of the standard Equi-NP Deletion transformation can supply *murder* with a subject, under identity with the subject of *expect*. [Hence, the gaps before *murder* in (3) and (4) could be filled EITHER by *WH*-Backing OR by the inverse of Equi-NP Deletion. But since in (3) there is no other gap for *WH*-Backing to fill, it MUST fill the gap before *murder* in (3). So the problem is solved for (3), though not yet for (4).]

(e) There is no transformation other than *WH*-Backing that could supply *murder* with an object in (4), (e.g., the inverse of the standard Object Deletion transformation does not apply to *murder*, nor does the inverse of the standard Tough Movement transformation, etc.). [Hence, the gap after *murder* in (4) cannot be filled except by *WH*-Backing. Therefore *WH*-Backing fills this gap, and the inverse of Equi-NP Deletion fills the gap before *murder*.]

This illustrates that for a *WH*-Backing transformation to apply correctly, it would need information about structures in the derivation of a sentence which are 'deeper' than the one on which it operates, i.e. structures which are generated only AFTER *WH*-Backing itself has applied. By contrast, the standard *WH*-Fronting rule is self-sufficient; it can apply correctly without 'looking ahead' to later stages in the derivation. The reason for this difference is that *WH*-Fronting parallels, while *WH*-Backing opposes, the direction of flow of information between structures like (2) and (3). Before *WH*-Fronting applies, the position of the interrogative pronoun indicates its syntactic and semantic role in the sentence. But this information is lost when all interrogative pronouns are moved into the same position at the front of the sentence. Thus, (2) contains more information (in this respect) than (3); (2) contains enough information to determine (3), but (3) does not contain enough to determine (2). Other transformations (e.g., Passive, Particle Movement) apparently involve no loss of information and hence determine a unique output when applied in either direction. An asymmetry in information content between two adjacent structural representations in a derivation thus gives some content to the notion of the direction of a rule.

Nevertheless, these observations do not in fact establish that standard syntactic derivations are correct and could not be replaced by their inverses. They do not even establish that a grammar of English must contain *WH*-Fronting rather than *WH*-Backing. The reason is this. It is true that *WH*-Backing could not apply correctly without 'looking ahead' to later stages of the (inverse) derivation. But the effect of 'looking ahead' can be achieved by means of a FILTERING device. That is, we could allow *WH*-Backing to apply freely, moving interrogative pronouns into incorrect positions in some derivations as well as into correct ones in others; then we could use later rules in the derivation (e.g., the phrase structure rules which define well-formed deep structures) to filter out the incorrect structures so generated— to discard derivations containing them. If, for example, *WH*-Backing were to move the interrogative pronoun in (3) into the position after *Jemima*, this derivation would subsequently be marked as improper by the rules defining well-formed deep structures (because *murder* would have two objects and no subject).

A filtering device is thus a way of reconciling a conflict between the direction of a derivation and the direction of flow of information. A derivation is discarded if it results from incorrect application of a rule at a stage when the information relevant to its correct application was not available. It might seem intuitively that a grammar in which the rules are sufficient to define the well-formed sentences of the language without the need for filtering devices is to be preferred over a grammar containing filters. But this intuition may well be nothing but a prejudice stemming from a particular interpretation of the word "generate," as in "generative grammar."

Technically, what makes generative grammar generative is that it recursively enumerates the infinite set of well-formed sentences of a language. ("Generate" contrasts here with a more traditional sense of "define," on which to give necessary and sufficient conditions for membership in a set is to define that set. A necessary and sufficient condition for membership in the set of mathematical theorems is that something should be a well-formed mathematical formula and true, but we cannot recursively enumerate this set.) But we also talk of generating a SENTENCE, or a derivation for a sentence. To generate something in this sense is to construct it. To use a test procedure (filter) to winnow out of the set of all strings those which are ill-formed would not count, in this special sense, as generating the well-formed sentences. (Also, to multiply each integer by two would be to generate the set of even integers, but to divide each by two and discard those for which the quotient was not a whole number would not count as generating—in this sense—the even integers.) Transformational grammars have been, for the most part, generative not only in the first sense but in this latter sense, too. But there seems to be no *a priori* reason why they should be.[1]

Notice that the contrast between 'constructive' rules and filtering devices holds both for syntactic transformations and for semantic rules such as projection rules. A filtering device can locally reverse the prevailing direction of a derivation, whether this is from syntactic structures to semantic representations or vice versa. It does so by rejecting a derivation part of which has already 'incorrectly' been constructed. In a body of rules deriving semantic representations from syntactic deep structures, a filter could determine the well-formedness of deep structures retroactively in terms of a property of the resulting semantic representations; in a body of rules deriving syntactic structures from semantic representations, a filter could determine the well-formedness of semantic representations retroactively in terms of a property of the resulting syntactic structures. To the extent that both the standard theory and generative semantics employ filters, the contrast between the directions of the 'semantic end' of their derivations is therefore not an absolute one.

1. Common terminology invites confusion. Note that "generative" in this special sense of "constructive" does not contrast with "interpretive." Just like phrase structure rules and syntactic transformations, interpretive semantic rules can contribute to the construction of well-formed derivations rather than to the discarding of ill-formed ones. Where "generative" is contrasted with "interpretive" (as in "generative semantics" versus "interpretive semantics"), a generative rule or a generative component of a grammar derives an infinite set of structures from a finite input. In current transformational grammars, the recursiveness of the grammar is embodied in the rules of the base; the phrase structure component is generative. By contrast, the syntactic transformations, the phonological rules, and semantic rules such as projection rules are all interpretive, since they simply define mappings from one infinite domain of representations to another. This is the sense in which generative semantics is distinctively generative—the recursive component of the grammar is the body of rules which define SEMANTIC structures. In a standard grammar, the semantic component is interpretive, because it is not semantic but syntactic structures that are generated by the phrase structure rules.

To add to the confusion, there is another sense of "interpretive" too, such that to interpret a structure is to provide it with a translation in some other vocabulary—e.g., the vocabulary of distinctive phonological features or a vocabulary of semantic primitives. In this sense, generative semantics grammars as well as standard grammars interpret the syntactic structures of a language.

Filtering devices were introduced quite early on. In *Aspects* (1965), Chomsky proposed that the identity between the head noun phrase of a relative clause construction and the noun phrase within the relative clause that is to become the relative pronoun should be established by a filter. The phrase structure rules and lexical insertion processes should apply quite freely to generate not only well-formed deep structures such as (5), but also deep structures like (6) which do not correspond to any well-formed sentence.

(5) I saw $_{NP}$ [the policeman $_S$ [Bert had kicked *WH*+a policeman]]

(6) I saw $_{NP}$ [the policeman $_S$ [Bert had kicked *WH*+a professor]]

Subsequently, the relative clause transformations would apply to (5) but would fail to apply correctly to (6), and the derivation containing (6) would therefore be thrown out. Many other filters have been proposed since. (See, for example, Perlmutter, 1971, and Postal, 1972.) Some of these can be exchanged for 'constructive' rules. For example, instead of Chomsky's filter analysis, relative pronouns could be directly generated as such in deep structures and subsequently supplied with content by an interpretive rule; (5) would then be produced by interpretation of a deep structure like (7), and (6) would never occur at all.

(7) I saw $_{NP}$ [the policeman $_S$ [Bert had kicked *WH*+*pro*]]

But it is doubtful that all filtering mechanisms (e.g., Perlmutter's surface structure constraints) could be analyzed away. And, as indicated, it is not clear whether, even if they could be, they should be.

Our goal is to narrow our characterization of grammars of possible human languages. At present it is too broad, for in many cases we can choose between positing a generative rule and positing a filter, and we do not yet know how to make this choice (or even to what extent it is a genuine choice). Excluding all filters would be one way, but it may not be the correct one. However, even though we may be uncertain how to FORMALLY EXPRESS the directionality of grammatical processes, we can at least ask of each one whether or not it is inherently directional, and if so what its direction is. And if the answer is not the same in all cases, we might go on to ask whether there are any properties common to those that have one direction rather than the other, whether there are any universal principles governing directionality. (It would presumably be significant if it were to turn out, for example, that grammars could be so organized that the only filters needed were the independently required phrase structure rules, or that all filters could be ordered after all 'constructive' rules.)

I have illustrated these points with rules which would normally be regarded as syntactic rather than semantic. This is because we know so little at present about the structures which constitute the 'semantic end' of derivations that it is difficult to say anything reliable about the directionality of the processes that interrelate them. But the kinds of question that we have just raised about syntactic rules must surely apply to semantic rules too.

Beginners often assume that the basic issue between generative and interpretive semantic theories is whether the meaning of a sentence determines its form or whether its form determines its meaning—this is the construal of the difference between 'semantically based' and 'syntactically based' grammars. The proponents of these theories quite properly resist these sweeping characterizations. Nevertheless, there may indeed be something to this question of what determines what. If we can establish the kinds of relation that can hold between the syntactic and semantic structures of a language, and if some of these relations have inherent directionality of the kind we have illustrated, then questions about direction of determination will not be empty. But two qualifications are important. First, there is no guarantee that there is a UNIQUE direction to relations between syntax and semantics; different aspects of the mapping (e.g., lexical decomposition and scope relations) might exhibit different asymmetries of information, and yet others might show no asymmetry at all. Secondly, as we have already observed, to the extent that both generative and interpretive theories employ filters, the different orders in which structures are generated in their respective derivations cannot be taken to constitute different empirical claims about which structures determine which.

Even in our present state of ignorance, we may tentatively conclude that the meanings of sentences do not contain information of a sort that will fully determine their syntactic structure. This would explain why generative semantics grammars apparently need to contain more filtering devices of various kinds than standard grammars. (An example is suggested at the end of Section 4.3.) But in the absence of an adequate theory of the status of filtering devices *vis-à-vis* 'constructive' rules, this cannot be regarded as a defect. Indeed, Postal (1972) has made a virtue of it. Perhaps it will turn out to be neither. Conceivably, the difference between the two kinds of formal mechanism will turn out to be a mere notational difference, and will fade into insignificance in the face of real empirical discoveries about directionality.

Finally, I must point out that the introduction of GLOBAL rules or filters (see G. Lakoff, 1970, 1971), which are sensitive simultaneously to more than one structure in a derivation, greatly complicates the picture presented so far, for it means that derivations are no longer linear. The issue here is which structures in a derivation are ADJACENT to which, in the sense that they are directly related by a rule of the grammar rather than standing in a more distant relation that is mediated by a sequence of other structures intermediate between them. Note that this is largely independent of the question of direction of derivation, for we can still ask which of two adjacent structures is derived from which. As we have observed (Sections 3.1 and 3.3) Katz claims that there is no direct relation between derived syntactic structures and semantic representations—the only connection between them is *via* deep structures. Both the extended standard theory and generative semantics deny this, and establish direct connections (by means of interpretive semantic rules and global constraints respectively) between certain derived syntactic structures and semantic representations. The difference between semantic rules which interpret derived structures, and global constraints which permit only certain relations to hold between semantic structures and derived structures, may itself turn out to be a mere notational difference. Both devices establish adjacency between semantic and derived syntactic representations. But the difference between both of these approaches on the one hand, and Katz's denial of adjacency on the other, surely cannot be discounted. Assuming that we can find independent empirical evidence for the structures which constitute derivations, it should be an empirical question (governed by the usual simplicity considerations) which of these structures is most closely related to which.

4.2. PROPERTIES OF THE MAPPING RULES

It was noted in Section 4.1 that if two grammars assign exactly the same derivation to a sentence but differ with respect to the sequence in which the structures constituting that derivation are constructed, there will inevitably be a difference in the operations that corresponding rules of the two grammars perform. A deletion rule in one grammar will correspond to an insertion rule in the other, and so on. This can serve as a basis for evaluating competing grammars if we have a theory of the types of rules a grammar may contain, for then we might be able to show that a rule of one proposed grammar is of an allowable type while the corresponding rule in the competing grammar is an 'impossible' rule.

Considerable effort has been expended in recent years towards developing such a theory for syntactic transformations. It has been proposed, for example, that a transformation moving a constituent to the right in a phrase marker may not move it out of the clause in which it appears (Ross 1967). It has been suggested that no transformation may move a constituent down into a lower clause (Chomsky 1965, Chapter 3). Note that these formulations of the constraints are ambiguous. We might want to say either that grammars may not contain transformations whose application could violate the constraints, or that grammars may contain such rules but the rules can apply only in contexts where they would not violate the constraints. The latter construal is arguably the correct one, but for our purposes it is sufficient to note that, either way, the constraints will exclude certain operations being performed by transformations.

Can these constraints on syntactic transformations (though admittedly still themselves under investigation) be applied to the mapping between syntactic and semantic structures to decide between competing theories about the rules that effect it? Is there any reason to believe that THESE rules should be governed by the same constraints as syntactic transformations? Generative semanticists have claimed that they should, that the rules that apply to structures containing semantic elements before lexical substitution occurs are of exactly the same kind as the transformations applying later in derivations to phrase markers containing lexical items. This is not a NECESSARY consequence of the direction of a generative semantics derivation, for there is no logical reason why the rules applying early in derivations should not differ in kind from the rules that apply later. But it is a natural position to take in view of the continuity of derivations from semantic representations through to surface structures. And it would clearly be impossible to maintain that all rules applying to structures containing semantic primitives are different in kind from all rules applying to structures containing lexical items if, as has been claimed, lexical items are not all inserted at the same stage of derivations. For there would then be some rules applying to structures with terminal elements of both kinds. Generative semanticists have therefore been eager to show that the processes which relate semantic and syntactic structures are subject to the same constraints as are the standard syntactic transformations.

McCawley (1973) has claimed that there could be no word *thork* meaning 'to give to one's uncle and,' i.e., no sentence of the form (8) meaning the same as (9).

(8) John thorked Harry 5000 yen.
(9) John gave to his uncle and Harry 5000 yen. (or, John gave 5000 yen to his uncle and Harry.)

He has also claimed (1971b) that there could be no word *flimp* meaning 'kiss a girl who is allergic to,' i.e., no sentence of the form of (10) meaning the same as (11).

(10) Bert flimped coconuts.
(11) Bert kissed a girl who is allergic to coconuts.

If these intuitions are correct, they are explained by the hypothesis that the collection transformations which gather semantic elements into complexes ready for lexical substitution are governed by the constraints on syntactic transformations. For there is a constraint (the Coordinate Structure Constraint, see Ross, 1967) which prohibits transformations from moving a conjoined constituent out of a conjunction, and there are constraints (the Left Branch Condition and the Complex Noun Phrase Constraint, Ross,

1967) that prohibit transformations from moving either the head noun phrase or any part of the *S* constituent out of the configuration

. The first constraint would prevent movement of the semantic elements *ONE'S UNCLE AND* out of the conjunction *ONE'S UNCLE AND HARRY*, in order to associate them with *GIVE TO*.[2] Therefore it would be impossible to generate the semantic complex *GIVE TO ONE'S UNCLE AND* under a single node, hence no lexical item could substitute for just this combination of semantic elements, and hence there could be no word *thork* with just this meaning. The other constraints would prevent any rule from moving *A GIRL WHO IS ALLERGIC TO* away from *COCO-NUTS* and into association with *KISS*. Therefore *KISS A GIRL WHO IS ALLERGIC TO* could never be generated as a single constituent that could be substituted for by *flimp*. In this way, familiar syntactic constraints apparently predict which aspects of the meaning of a sentence can, and which cannot, be coded into single lexical items.

This is a very ingenious form of argument, and the distinction between possible and impossible words could prove a rich source of data for testing semantic theories. But there are at least two problems that it faces. One is that it demands intuitions subtle enough to distinguish between a word's being impossible in some language because that language HAPPENS NOT to contain any rules that would collect up the necessary semantic elements, and a word's being impossible in the stronger sense that the grammar COULD NOT contain such rules because they would violate general constraints on possible rules. Only the latter cases would constitute data for arguments like McCawley's.

A second point is that many words, real or hypothetical, can be paraphrased in more than one way. There is therefore more than one plausible candidate for the semantic representation of such a word. If *kill* means 'cause to die,' it also means 'cause the death of.' The constraints on transformations might conceivably rule out the derivation of a word from its semantic representation if cast in one form, but not if cast in the other. So no clear predictions about possible words follow unless there is some way of establishing what the precise form of an underlying semantic representation is.

Even allowing for these uncertainties, there appear to be counterexamples to the generative semantics hypothesis. There are verbs in English which are most naturally paraphrased by the verb, first noun phrase and preposition of the construction (4-4).

---

2. The elements that the movement rules apply to are in capital letters to indicate that they are semantic elements, not lexical items. But, as usual, I do not mean to imply that the meanings of the words *uncle*, *kiss*, *coconut*, etc. are truly unanalyzable.

(4-4)

```
                    VP
           ┌────────┴────┐
         V              NP
                   ┌─────┴──────┐
                  NP          PrepP
                          ┌─────┴────┐
                        Prep        NP
```

For example *weigh* in one sense means 'determine the weight of'; *locate* can mean 'determine the position of'; *solve* means 'find the solution to'; *substitute for* can mean 'take the place of'; *crown* in its colloquial sense means 'strike the head (crown) of.' (Also, *kill* means 'cause the death of'.) If these paraphrases do mirror the prelexical structures from which the words would be derived in a GS grammar, then the collection transformation that groups together the relevant semantic elements would violate a constraint on transformations. This constraint is the Left Branch Condition, and it prohibits the extraction of the noun phrase on the left branch of the construction   NP   This constraint applies to syntactic transfor-

```
        NP
```

mations to prevent the derivation of sentences such as (12) and (13).

    (12) *The weight, I determined of the box (but the size I didn't).
    (13) *The weight of, I determined the box (but the size of I didn't).

By contrast, the sentences (14) and (15) are grammatical, since what has been extracted is a right-branching *NP* in (14), and the whole complex *NP* in (15).

    (14) The box, I determined the weight of (but the barrel, I didn't).
    (15) The weight of the box, I determined (but the size of the lid, I didn't).

What we have argued is that there is at least one case in which constraints on possible words do not match constraints on syntactic transformations. If the argument is valid, it falsifies the GS claim that the whole derivation from semantic structures to surface syntactic structures is effected by rules of the same formal type.

    Another argument that the rules of generative semantics do not conform to the definition of possible transformations has been given by Chomsky (1972a). In a GS grammar, quantifiers are represented in underlying structures as the predicates of higher clauses (as are auxiliary verbs and adverbs, see Section 3.2). The grammar must therefore contain a Quantifier Lowering transformation which will move the quantifiers down into their proper surface positions. This transformation will convert an underlying structure of the form (4-5) into the derived structure (4-6).

(4-5)

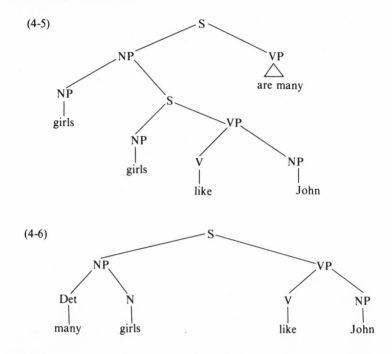

(4-6)

Chomsky pointed out that this Quantifier Lowering transformation violates a proposed constraint that transformations may not move a constituent of one clause down into a lower clause. An absolute veto on lowering rules may be too strong (see Chomsky, 1973, for discussion); but even in weakened form, the constraint would appear to exclude Quantifier Lowering, Adverb Lowering and possibly other rules needed for generative semantics analyses.

The conclusion that these rules must be of a type distinct from standard syntactic transformations is of course no stronger than the empirical support for the syntactic constraint on lowering, which in turn depends on a number of other issues in syntax. But this is an interesting form of argument. Many of the constraints on transformations appear to be symmetrical; typically, if no transformation may move a constituent out of some configuration, then no transformation may move a constituent into it either. Hence, if a given rule violates one of these constraints, the inverse rule in a grammar with the opposite direction of derivation would also violate the constraint. But this is not the case with lowering rules, for the inverse of a lowering rule is a raising rule; and transformations which raise constituents into higher clauses (e.g., Subject Raising, *WH*-Fronting) are accepted, and for good reason, by all current theories. Changing the direction of derivation may thus exchange an impermissible rule for a permissible one.

There is another reason for being suspicious of the lowering rules which are characteristic of the generative semantics treatment of semantic scope relations. A very strong form of argument for the existence of a transformation consists in observing that a surface structure contains an incomplete clause, e.g., a verb with no subject, a transitive verb with no object, a sequence of noun phrases with no verb to relate them.

(16) John wants *to sleep.* (no subject)
(17) The man *I slugged* was charming. (no object)
(18) John likes apples and *Mary bananas.* (no verb)

The postulation of transformations that delete constituents or move them away from their original positions explains the existence of these partial clauses. But there is no evidence of this kind for rules like Quantifier Lowering or Adverb Lowering. There are no remnants in the surface structures of sentences like (19) and (20) of the clauses from which the quantifier and the adverb are supposed to have been derived.

(19) Many people hate spinach.
(20) Obviously he was drunk.

There may be more than one way of accounting for this. Perhaps lowering rules are subject to a special constraint requiring them to leave no incomplete clauses behind (though why should there be such a constraint?). Or perhaps it is a straightforward consequence of the structural simplicity of clauses at the stage at which the lowering rules apply. For example, if the copula is not present at this stage (see Section 3.2), lowering *many* or *obvious* would not leave behind an incomplete predicate. But it is also possible that there are no traces of lowering rules because there are no lowering rules. If the scope of quantifiers and adverbs is treated instead by interpretive rules, it is automatically predicted that though there can be incomplete clauses in surface structures due to the operation of syntactic transformations, there can be no incomplete clauses resulting from the rules which handle quantifier and adverb scope.

We have considered arguments for and against the claim that the rules which map semantic structures onto more superficial syntactic structures in a generative semantics grammar are of the same type as syntactic transformations. Whether or not this claim turns out to be true, at least a claim has been made; the character of the mapping rules has been specified. It is less clear that any constraints on the nature of possible interpretive rules follow naturally from the current interpretive semantic theories. The projection rules of Katz's theory, for example, are part of a component of the grammar quite distinct from the syntactic component, and hence there seems to be no reason why they should be similar to syntactic transformations. They do in fact differ from syntactic transformations in a number of respects. So do some of the interpretive rules of Jackendoff's theory. For example, the rules which apply to derived structures and have as output a table of coreference do not conform to the standard definition of syntactic transformations as rules that map phrase markers into phrase markers.

Nevertheless, some of the rules for interpreting derived structures that have recently been formulated apparently do obey the same constraints as syntactic transformations. For example, Fiengo and Lasnik (1973) have examined constraints on the interpretive rule that finds an antecedent for the phrase *each other* in sentences like (21) and (22).

(21) The men wanted each other to hit Mary.
(22) *The men shouted that each other had hit Mary.

The antecedent of *each other* can be the noun phrase *the men* in (21) but not in (22). (Since *each other* has no other possible antecedent in (22), the sentence is unacceptable.) A generalization that emerges is that the antecedent of *each other* may not be outside the clause in which *each other* appears if (i) *each other* is the subject of the clause, and (ii) the clause contains a complementizer (such as the word *that* in (22). This constraint parallels a constraint on syntactic movement transformations, which stipulates that the subject of a clause with a complementizer may not be moved over the complementizer and out of its clause. For example, the *WH*-Fronting transformation may move the subject out of the complement clause in (23), which has a structure like (21); but it may not move the subject of the complement in (24), which has a structure like (22).

(23) Who did the men want to hit Mary?
(24) *Who did the men shout that had hit Mary?

Given that neither syntactic transformations nor the postulated semantic interpretation rule can apply across the complementizer, what does this show? It might be claimed to show that it is wrong to capture the relation between *each other* and its antecedent by means of an interpretive rule, i.e., that since this relation exhibits the same limits as syntactic transformations, it must be expressed by a syntactic transformation.[3] This would be to take a rule's obedience to the constraints on syntactic transformations as the criterion for its BEING a syntactic transformation.

However, we do not conclude that there is no formal distinction between syntactic rules and phonological rules on the grounds that both

---

3. The syntactic transformation might be a kind of pronominalization rule, reducing a full noun phrase such as *the men* to *each other* in the context of an appropriate antecedent. Or it might be a movement transformation which derives a sentence like (21) from a structure of the form *Each man wanted the other to hit Mary*. This is proposed by Dougherty (1970).

apply cyclically. Similarly, it might simply be acknowledged that the constraints apply equally to syntactic transformations and to at least SOME interpretive rules. To give substance to this proposal, it would then be necessary to provide some principled distinction between those semantic rules which are subject to the constraints and those which are not. Chomsky (1975, Chapter 3) offers a suggestion, but its validity has yet to be thoroughly explored.

The possibility that the semantic rules themselves may not constitute a single natural class is easily overlooked in the business of comparing semantic rules with syntactic rules. But semantic rules do now appear to be shaking out into distinct types. For example, the lowering rules of generative semantics have been proposed primarily to deal with scope relations, whereas the rules that collect semantic elements into complexes ready for lexical substitution tend to raise constituents into higher clauses. The extended standard theory also distinguishes, though in a different way, between scope phenomena and the internal semantic analysis of lexical items (see Section 3.3). If this distinction stands up to further observation, then one more piece of the jigsaw puzzle will have slipped into place. It would be especially interesting if this difference turned out to be correlated with obedience to the constraints on syntactic transformations, or with other properties of rules, such as directionality. It would then be clear that there were at least two distinct types of rule in semantics, each narrowly constrained but in different ways.

4.3. THE LEVEL OF DEEP STRUCTURE

The different directions that current linguistic theories impose on the syntax-semantics mapping are in part logically related to the different claims these theories make about the level of deep structure. A grammar with an interpretive semantic component MUST recognize a significant level of structure intermediate between the semantic and surface structure levels, because the direction of the derivation reverses somewhere in the middle. (This is so whether the interpretive rules apply only to deep structures or to derived syntactic structures as well.) A generative semantics grammar, whose derivations are unidirectional from semantic structures through to surface structures, need not (though it could) admit an intermediate linguistic level. As we noted in Section 3.2, generative semanticists have in fact claimed that no such level exists.

There are two ways of characterizing this difference between the theories. Which one we opt for is unimportant because it is simply a matter of terminology. But each serves to emphasize a different aspect of the theoretical dispute. One way to state the difference between the theories is to say that the standard theory does, and generative semantics does not, require grammars to define a level of deep structure. This account takes deep structures to be defined by their internal properties, e.g., their terminal elements must be morphemes, not semantic primitives. Generative semantics does not recognize a level of deep structure in this sense. Another way to state the difference is to say that BOTH theories recognize a level of deep structure, but that generative semantics does, and the standard theory does not, identify this level with the semantic level. This account takes the defining property of deep structures to be that they are the input to the transformational component, and that they themselves are directly generated (by phrase structure rules or the like) rather than being derived indirectly by the transformation of some other structures. Generative semantics does recognize a level of deep structure in this sense. Indeed, since transformational rules must transform SOMETHING, any transformational grammar must contain such a level.

Questions about deep structure in the two senses interact, but I will separate them as far as possible. To decide which theory is correct about deep structure in the first sense, we must determine whether there is empirical motivation for a level of linguistic structure intermediate between the semantic level and the surface structure level, or whether, conversely, there are generalizations about languages that will be missed if grammars are required to meet such a level. To determine which theory is correct about deep structures in the second sense, we must determine whether semantic representations and/or standard syntactic deep structures are of the kind that can be directly, nontransformationally, generated. In *Syntactic Structures*, Chomsky showed that there are structures which cannot (or cannot naturally) be generated by phrase structure rules, but which can be derived transformationally from other structures which are so generated. This was a major argument in favor of transformational grammars over grammars containing only the equivalent of phrase structure rules. Since it is fairly well established that standard deep structure configurations can be generated by phrase structure rules[4], the important question here is whether or not SEMANTIC structures can be directly generated.

Let us take the first of our two questions first. Certain facts about sentences are expressed in the syntactic deep structures of a standard grammar. In a GS grammar, these facts have to be captured in other ways. The fundamental constituency relations (the fact that a complex sentence is built up out of simple sentences, and that a simple sentence contains a verb and some number of noun phrases) are captured in the usual fashion by means of labeled tree diagrams, though these diagrams double as representations of meaning. The underlying structures of generative semantics are, however, less highly articulated in some respects than standard deep structures. They contain no prepositions; adjectives and predicate nominals have the same distribution as verbs; auxiliary verbs are not structurally

4. This is an oversimplification if transformational filters are necessary. See Section 4.1.

distinguished from main verbs; and so on. As we have seen (Section 3.2), some structural differentiation is introduced by the transformations, e.g., the transformation introducing a copula before adjectives and predicate nominals but not before main verbs. Other information contained in standard deep structures is captured in a GS grammar by selection restrictions. For example, the proper sequence of auxiliary verbs in English is determined in a standard theory grammar by a phrase structure rule.

(25) Aux ———→ Tense (Modal) (*have* + EN) (*be* + ING)

In a GS grammar, with auxiliaries analyzed as the main verbs of higher clauses, the sequence of auxiliaries must be captured instead by selection restrictions between the verb of one clause and the verb of the clause beneath it (i.e., 'verb-verb restrictions,' see McCawley, 1971).

Positive support for the standard theory would consist of a demonstration that there are further generalizations about sentence structure which are captured by standard deep structures but which cannot be captured by any of the representations or rules of a generative semantics grammar. Chomsky's observations about derived nominals in English (see Section 3.3) are intended as a demonstration of just this kind. Though derived nominals and sentences are related in meaning, and have certain structural similarities, they also exhibit structural differences. Chomsky's claim is that these differences can be stated only at a level less abstract than the semantic level, a level at which the formal properties of an expression are captured at the expense, if need be, of its semantic properties.

How could this argument against generative semantics be countered? A crucial question is whether there must be any identifiable LEVEL in derivations at which the syntactic properties of nominals are established. Might they not instead be introduced gradually in the course of a continuous derivation from sentential semantic representations to nominal surface structures? GS grammars do not distinguish any nouns from verbs in underlying structures, so they must in any case contain transformations that convert verbs (or members of a nondifferentiated category of 'predicates') into nouns at some stage in derivations. If these transformations were also responsible for producing derived nominals, then all subsequent transformations would treat derived nominals in the same way as ordinary noun phrases; this would explain why derived nominals differ from sentences in just the ways that ordinary noun phrases do.

An appropriate ordering of the transformations concerned could even turn this to positive advantage. If the nominalizing transformations were ordered before lexical insertion, Chomsky's observations about the semantic differences between derived nominals and their corresponding verbs could be accommodated. Though there is a semantic relation between *destroy* and *destruction*, it is not the same as the relation between *prove* and *proof*, and neither is exactly like the relations between *do* and *deed*, *laugh* and *laughter*, *transform* and *transformation*, etc. This diversity requires that the noun and the verb be substituted for slightly different complexes of semantic elements, and this is possible if the lexical nouns and verbs are substituted after a semantic noun/verb distinction is established. (By contrast, the semantic relation between gerundive nominals and their corresponding verbs is quite uniform. Therefore the transformation that produces gerundive nominals should apply AFTER lexical insertion.) Furthermore, by ordering the formation of derived nominals after such transformations as Passive and Equi-NP Deletion, it would be explained why Passive and Equi-NP Deletion apply within nominals as well as within sentences. By ordering the nominal forming rule before transformations like Subject Raising, it would be explained why Subject Raising applies only to sentences and not to derived nominals.

Chomsky's arguments for the standard theory's level of deep structure have not so far been strongly challenged along these lines. Perhaps no one has been able to establish an ordering of transformations which would meet all of these requirements. But the standard theory also has no obvious explanation of which transformations do apply to noun phrases as well as to sentences, and which do not. At present, each transformation must be specifically formulated to indicate whether its domain is defined by S nodes only, or by both NP and S nodes. The extended standard theory would obviously be in a stronger position if some principled distinction between these transformations could be established, perhaps by appeal to general constraints on the applicability of certain types of transformation

In another line of defense of the standard theory's level of deep structure, Jackendoff (1969, discussed in Chomsky, 1972a) has maintained that some very gross generalizations about sentence structure are obscured by the derivation of sentences from their semantic representations. A sentence consists of a noun phrase and a verb phrase. Virtually any noun phrase, regardless of its internal structure (e.g., regardless of whether or not it contains a determiner) can co-occur with virtually any verb phrase, regardless of its internal structure (e.g., regardless of whether or not it contains an auxiliary verb). But the interpretation of the various combinations differs. Jackendoff notes that the sentence (26) is generic, while the sentences (27) and (28) have only a specific interpretation.

(26) A beaver builds dams.
(27) That beaver builds dams.
(28) A beaver is building a dam.

If these three sentences were derived from structures representing their meanings, they would therefore have to be derived from distinct, and in all likelihood very different, underlying structures. It would then be merely a coincidence that their derivations subsequently converge on such similar structures. But a standard theory deep structure level, imposing tight structural constraints on sentences regardless of their meanings, would explain the existence of syntactic regularities holding across semantically dissimilar sentences. The base rules of a standard grammar provide a highly restricted set of deep structures which the language must use for the expression of an enormously wide range of meanings. They impose a sort of 'wasp waist' in the middle of derivations, in contrast to the diversity of both surface structures and meanings.

There are also arguments AGAINST the standard level of deep structure. These have been likened to Halle's argument (Halle, 1959, discussed in Chomsky, 1964) against the taxonomic phonemic level. Russian obstruents become voiced in certain contexts, but this voicing is contrastive ('phonemic' in the taxonomic sense) for some obstruents and not for others. Because of this, obstruent voicing cannot be stated as a single general rule as long as phonological derivations must respect the taxonomic phonemic level. Instead, there must be two distinct obstruent voicing rules—one which applies in the derivation of phonetic representations from taxonomic phonemic representations, and another which applies in the derivation of taxonomic phonemic representations from morphophonemic representations. Halle's point was that giving up the taxonomic phonemic level permits these two rules to be collapsed into a single and much more general rule. It thus results in a simplification of the grammar, a simplification which reflects the fact that a genuine generalization about the language has been captured.

Bach (1968) has argued that recognition of the standard level of deep structure would, in a similar way, obstruct the statement of a generalization about opaque contexts. In Section 2.6, we considered opaque constructions with emphasis on the failure of substitutivity of coreferential expressions. Another striking property of opaque constructions is that they permit a nonreferential, or NONSPECIFIC, interpretation of indefinite noun phrases. The sentence (29), for example, has a nonspecific interpretation on which it can be true even if there is no PARTICULAR eraser that Mary is looking for.

    (29) Mary is looking for an eraser.

(In fact, like all such examples, (29) is ambiguous. It also has a specific interpretation according to which there IS some particular eraser that Mary is looking for.)

Nonspecific noun phrases are generally found in complement clauses, as in (30) and (31).

    (30) Mary hopes that she brought an eraser.
    (31) It was obvious that Mary had brought an eraser.

They also occur in single-clause sentences containing certain adverbs and modal verbs.

(32) Obviously Mary has brought an eraser.
(33) Mary may have brought an eraser.

It is important to Bach's argument that sentences like (32) and (33) are derived from underlying complement constructions in a generative semantics grammar. Nonspecific noun phrases are NOT normally found in single-clause sentences such as (34) and (35).

(34) Mary brought an eraser.
(35) Mary found an eraser.

(If Mary brought or found an eraser at all, then there is some specific eraser that she brought or found. It is possible to look for a nonspecific eraser, but it isn't possible to find one.) The verb *look for* is unusual in this respect, for as the nonspecific interpretation of (29) shows, it is opaque even in a single-clause sentence.

The verb *look for* is thus an apparent exception to what would otherwise be a valid generalization about the syntactic properties of opaque contexts: all and only those sentences that contain a complement clause (at the deep structure level) have opaque interpretations. The exception can be eliminated only if a sentence like (29) is derived from an underlying complement construction. It is this that Bach proposes, and for obvious semantic reasons he takes the structure underlying (29) to be the same as the one that underlies the sentence (36).

(36) Mary is trying to find an eraser.

The *look for* sentence might be transformationally derived from this structure by the conversion of one sequence of lexical items into another. Or, as current GS theory proposes, the underlying structure might contain not the English lexical items *try* and *find* but the semantic elements which represent the meanings of these words (e.g., *TRY* and *FIND*). If Predicate Raising applies to combine these semantic elements under a single node in the prelexical phrase marker (see Section 3.2) the lexical item *look for* can be substituted for them. In either case, the transformational derivation of *look for* from a complement construction would violate the standard theory's conception of the level of deep structure, at which the morphological integrity of lexical items must be preserved. (Note that if *obviously* is derived from *it is obvious that*, as Bach assumes, this already involves tampering with lexical items. But at least in this case there is a morphological relation between *obvious* and *obviously*.)

Bach's conclusion is that, in order to capture the generalization about the distribution of nonspecific noun phrases, the standard level of deep structure must be abandoned. But this argument has more than one weakness. For one thing, the generalization could be preserved in a way compatible with the standard deep structure level if *look for* were derived not from *try to find* but from *look (for) to find* or *look (for) to have*. This derivation would involve only DELETION, not the substitution of one lexical item for others (or for semantic elements). In support of this solution, we may note that the verb *look* does take complements, at least archaically, as in (37).

(37) He is looking to cause trouble.

And the deletion might be merely an instance of a more general phenomenon which relates such sentences as those in (38) and (39).

(38) (a) Mary wants an icecream.
    (b) Mary wants to have an icecream.
(39) (a) Mary is hoping for a new briefcase for Christmas.
    (b) Mary is hoping to get a new briefcase for Christmas.

More importantly, there is really no parallel between the case of *look for* and Halle's argument about obstruent voicing in Russian. It is true that unless *look for* is derived from a two-clause construction, two principles will be needed to predict the distribution of nonspecificity—the general principle governing complement constructions, and a special principle covering *look for* and a handful of similar examples. But against this extra semantic rule must be set the extra syntactic rule which would be needed, on Bach's proposal, to derive *look for* from a complement construction. A simplicity argument therefore does not go through. With the level of taxonomic phonemic structure, there must be two voicing rules; without it there can be one. But with or without the standard deep structure level, there must be two rules to account for the distribution of nonspecificity. (For arguments of a similar type but based on different data, see McCawley, 1968b, and G. Lakoff, 1968; these are discussed in Chomsky, 1970b.)

Let us turn now to the second question about deep structure that we posed at the beginning of this section. If by deep structures we mean those structures which are directly generated and serve as input to the transformational component, then both interpretive and generative semantic theories admit a level of deep structure. The crucial question for generative semantics is whether semantic structures can be directly, nontransformationally, generated. This question has rarely been explicitly raised, but there are indications that the answer is negative.

In GS underlying structures, quantifiers appear as higher predicates, and their relative scope is signaled by their relative height in the phrase marker (see G. Lakoff, 1965). The sentence (40) is scope-ambiguous.

(40) Some boys like many girls.

On one of its readings, the quantifier *some* has scope over the quantifier *many*; the sentence means 'There are some boys such that for each one there are many girls that he loves'. (Each of these girls, however, might be loved by only one boy.) On this reading, (40) would be assigned the underlying semantic structure (4-7).

(4-7)

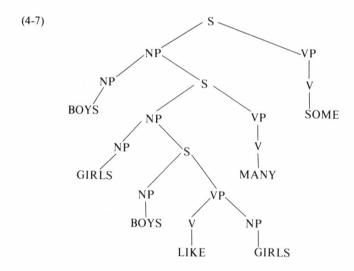

On the other reading of (40), it is *many* that has the wider scope. The sentence means 'There are many girls such that each is loved by some boys.' (In this case, each of the girls must be loved by MORE than one boy.) The underlying semantic structure for this reading of (40) would be (4-8).

The position of a quantifier in the underlying phrase marker thus specifies its semantic scope. But notice that in order to gain the freedom to vary the relative positions of quantifiers according to their scope, the quantifiers have had to be separated from the noun phrases in which they appear in surface structures. The words *some* and *boys*, or *many* and *girls*, are not grouped together as a single constituent in the underlying structures (4-7) and (4-8). This separation of quantifiers from the nouns they modify

(4-8)

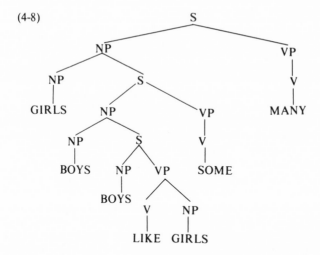

makes it very difficult to capture certain generalizations about semantic structures.[5]

One generalization is that, at the semantic level, each noun must have one and only one quantifier (or other determiner). A semantic representation such as (4-9), which lacks a quantifier for one of its nouns, has to be regarded as ill-formed; it does not represent a coherent meaning.

(4-9)

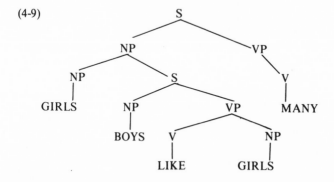

To say this is NOT to deny that a noun can appear without a determiner in SURFACE STRUCTURES, as *boys* does in sentence (41).

(41) Boys like many girls.

5. An alternative analysis might separate the noun phrases as a whole from the sentential frame in which they appear, and order these noun phrases so as to represent their relative scope. A different but comparable problem would afflict this proposal.

But even this sentence must be represented as having a quantifier for the noun *boys* at the level of semantic representation. This is because (41) exhibits exactly the same kind of scope ambiguity as the sentence (40). And quantifier scope ambiguities must be captured at the semantic level by the relative positions of TWO quantifiers. (This general principle is accepted by virtually all semantic theories, even those which disagree with Lakoff's analysis of quantifiers as the verbs of higher clauses.)

What we have established is that (4-9) is not a correct semantic representation for any sentence. In particular, it is not the proper semantic representation for sentence (41). If (4-9) were ever generated at the semantic level, it is hard to see how the transformations could fail to convert it, incorrectly, into (41). But it is equally hard to see how to prevent (4-9) from being generated at the semantic level as long as the semantic level is identified with the deep structure level, and is defined by phrase structure rules or their equivalent. The problem is that phrase structure rules cannot impose constraints across widely separated constituents such as the quantifiers and nouns of GS semantic representations. The semantic representation (4-9) needs another quantifier in another higher clause, because it contains TWO nouns in its lowest clause. To state this dependency across clauses by means of phrase structure rules, one would have to resort to powerful context-sensitive mechanisms. These are not needed for the generation of STANDARD deep structures. Well-formedness conditions on GS deep structures, which represent meaning, thus appear to be considerably more complex than those on standard deep structures, which do not.

The significance of this extra complexity becomes apparent when we compare a standard theory treatment of the same data. A standard grammar would generate deep structures in which a noun and its quantifier are adjacent and form a single constituent. The dependency between quantifier and noun would thus be a very local one, and it could be captured by a simple phrase structure rule.

(42) NP ⟶ Q . N
(Noun Phrase is rewritten as Quantifier followed by Noun)

Of course, the structures generated by a base component containing this rule could not serve as representations of meaning, for quantifier scope ambiguities would not be resolved; both readings of an ambiguous sentence like (40) would have the same representation, in which the quantifier appears directly before the noun it modifies. Therefore these standard deep structures would have to be associated with semantic representations by means of interpretive rules. Conceivably, though by no means necessarily, these semantic representations would be exactly like Lakoff's. The important point is that the well-formedness conditions on semantic representations which use quantifier position to indicate quantifier scope apparently CAN be stated in a standard grammar which derives these structures INDIRECTLY by operations over nonsemantic deep structures. Suitable interpretive rules could derive the semantic representations (4-7) and (4-8) from the deep structure of sentence (40). In interpreting the generic noun phrase *boys* in sentence (41), they could supply a quantifier at the semantic level. And the ill-formed semantic representation (4-9) would never be produced, because the phrase structure rules would generate no deep structure from which it could be derived.

To summarize: a set of phrase structure rules (especially context free phrase structure rules) defines a heavily restricted set of linguistic structures. It is the fundamental premise of transformational grammar that the set of surface structures of a natural language is not such a set. It now appears that the set of semantic representations is also not such a set. Like surface structures, however, semantic structures can be derived FROM structures that meet phrase structure conditions, by means of rules which can alter the configurations of constituents. These rules, the interpretive semantic rules of a standard or extended standard theory grammar, must of course be formulated in detail. (See Kroch, 1974, for some proposals within the extended standard theory; Kroch's interpretive rules apply to derived structures rather than to deep structures as implied in the simplified discussion above.) New problems might arise in the course of developing these rules, indeed we might all be wrong about the proper way to represent quantifier scope. So the observations presented here are not immune to the results of further research, but they do provide a *prima facie* argument for the existence of a level of syntactic deep structure distinct from, and shallower than, the semantic level.

Nevertheless, as so often in linguistics, there is a way around the argument, and it relies on the interchangeability of filters and rules discussed in Section 4.1. Generative semantics takes the initial, nontransformational, stage of a derivation to be the semantic representation, and the quantifier argument does not really preclude this. All that it shows is that the phrase structure rules which build up well-formed semantic representations will also, unless restricted in complex ways, generate some ill-formed semantic representations which must not be transformed into surface sentences. But these incorrect semantic structures need not be excluded at the semantic level; derivations that begin with them could be filtered out at a later stage— presumably when the quantifiers are lowered into position next to the nouns they modify, since it is at this stage that the quantifier-noun dependency can be stated most simply. The 'source' of GS derivations would still be semantic structures, though some of the well-formedness conditions on those structures would be imposed at a later derivational stage which in important respects resembles the standard level of deep structure. Whether this would actually be tantamount to admitting the reality of the standard deep structure level would then depend on whether this and other filters needed in a GS grammar turn out to apply at the SAME stage of derivations, a stage that would qualify as a genuine linguistic LEVEL. This question is an extremely significant one for the decision between generative semantics and the standard theory. Recognizing its importance is itself a step forward; finding the answer to it is likely to prove a much more arduous task.

4.4. CUMULATIVE VERSUS NONCUMULATIVE DERIVATIONS

We have been focusing on differences between the derivations defined by different theories, trying to extract different predictions which could be put to an empirical test. But some differences between them apparently have no empirical consequences. One example is the 'cumulativeness' of Katz's semantic derivations compared with the 'noncumulative' character of generative semantics derivations.

A semantic derivation on Katz's theory begins with an underlying phrase marker with readings associated with its lexical items. It ends with a semantically interpreted underlying phrase marker (SIUPM). This is the same syntactic phrase marker, except that it now has readings associated with all of its nodes. A SIUPM (as observed in Section 3.1) is a multidimensional tree structure; a node dominates both a sequence of syntactic nodes indicating the syntactic composition of the phrase, and also a set of readings indicating its semantic content. The function of the projection rules is to develop readings which can be attached to higher nodes in the phrase marker, nodes which already dominate syntactic configurations. In this respect, the projection rules are quite unlike the familiar syntactic transformations. And SIUPMs are quite unlike the two-dimensional tree structures (with or without additional indicators of focus, etc.) which are the semantic representations in a generative semantics grammar.

However, Katz (1972, Chapter 8) has claimed that the prelexical derivations of generative semantics (insofar as 'prelexical' is well-defined) are simply the inverses of the semantic derivations defined by his own projection rules. In making the comparison, Katz compares GS semantic representations with his SENTENCE READINGS, not with SIUPMs. In Section 5.4 we will investigate the relations between all three types of structure (SIUPMs, sentence readings, and GS semantic representations) in more detail. Here we are concerned with a difference between Katz's projection rules and the transformational rules used in the corresponding part of GS derivations.

To illustrate the cumulativeness of Katz's semantic derivations, let us consider the derivation of the sentence (43).

(43) Harry reminds me of Fred Astaire.

After lexical insertion, the standard theory deep structure phrase marker for this sentence would be (4-10).[6]

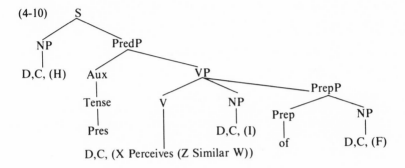

Lexical items are represented as complexes of phonological, syntactic and semantic specifications. Since they are not relevant to the present discussion, I have merely indicated the phonological and syntactic specifications in (4-10) with the abbreviations D and C respectively. The semantic representations of *Harry*, *me* and *Fred Astaire* have been abbreviated by (H), (I) and (F) respectively, since their internal structure is not relevant here. The semantic representation of *remind* is given in full; it appears under the verb node as $(X$ *Perceives* $(Z$ *Similar* $W))$. This a complex semantic marker, and contains the categorized variables X, Z and W which mark the positions into which the readings of the direct object, the subject, and the prepositional object respectively are to be inserted by the projection rule (see Section 3.1).

The projection rule works up from the bottom of the phrase marker. It first substitutes (I) and (F) for X and W respectively in the reading for the verb, and attaches the derived reading to the VP node. The result is (4-11).

6. The semantic analysis of the verb *remind* which is represented by (4-10) is an analysis given in Postal (1970), which Katz has simply recast in the notation of his own theory for the purposes of comparison with a GS derivation. This is convenient, for if both theories agree on what the word means, then differences between the formal mechanisms for treating that meaning will stand out more clearly. But in fact Katz does not endorse Postal's account of the meaning of *remind*; he uses it only for illustration.

(4-11)

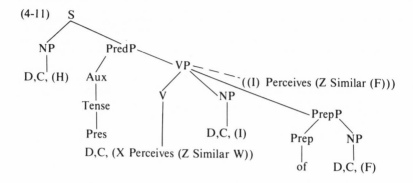

If we ignore the Tense constituent, the next and final step is the substitution of the subject reading (*H*) for the categorized variable *Z* in the reading for the *VP*, to give a reading for the *S* node. The result is (4-12).

(4-12)

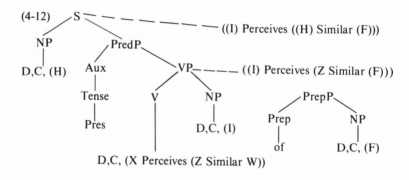

This derivation is cumulative in the sense that the output of each projection rule is added to the structure input to it. It may be compared with the apparently equivalent but NONcumulative derivation (4-13). Here, the derived reading for a constituent, produced by the projection rule, is SUBSTITUTED for the structure that the node previously dominated. The result is not a SIUPM but simply a sentence reading.

We can get a sense of the difference between these two semantic derivations by observing that the cumulative derivation (4-10)–(4-12) would be analogous to a syntactic derivation in which the output of each transformation did not replace the input but combined with it to. form a multi-dimensional phrase marker. It is as if the Passive transformation, for example, were to transform the structure (4-14) (a) into the structure (4-14) (b).

(4-13) (a) as in (4-10)

(b)

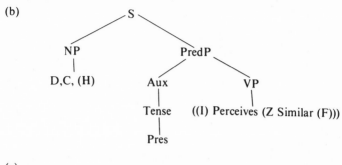

(c)

(4-14) (a)

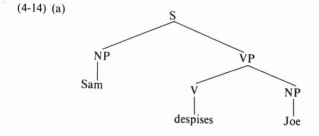

(b)

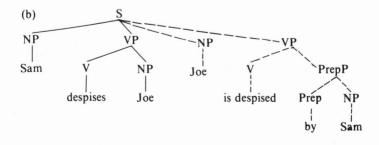

Each subsequent transformation would add a further dimension to the structure, and the final result would be a 'surface structure' which would encapsulate the whole of the syntactic derivation. This is not the way in which syntactic derivations are normally conceived.[7] If the semantic part of derivations is to be cumulative, it will therefore be very different from the syntactic part of derivations. Let us consider whether there is any justification for this.

First, it might be argued in favor of cumulative derivations that the adding of derived readings to the phrase marker to produce a SIUPM is a natural way to express the fact that the semantic component is interpretive—it adds an interpretation to what is already there in the phrase marker. In Section 4.1 (footnote 1) we distinguished several senses of "interpret". Projection rules are interpretive (as syntactic transformations are) in the sense that they do not construct an infinite set of structures out of a finite input, but map the structures of one infinite set into those of another. In THIS sense, the interpretiveness of projection rules cannot be taken to justify cumulative derivations—unless we are also prepared to argue from the interpretiveness of syntactic transformations that cumulative SYNTACTIC derivations are necessary. In a more ordinary sense of "interpret," projection rules are interpretive in that they provide interpretations (meanings) for sentences. But this too does not necessitate cumulative derivations; a meaning can be assigned to a sentence by associating the deep structure with a sentence reading just as well as by attaching the sentence reading to the deep structure phrase marker.

A different defense of SIUPMs might be that they are needed because some semantic properties and relations cannot be defined over sentence readings alone but require reference to deep structure phrase markers too. This point will be discussed in more detail in Section 5.4. For now, we may simply note that even if this is true, it is inconclusive. Some syntactic properties of sentences are defined over deep (and perhaps intermediate syntactic structures as well as over surface structures, and this is not taken to necessitate cumulative syntactic derivations. Nothing is LOST in a noncumulative derivation, as long as definitions of syntactic and semantic properties are given access to all stages of the derivation and not just to its final output stage. The same point applies to the provision of readings for the constituents within a sentence. A SIUPM clearly does contain constituent reading as well as a sentence reading, but this does not make cumulative derivation superior to noncumulative ones. It is true that in the noncumulative derivation (4-13), information about the meanings of constituents (e.g. the VP constituent) is not present at the final stage (c). But it is present a stage (b).

Our arguments so far do not establish that cumulative derivations ar incorrect. Rather, they suggest that they are a mere notational variation o

7. But see the discussion of 'trace theory' in Chapter 6.

noncumulative derivations in which definitions of semantic properties have access to intermediate structures in the derivation. However, there is one substantive difference between the two types of derivation, and it is a difference which militates in favor of noncumulative derivations.

A theory permitting only noncumulative derivations has built into it the restriction that the operation of each rule is governed solely by the output of the previous one and not by prior structures in the derivation. Katz's projection rules do not, as a matter of fact, utilize information from prior structures of the semantic derivation, e.g., information about constituents whose readings have already been amalgamated into derived readings for higher constituents. (This is why it was POSSIBLE to convert the cumulative derivation (4-10)–(4-12) into the noncumulative derivation (4-13), in which constituents are deleted as their readings are amalgamated.) To insist on noncumulative derivations would convert this mere fact about Katz's derivations into an explicit restriction, just as in the case of syntactic derivations. And this would be one more contribution to the general goal of an explicit characterization of the bounds on possible grammars of human languages.

Global rules, which are allowed in a GS grammar, are not restricted in this fashion; they may use information from structures other than the immediately preceding one in the derivation. But Katz's theory explicitly prohibits global rules; and for this constraint to have any force, his theory obviously must also prohibit anything that is equivalent to global rules. So it should prohibit cumulative derivations in which, in principle though not in fact, every rule has access to all earlier structures in the derivation. (Then, if further research should show that global rules ARE essential in the description of natural languages, this would stand out very clearly. As always, there is more to be learned from a very restrictive theory, even if it should eventually prove to be false, than from an over-permissive theory.)

If, for these reasons, we do reject Katz's cumulative derivations (and therefore SIUPMs too), the similarities with GS derivations become much more obvious. The GS derivation proposed by Postal (1970) for the sentence *Harry reminds me of Fred Astaire* is (4-15). (The noun phrases in these structures have not been translated into semantic elements, since their internal semantic structure is not relevant to the discussion.) In this GS derivation, the underlying structure (a) is transformed into (b) by a Noun Phrase Raising transformation; (b) is converted to (c) by the Predicate Raising transformation; (c) becomes (d) by the Psych Movement transformation, which interchanges 'subject' and 'object' noun phrases in much the same fashion as the Passive transformation; (d) is transformed into (e) by the transformation that promotes one noun phrase into subject position. The verb *remind* will then be substituted for *STRIKE SIMILAR* by the lexical insertion rule.

The similarity with Katz's derivation (with the direction inverted) is obvious. It becomes clearer still if we exchange the parenthesization in

(4-15) (a)

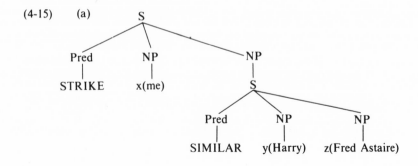

(b)

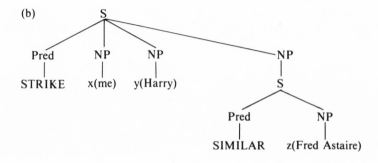

(c)

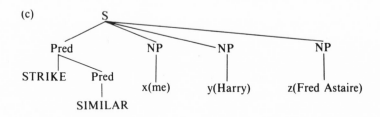

(d)

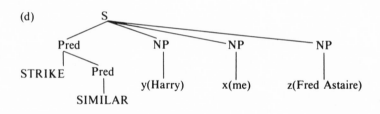

(e)

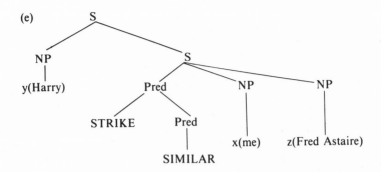

Katz's readings for branching structure (by an algorithm discussed further in Section 5.4). Katz's derivation (4-10)–(4-12) would then take the form (4-16).

(4-16)   (a)

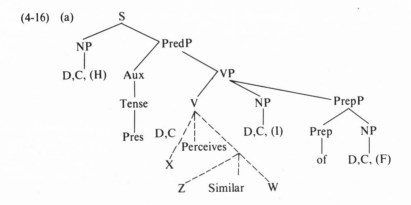

(b)

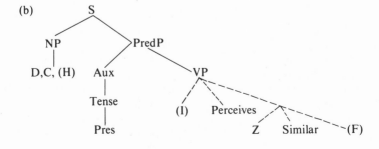

(c)

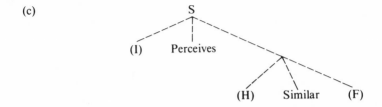

I do not mean to imply that (4-16) is exactly identical with the GS derivation (4-15); there do remain differences between them. One obvious one is directly related to the difference in direction of derivation. Like GS transformations, Katz's projection rules make structural changes. But unlike GS transformations, the changes that the projection rules make are already implicit in the reading of the verb. For example, the reversal of the readings of *Harry* and *I* is determined by the categorized variables in the reading of *remind*. Because of the direction of its derivations, GS must allow the rules that make structural changes to apply freely, and then make the choice of lexical items depend on what changes have occurred. Because of the opposite direction of his derivations, Katz has to make the structural changes that occur dependent on the lexical items; the appropriate changes differ from verb to verb, and are coded into the lexical reading for each verb by means of its categorized variables. (See the comparison of Fillmore's theory with Gruber's in Section 3.4.) How significant this difference is has not been established, though at first sight it looks as if there may be fewer degrees of freedom in the GS approach which requires the relation between word meanings and sentence meanings to be characterizable by general rules.

Other differences between the derivations, differences in the semantic representations themselves, are discussed in Section 5.4. The purpose of this section has been to clarify and compare the operation of the syntax-semantics mapping rules of the two theories. The two types of rule may be formally constrained in different ways (see Section 4.2), and the direction of derivation is at least superficially different. But both sets of rules serve essentially the same function; what is common to both theories is the recognition that the configuration of semantic elements in the meaning representation of a sentence may differ from the configuration of its lexical items. (Arguments for this are presented in Section 5.3.) In the earliest versions of Katz's theory, before the introduction of complex semantic markers containing categorized variables, the projection rules merely trans-lated constituents into semantic elements. Now, just like the corresponding transformational rules of generative semantics, they also alter the relative positions of constituents. And once Katz's derivations have been rendered noncumulative, as we have argued that they should be, we see that both kinds of rules define quite similar semantic derivations.

5
Semantic Representations

We have compared semantic theories so far with respect to the form and mode of application of the rules which associate semantic representations with other structural representations in the derivations of sentences. Now we turn to the properties of the semantic representations themselves. In a sense this is to put the cart before the horse, though it simplifies exposition to do so. But let us pause briefly to consider the relation between the issues of the previous chapter and those that will be our concern in this.

At a very general level, we would expect some interdependence between claims about semantic representations and claims about the overall organization of grammars, in particular the relation between semantics and syntax. One example of this that we considered in Section 4.3 is that discoveries about the structural properties of semantic representations can have implications for whether or not those representations can be generated by phrase structure rules. Another example is the GS claim that there is no level of syntactic deep structure distinct from the semantic level, and that the 'semantic rules' of the grammar are therefore really syntactic transformations. This requires that semantic representations must take the form of syntactic phrase markers. Nevertheless, there are some degrees of freedom. For example, even if it should turn out that semantic representations do have the form of syntactic phrase markers, this would not force us to the conclusion that semantics is generative. For there is nothing in principle to prevent a grammar from assigning semantic representations of this kind by means of interpretive rules (of an appropriate sort) which apply to standard deep structures.

At the level of particular rules, the relation between rules and structures is very close. Grammatical rules are structure-dependent, i.e., whether and how a rule applies to a grammatical representation that is input to it depends on the internal structure of that representation. Hypotheses about semantic representations therefore inevitably interact with hypotheses about the rules that generate them and interrelate them with other structures in a derivation. In constructing a grammar for a language, we have to juggle both at once. Typically, what comes first is evidence about some grammatical representations; certain properties of expressions are observed which must be formally captured. Then rules must be formulated which will associate these representations with representations of other properties of the expressions. Very often it turns out that the rules can be simplified if the relation between the two levels of representation is broken down into a sequence of smaller steps, each the responsibility of a single rule. Each of these rules then determines an intermediate representation in the derivation.

Semantic representations are not intermediate structures; they stand at one end of derivations and thus constitute one of the points at which the grammar connects most closely with empirical observations about the language. Therefore, the more we can determine about the meanings of expressions and how they should be formally represented, the more we can constrain the rather murky area in the middle of derivations over which there is so much disagreement.

In this chapter, we will develop some minimal requirements on any adequate system of semantic representation, based on some quite general observations about the kinds of fact that semantic representations must represent. The questions we will be concerned with include: What are the minimal elements of meaning and in what combinations do they occur? How do word meanings relate to each other? How do word meanings add up to sentence meanings? Later in the chapter, we will address some of the problems involved in evaluating alternative systems of semantic representation, all of which meet the minimal requirements.

5.1. THE SEMANTIC PRIMITIVES

The meaning of a sentence cannot be regarded as monolithic. It is only by treating a sentence meaning as composed somehow out of the meanings of smaller constituents that we can characterize the meanings of the infinite range of nonsynonymous sentences in a language. But a language contains only a finite number of morphemes, and the meaning of a morpheme therefore could in principle be represented as a single, unanalyzable entity. Nevertheless, most current semantic theories, and many traditional ones too, analyze meanings into 'smaller' component meanings, and assign to a lexical item a semantic representation consisting of a complex of semantically primitive elements. (Some examples, from both interpretive and generative semantics, were given in Chapter 3.)

The motivation for a componential (decompositional) approach to the meanings of lexical items is this. If the meaning of a lexical item, for example *father*, were not analyzed into components, a grammar would have to simply list the semantic properties and relations of that item as independent facts: that *father* is synonymous with *male parent*; that it is antonymous with *mother*; that *male father* is redundant; that *deciduous father* is anomalous; that *female father* is contradictory; and so on. This would be descriptively uneconomical and, more importantly, would miss the fact that these properties are NOT independent of each other. There could be no word synonymous with *elephant*, antonymous with *raspberry*, redundant with *oxidized*, contradictory with *sad* and entailing *archeological*. A componential approach to meaning guarantees this, for all the semantic properties of an item are determined on the basis of the same fixed set of meaning components. Recognizing components of maleness and parenthood in the meaning of *father* SIMULTANEOUSLY explains (given suitable componential analyses of other words) the contradictoriness of *female father*, the antonymy of *father* and *mother*, and so on. The componential analysis of a lexical item is idiosyncratic, but the properties of the item can be determined from this analysis by general principles and need not be independently listed.

The question of how far the extraction of semantic components can or should be taken (how 'delicate' the meaning analysis should be) has often troubled linguists. Should we extract only those components (e.g., animateness, maleness, abstractness, causation) which recur throughout the vocabulary of the language and which can plausibly be regarded as universal? Wouldn't this mean stopping short of the point at which all nonsynonymous words are assigned distinct componential analyses? If so, how else could we capture the nonrecurrent, idiosyncratic 'remainders' of word meanings which serve to distinguish nonsynonymous words? If we were to analyze these into components too, wouldn't we be in danger of postulating more meaning components than there are words in a language to be analyzed?

These questions are presumably what lie behind the distinction between semantic markers and distinguishers that was drawn in the early stages of Katz's theory. Katz and Fodor (1963) wrote:

> Semantic markers are the elements in terms of which semantic relations are expressed in a theory. . . . the semantic markers assigned to a lexical item in a dictionary entry are intended to reflect whatever systematic relations hold between that item and the rest of the vocabulary of the language. On the other hand, the distinguishers assigned to a lexical item are intended to reflect what is idiosyncratic about the meaning of that item.

An illustration of this distinction is the dictionary entry (5-1) for *bachelor* (see Section 3.1).

(5-1)

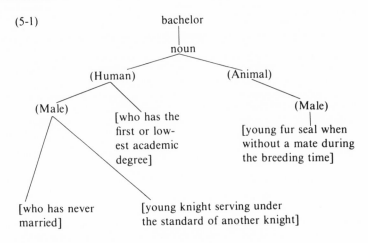

The elements in parentheses are semantic markers; those in square brackets are distinguishers. Notice that the only components represented by semantic markers are the concepts of maleness, humanness, and animalness, which are components of a great many other words in English and other languages as well. But these semantic markers alone hardly begin to distinguish the four senses of *bachelor* from each other.

The Katz and Fodor characterization of distinguishers was taken to imply (i) that a distinguisher can appear only once in the dictionary of a language, i.e., that it represents part of only one sense of one lexical item, and (ii) that selection restrictions (which encode semantic *relations* between parts of sentences) may not refer to distinguishers but only to semantic markers.

These claims have been criticized. Conclusion (i) is obviously untenable if there are synonymous lexical items in a language whose meaning must be represented with a distinguisher, since then the distinguisher would appear twice in the dictionary. Also, the existence of the English word *spinster* means that the distinguisher [*who has never married*] in the Katz and Fodor dictionary entry for *bachelor* would have to be converted to a semantic marker. Even the highly idiosyncratic and unsystematic concept of being without a mate during the breeding season would have to be represented by a semantic marker if there were also a word in English meaning, for instance, a young male rabbit without a mate during the breeding season.

Conclusion (ii) also leads to the reanalysis of many of the original distinguishers as markers. Katz and Fodor themselves presented one potential example. Suppose a sentence like *The old bachelor finally died* is regarded by English speakers as having only the 'unmarried' sense of *bachelor* and not the 'young knight' sense. Then the information that a bachelor knight is necessarily young would have to be encoded by a marker and not by a distinguisher, since this information would then be interacting with a selection restriction to disambiguate the sentence. In Katz and Postal (1964), the marker (*Young*) was in fact adopted. Bolinger (1965) has demonstrated that, with a little ingenuity, virtually any aspect of the meaning of a word can be shown to be relevant to the disambiguation or anomaly of some expression, with the consequence that it must be represented by a semantic marker.

Obviously, if a decompositional analysis is to capture ALL the semantic properties and relations of a lexical item, the decomposition must be very fine-grained. (We may dispense with the objection that the result might be more semantic components than lexical items in the language, by observing that this would be no defect; the purpose of extracting semantic components is to reveal meanings and meaning relations, not to reduce the size of the vocabulary. A phonological feature analysis would not be invalidated by the discovery that there are more features than phonemes in some language.) Nevertheless, as the compositional analysis becomes finer-grained, the role of the Katz and Fodor distinguishers becomes smaller and smaller until, we might suspect, it reaches vanishing point.

Katz (1972, Chapter 3) has recently offered a defense of distinguishers, in which he refines, or perhaps changes, the early definition.

> Distinguishers can be regarded as providing a purely denotative distinction which plays the role of separating lexical items that would otherwise be fully synonymous. Unlike semantic markers, which represent conceptual components of senses of lexical items and expressions, distinguishers mark purely perceptual distinctions among the referents of conceptually identical senses.

The specification of the meanings of 'perceptual' words like the color adjectives has long been problematic. Typically, we learn the meanings of these words not by being given definitions in the dictionary sense, but through ostensive definition, by being shown red things and green things and being told that these are called "red" and "green." These two words differ in their extensions, the classes of things to which they apply. The extension of *red* includes ripe tomatoes and embarrassed faces; the extension of *green* includes healthy grass and unhealthy faces. Yet there does not seem to be any CONCEPTUAL difference between the two words to which the difference in extension can be ascribed. It is this kind of difference in extension or denotation, not correlated with a conceptual difference, that Katz now uses distinguishers to represent.

With this new characterization of distinguishers, the contrast between markers and distinguishers as different theoretical entities can no longer be motivated by appeal to the different roles they play in the grammar. For one thing, distinguishers as well as markers must be able to appear in more than one lexical entry. (As Katz observes, the fact that scarlet things are red is an analytic truth, i.e., the concept of being scarlet includes the concept of being red. To capture this, the reading assigned to *scarlet* must include the reading assigned to *red*. Hence, both readings will contain the same distinguisher.) Also, selection restrictions must be allowed to take account of distinguishers as well as of semantic markers. (The adjective *flaming*, for example, can modify only color words in the red-orange-yellow range; the phrase *the flaming blue of her eyes* is anomalous. So this selection restriction needs access to the distinctions between different color words, and these are encoded by distinguishers.)

If the semantic theory is to persist in drawing a formal distinction between markers and distinguishers, this must therefore be justified either by the fact that some contrasts are perceptual and some are conceptual, or by the existence of purely denotative contrasts. Perhaps these two classifications are equivalent, though it is not obvious that they must be. In any case, the perceptual/conceptual distinction does not seem to constitute a very telling argument in favor of distinguishers. It is also very hard to draw. (Katz implies that redness is perceptual but that roundness is conceptual, since the latter is identifiable in more than one sensory mode.) However, the existence of differences in denotation not correlated with differences in meaning does call for special treatment, for the traditional assumption has been that denotation is DETERMINED BY meaning.

It is arguable that this problem is a quite general one, not limited to words which designate properties that we would be inclined to call perceptual. Once we have factored out a component that can be represented by the marker (*Colored*), there seems to be nothing more we can say about the MEANING of the word *red*, though we must still distinguish its denotation from those of *green* and *purple*. But also, once we have factored out (*Animal*) and perhaps (*Mammal*), there seems to be nothing more we can say about the MEANING of the word *cow*. Of course, cows differ from horses and dogs and camels in some quite familiar ways, but it is no part of the MEANING of *cow* that cows say "moo," and give milk, and look thus-and-so. These are not NECESSARY truths about cows; a cow that did not say "moo" would still be a cow, and so would one that did not give milk or was purple or looked like a horse. Another example is the word *chair*, for which Katz has given the dictionary entry (1).

(1) (Object), (Physical), (Non-living), (Artifact), (Furniture), (Portable), (Something with legs), (Something with a back), (Something with a seat), (Seat for one)

There are modern chairs that show that not all of the properties Katz ascribes to chairs are analytically tied to the concept of being a chair. But if it is NOT part of the meaning of *chair* that chairs have backs, are portable and so on, how can its meaning distinguish its denotation from that of *couch*, *stool, bench*, and other related words?

These examples show that even without being sceptical of the GENERAL notion of an analytic truth, one can be distrustful of many of the putative analytic relations that have often been claimed to hold between concepts. This poses a serious problem for decompositional theories of meaning. If the meaning of *cow*, for example, is analytically related only to the concepts of being an animal and being a mammal (arguably not even to these), then there are too few analytic connections between the meaning of *cow* and other concepts to permit a complete decomposition of the meaning of *cow* into a complex of more primitive concepts. If we were to insist on a decompositional approach to meaning, the only way to keep separate the words *cow, horse, dog*, etc. would be to adopt theoretical constructs (which we might want to call distinguishers) such as [*Bovine*], [*Equine*], [*Canine*], whose sole function is to record the fact that the words have different extensions.

The implication is that the meaning of a word is sometimes pretty threadbare, that (contrary to commonly received views) it does not even in principle determine the extension of the word. If this is so, then a specification of the meaning of a sentence will not always provide a complete account of its truth conditions. These conclusions are important to the conception of meaning, so let us review the structure of the argument. First, there are empirical facts (intuitions about analyticity) which preclude excessively 'delicate' decompositions of certain word meanings; many properties that we all associate with cows, that standard reference dictionaries associate with cows, and perhaps that we use for actually identifying cows in typical cases, are not analytically tied to the property of being a cow. Hence they cannot be used to distinguish the property of being a cow from the property of being a horse, etc. At the extreme, the property of being a cow could not be further semantically analyzed at all; it would have to be one of the primitive elements of the semantic system. The conclusion would be that the primitive elements of the system are sometimes quite large, 'word-sized' ones.

If the argument ended here, it would be important but it would not threaten traditional views of meaning and reference. We could simply accept that one of the primitive concepts is bovinity. Like all concepts, it determines an extension. Of course, there is the problem of saying HOW it does this, but in this respect bovinity is no more problematic than 'thinner' concepts such as the concept of being an object, the concept of being animate, and so on. However, Katz's new definition of distinguishers suggests we should press further, and consider whether there is any sense in which bovinity is a concept at all, or whether it is merely a direct characterization of an extension. In other words, we might wonder whether the meaning/reference distinction really applies in this case. Katz's claim that there are "purely denotative distinctions" between words "that would otherwise be fully synonymous" certainly raises this question. He apparently intends that *cow* and *horse*, or at least *red* and *green*, are not fully synonymous and yet that they differ only denotatively—matters of meaning and reference are not distinguished.

We will return to this matter in Chapter 6. Here I wish to turn to a slightly different problem that afflicts a decompositional approach to word meaning. It also leads to the conclusion that the minimal concepts are larger than they have been taken to be. The tacit assumption seems to be that a word meaning can be broken up into a number of independent parts and that all semantic properties and relations can be characterized by appeal to these independent bits of meaning and the ways in which they combine. This model implies that given, for example, that it is analytic that all red things are colored, then the concept of being colored is one component of the concept of being red. It is only ONE component, for to say that something is red is to say more than that it is colored. So now at least one other component of the meaning of *red* must be identified. Let us assume, just for convenience, that there is only one, i.e., that no further analysis is possible. For this component to be independent of the coloredness component, it must consist of the concept of redness-but-not-necessarily-coloredness. But there surely is no such concept (or even percept). There is no property R which does not itself contain the property of being colored, such that being red = being colored + R.

What this means is that, quite apart from worries about conceptual/perceptual or meaning/reference distinctions, lexical decomposition cannot capture ALL semantic relations. Since we cannot admit components which are internally incoherent, we cannot capture the fact that redness necessarily implies coloredness by factoring redness into two parts, coloredness and something else. (Notice the similarity with morphology: *cranberry* contains the morpheme *berry*, but factoring this out would require admitting *cran* as a morpheme too.)

Representing the meaning of *red* by means of the semantic marker (*Colored*) plus a distinguisher thus looks feasible only as long as we do not ask what property the distinguisher expresses. What must be faced is that the ultimate components of meaning are atomic in the sense that they are not themselves fully decomposable into other smaller components, but are nevertheless internally complex in the sense that they CONTAIN other smaller components. Though the concept of being colored cannot intelligibly be SUBTRACTED from the concept of redness, it is nevertheless contained therein, and this fact must somehow be recorded. This is the sense in which decomposition stops short before all significant semantic relations have been captured. At least some relations between concepts must be captured in a different fashion.

Now it turns out that containment relations between the minimal semantic components are already implicitly acknowledged in Katz's theory.

They are expressed by REDUNDANCY RULES (or "category inclusion rules"). These were introduced by Katz and Postal (1964) to state certain regular dependencies between semantic markers in word readings. For example, any reading which contains the semantic marker (*Human*) must also contain the marker (*Physical Object*). This is equivalent to saying that it is analytic that humans are physical objects, that the concept of being a physical object is contained within the concept of being human.

In the earliest versions of Katz's theory, there were no semantic redundancy rules. Dictionary entries were hierarchically structured. To capture the dependency between semantic markers, (*Human*) would appear lower on the hierarchy than (*Physical Object*), indicating that the feature (*Human*) could only properly be applied to those things with the feature (*Physical Object*). But subsequently, these hierarchies were abandoned, for reasons very similar to those which Chomsky gave in *Aspects* (1965, Chapter 2) for dropping a hierarchical treatment of syntactic features in favor of a cross-classification system.

Consider the male/female and human/nonhuman distinctions. These both divide the domain of animate things (or animals, depending on what we say about plants, etc.). They divide it in different ways, but neither division is in any sense 'prior' or 'superior' to the other. In fact they cross cut each other; there are four categories—male humans, female humans, male nonhumans and female nonhumans. In the Katz and Fodor dictionary entry (5-1) given at the beginning of this section (*Human*) is above (*Male*). But this entry is no better motivated than the alternative (5-2), in which (*Male*) is above (*Human*). In (5-1), the marker (*Male*) had to appear twice; in (5-2), the marker (*Human*) has to appear twice. These duplications reflect the fact that there is a cross-classification of lexical items by semantic markers that is not being properly represented in these hierarchical structures.

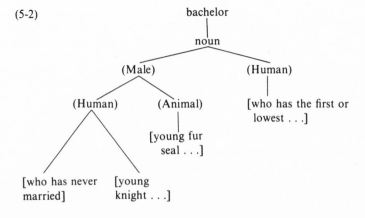

(5-2)

It is for this reason that Katz's readings now consist of unordered sets of semantic markers, distinguishers and selection restrictions. Some dependencies between markers do exist, as for example between (*Human*) and (*Physical Object*). But since a full hierarchy is impossible, these dependencies are now simply listed in the form of redundancy rules such as those in (2).

(2) (a) (Human) ⟶ (Physical Object)
    (b) (Furniture) ⟶ (Artifact)

These rules are called redundancy rules because they permit the omission from dictionary entries of semantic markers whose presence is fully determined, such as (*Physical Object*) in the context of (*Human*). But their real importance is not that they conveniently shrink dictionary entries, but that they capture relations—containment relations—between the primitive elements of the system. The concept of being a physical object is CONTAINED IN the concept of being human. (Equivalently, *is human* entails *is a physical object*.)

A theory which employs semantic redundancy rules implicitly acknowledges that the decompositional approach to meaning is unable to capture ALL relations between meanings. The relation between (*Human*) and (*Physical Object*) is not treated by decomposing the concept of being human into the concept of being a physical object plus some further concept(s). We can see that this is so by observing that if the concept of being human WERE regarded as decomposable, then the theory would have no cause to employ the marker (*Human*) or the redundancy rule at all. Instead of (*Human*), the theory would employ (*Physical Object*) together with some additional marker(s) representing the other component(s) of the concept of being human.

So, as it turns out, the machinery of redundancy rules offers us a solution to the problem posed by the meanings of words like *red*, a problem which the mere postulation of distinguishers did not solve. Our aim is to state that part of the meaning of *red* is the concept of being colored, without thereby committing ourselves to there being any OTHER identifiable component of the meaning of *red*. To do this, we can assign to *red* simply the marker (*Red*), and use the redundancy rule to indicate that the concept represented by this marker includes the concept of being colored.

(3) (Red) ⟶ (Colored)

Apart from the fact that they express relations between universal semantic elements rather than between actual lexical items of the language under study, the redundancy rules would now be functioning just like the MEANING POSTULATES in the work of Carnap (1947) and subsequently of other logicians. The arrow in the redundancy rule can be read as indicating analytic entailment. These rules are thus inference rules; they express analytic entailment relations between words, though WITHOUT translating the words into formulae which represent COMPLETE DECOMPOSITIONS of their meanings. Meaning postulates are just like other inference rules in a logical system, though they are more restricted since they apply only to particular predicates. (And they may be assigned a special status if it is considered important to distinguish between logical implications and analytic entailments).

Recently, Katz and Nagel (1974) have argued against meaning postulates, apparently without realizing that Katz's own theory admits them or at least something closely akin to them. Their argument is fundamentally that meaning postulates do only what lexical decomposition does, and do it less well in various ways. But we have seen that there is something that meaning postulates can do that decomposition cannot, and this is to capture 'one-way' relations between concepts. Decomposition of a word meaning demands that sufficient as well as necessary conditions can be given for that word to be true of something. The components extracted must add up to the full meaning of the word. To put it loosely, not only must the word entail each component, but the components must between them entail the word. Decompositions can thus be viewed as one special case of meaning postulates, the case in which the postulates happen to exhaust the meaning of the word. Because the decomposition approach can only handle 'two-way' entailments, it is inherently less powerful than the meaning postulate approach. Some examples do seem to demand this extra power, but since any proposed increase in the power of linguistic theory must be scrutinized very carefully, the question of whether, and how extensively, meaning postulates are to be employed will no doubt be with us for some time to come.

Since meaning postulates are apparently required for examples like *red/colored*, it might be suggested that they should be the ONLY device in a grammar for capturing meaning relations. That is, even a word like *kill*, whose meaning is supposed to be decomposable into the concepts of causing and dying, would have a dictionary entry whose semantic component contained only meaning postulates. The only difference between *red* and *kill* would then be that in the latter case, the meaning postulates would represent bidirectional entailment. It is worth observing that if a case for this position could be established, it would profoundly affect the conception of a semantic representation.

Decomposition lends itself naturally as a TRANSLATION mechanism. Sentences of a natural language like English can be translated into a 'language' of semantic representation, whose vocabulary is restricted to only the ultimate, irreducible component meanings. This is the source of the by now traditional conception of a semantic representation as an ANALYSIS, an explicit display of the atomic concepts which are the building blocks of the larger meaning that is to be represented. By contrast, meaning postulates (at least insofar as they are not bidirectional) do not provide a basis for this kind of translation. We have proposed the meaning postulate $(Red) \rightarrow (Colored)$, but the English word *red* obviously cannot be TRANSLATED by the semantic marker $(Colored)$ without loss of important semantic information. The most that is possible is a translation of *red* into (Red). That is, language-specific words can still be represented by language-neutral universal semantic symbols, but the translation would not be any more DETAILED or explicit than the expression it translates. The most abstract level of representation provided by the grammar would thus be less abstract than is implied by decompositional theories. (Under a psychological interpretation of grammars, this difference between the two approaches should presumably be significant. See J. D. Fodor, J. A. Fodor, and Garrett, 1975.)

A move of this kind, away from the traditional level of semantic representation, might appear to involve loss of descriptive capacity, since containment relations between word meanings would no longer be captured at this level. What we have argued, however, is that these relations do not after all demand the more abstract, analytic traditional representations. They could be captured instead by the application of meaning postulates to much less abstract representations. However, it does remain to be shown that meaning relations other than entailment, such as ambiguity, redundancy, anomaly, and so on, can be adequately treated in a semantic system without lexical decomposition.

Lakoff (1970) has argued that meaning postulates are necessary, but he proposes a mixed system. He retains lexical decomposition mechanisms to account for certain facts, such as that the sentence *John killed Bill* entails that John caused something. This sentence would be derived from an underlying structure in which *JOHN* is the subject of *CAUSE*. On the other hand, the fact that this sentence entails that Bill died (i.e., that what was caused must actually have taken place), is to be captured by the meaning postulate (4).

(4) CAUSE $(x,S) \longrightarrow S$

Similarly, the word *convince* as in *Sam convinced Tom that he's neurotic* is to be decomposed into *CAUSE TO BELIEVE*. But the fact that the sentence *Sam required Tom to leave* entails that Sam permitted Tom to leave is to be stated by the meaning postulate (5).

(5) REQUIRE $(x,y,S) \longrightarrow$ PERMIT (x,y,S)

Lakoff suggests a number of criteria for deciding which of the two formal mechanisms to use in a given case. For example, he argues that where the relation between an expression and its meaning is governed by constraints like those on syntactic transformations (see Section 4.2), this relation must be expressed by decomposition. That is, it must be captured in the derivation of the expression, which is defined by the rules of the grammar, and not by meaning postulates, which are inference rules holding over structures output by the grammar. The inference rules are assumed not to be subject to syntactic constraints. Also, meaning postulates are assumed to apply only to semantic elements and not to language-specific lexical items. Therefore, when a semantic relation holds between two lexical items despite other variations in their meanings, this relationship must be treated in the grammatical derivation, i.e., by decomposition. Lakoff's examples are *come* and *bring*, as in *come/bring home*, *come/bring up for discussion*, *come/bring to* (of someone who has fainted). The conclusion is that *bring* should be decomposed into the universal semantic element *CAUSE* and the English lexical item *come*.

I will not attempt an evaluation of all of Lakoff's arguments here. It is not clear that the boundary between decompositional rules and meaning postulates must lie exactly where he claims that it does, but this line of research is undoubtedly important. Once it is recognized that meaning postulates are needed in linguistic descriptions, their proper domain must be precisely determined. It may well turn out to be quite considerable.

5.2. ORGANIZATION OF THE DICTIONARY

Every grammar of a language must contain a dictionary which records the associations of phonological, syntactic, and semantic properties which constitute the lexical items of the language. The form that dictionary entries must take interacts with the nature of the lexical insertion process, with how the lexical items get into phrase markers. Also, given that sentence meanings are composed of word meanings, the properties of the semantic specifications in dictionary entries interact with the properties of semantic representations of sentences. Many of the issues that arise in connection with dictionary entries are therefore discussed elsewhere in this book. Here I shall only give examples of dictionary entries proposed in current semantic theories, and raise one question of organization.

In a generative semantics grammar, a lexical item is substituted for a constituent of a phrase marker whose terminal elements are semantic primitives. A dictionary entry must therefore associate a phonological feature matrix and any idiosyncratic syntactic features of the lexical item with some partial phrase marker which represents the meaning. For *kill*, for example, this might be (5-3).

(5-3)

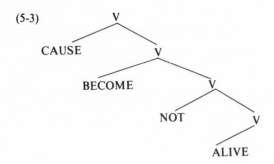

Such a dictionary entry defines a substitution transformation. The structural description of the transformation is the structure (5-3) together with certain contextual specifications such as that *kill* takes a direct object, does not take a complement, etc. This is substituted for by the phonological representation of *kill*, together with any idiosyncratic syntactic features that are needed to govern the behavior of *kill* under post-lexical transformations (see McCawley, 1968a).

Examples of dictionary entries on Katz's theory have already been given, but I repeat here in (5-4) the entry for (or rather one reading for) the verb *chase*.

(5-4)

(((Activity)(((Physical))((Movement)((Speed)$^{(Fast)}$(Following $^{[NP,VP,PredP,S]}_{X<(Object)>}$)))((Purpose)

((To catch $^{[NP,VP,PredP,S]}_{X<(Object)>}$))))) $^{[NP,S]}_{X<(Human) v (Animal)>}$)

This, together with phonological and syntactic feature specifications, would be inserted into a standard deep structure phrase marker by a lexical insertion transformation of the kind defined by Chomsky in *Aspects*, i.e., the whole complex of semantic, syntactic, and phonological specifications is substituted for the dummy terminal symbol Δ.

Jackendoff (1972, Chapter 2) gives (5-5) as the dictionary entry for the verb *open* in its causative sense.

$$(5\text{-}5) \quad \begin{bmatrix} Open \\[1ex] +V \\[1ex] +[NP^1 \underline{\hspace{2cm}} NP^2] \\[1ex] CAUSE\ (NP^1, \begin{bmatrix} CHANGE \\ physical \end{bmatrix} (NP^2,\ NOT\ OPEN,\ OPEN)) \end{bmatrix}$$

The bottom line of (5-5) expresses the meaning of the verb. The super-scripted *NP* symbols in this line relate to those in the line above, which specifies the syntactic context into which the verb can be inserted in deep structures. They thus perform the same function as Katz's categorized variables: they indicate which syntactic constituents have their readings inserted into which position in the reading for the verb. The semantic elements *CAUSE* and *CHANGE* are relational, and their arguments are listed in parentheses after them. $\begin{bmatrix} CHANGE \\ physical \end{bmatrix}$ has the three arguments NP^2, *NOT OPEN*, and *OPEN*. The first argument indicates what undergoes the change, and the others indicate its initial and final states. *CAUSE* has two arguments corresponding to the agent and the event caused, which are respectively NP^1 and the whole of $\begin{bmatrix} CHANGE \\ physical \end{bmatrix} (NP^2,\ NOT\ OPEN,\ OPEN)$.

Besides this representation of FUNCTIONAL structure, Jackendoff's dictionary entries for some words also contain a semantic marker called a MODAL OPERATOR together with a specification of its scope. These will determine the range of modal structures assigned to sentences in which the word appears. (See Section 5.5 for more details.)

Apart from the obvious differences illustrated in these entries, there have been divergent proposals about the individuation of lexical items, and hence about the individuation of dictionary entries. McCawley (1968b) has claimed that an ambiguous word should be regarded as constituting two (or more) distinct lexical items, each with its own dictionary entry. This would be to individuate lexical items by their semantic properties as well as by their phonological and syntactic characteristics. Katz, on the other hand, assumes that an ambiguous word such as *bachelor* constitutes a single lexical item with a single dictionary entry. This entry would contain two (or more) distinct readings. Thus, Katz would individuate lexical items by their form but not by their meaning. A third possibility, which runs counter to normal terminology and which apparently no one has proposed, would be that lexical items are individuated *solely* by their meanings. For example, there would be one dictionary entry pairing the phonological forms of both *rock* and *stone* with a representation of their common meaning; and this would be distinct from the entries for each of the other senses of *rock* and *stone*. What must be determined is whether or not there are any empirical consequences of these different assumptions.

First let us consider two points that might appear to be relevant to the choice between these proposals, but which in fact are not. One explanation of Katz's conception of dictionary entries may lie in a view of the dictionary as a source of readings for lexical items whose phonological and syntactic properties are already specified in syntactic phrase markers. The first step in semantically interpreting a phrase marker is to associate with each lexical item in it the set of readings assigned to that item in the dictionary. It might appear that this dictionary look-up procedure would be facilitated if lexical items were grouped in the dictionary on the basis of their phonological and syntactic properties. By contrast, in a GS derivation, the phonological and syntactic properties of lexical items are substituted for representations of their meanings. A grouping of lexical items in the dictionary on the basis of their meanings might therefore seem natural.

It is very doubtful that the kind of simplicity measure on which such arguments are based is the kind that genuinely contributes to the value of a grammar. In a PERFORMANCE model, it is true, we do need to specify how appropriate lexical items are accessed. But a grammar is not a model of performance; and the GRAMMATICAL rules which insert either readings or phonological matrices into phrase markers would be essentially the same however the dictionary was organized, however difficult it was for these rules to 'find' the appropriate entities to insert.

Secondly, it might appear that the difference between Katz's proposal and the GS proposal about dictionary entries connects with their different approaches to sentence ambiguity. Katz assigns ALL possible readings simultaneously to the lexical items in a phrase marker, and the projection rules derive a single semantically interpreted phrase marker in which ALL possible readings of the sentence are simultaneously represented. Generative semantics captures the ambiguity of a sentence by assigning it two or more distinct derivations from distinct underlying phrase markers, in each of which a single 'reading' is associated with the S node. But these aspects of the two theories are also logically unrelated to the organization of the dictionary. A set of readings could be assigned to an item in a phrase marker even if the readings were not all combined into a single dictionary entry. And readings could be assigned one at a time to items in phrase markers even if a dictionary entry contained more than one reading. Furthermore, it is far from clear that the difference of approach to sentence ambiguity itself has any empirical consequences (see Section 5.4).

An empirical role for the association in the dictionary of different senses of a lexical item was proposed by Weinreich (1966). He suggested that this should be used to capture cases of "lexicologically interesting polysemy," such as that between *land* meaning 'country' and *land* meaning 'real estate.' These cases would thereby be contrasted with cases of "fortuitous homonymy", as between the two senses of *rock* ('mass of stone' and 'rocking motion') which would be assigned distinct dictionary entries. This would certainly be a natural way of capturing such a distinction formally, but there is no agreement at present as to whether there exists such a distinction to be captured, or whether instead there are simply all degrees of partial relatedness between lexical items. Connected with this issue is a host of questions about the proper individuation of word meanings (such as when a meaning has been metaphorically extended and when a word actually acquires a new meaning) which have been given little attention by generative linguists.

In at least one area, however, the issue is a pressing one. A GS grammar expresses the semantic relations between morphologically related lexical items (e.g., between causative and inchoative verbs) by deriving one from another transformationally. A standard theory, operating with a relatively shallow level of deep structure, cannot capture these relations in the transformational derivation, and so must express them in the dictionary. That such items must be related somehow is clear, for the fact that a pair of words like *destroy* and *destruction* share certain semantic properties is surely no accident, even from a synchronic point of view. This relatedness between items presumably does contribute to the real simplicity of a grammar; a language containing *destroy* and *destruction* is in some sense simpler than a language in which *glog* is the noun corresponding to *destroy*.

Chomsky (1970b) suggested capturing the relation between words like *destroy* and *destruction* by assigning them a single dictionary entry, neutral between a noun and a verb. Their common phonological, syntactic, and semantic properties would than have to be listed only once in the dictionary. However, idiosyncratic semantic properties must also be associated with the two syntactic roles. The noun and the verb do not mean the same; and, as Chomsky himself has stressed, the difference between their meanings is not fully predictable on the basis of their syntactic categories. As noted in Section 4.3, the semantic relation between *destroy* and *destruction* is not exactly the same as the relation between *believe* and *belief*, *marry* and *marriage*, and so on.

Jackendoff (1975) has proposed that the verb and noun should each be assigned a separate dictionary entry, and that the overlap between their semantic and syntactic properties should be captured by redundancy rules relating the two entries. (Note that these would be rather different from the redundancy rules discussed in Section 5.1, which relate semantic markers to semantic markers.) How these proposals are to be implemented in detail, and their merits relative to each other and to the transformational approach of generative semantics, still remains to be seen.

There has been some scepticism about the ability of a GS grammar to deal with complicated word meanings. The appeal of a lexical rule substituting *kill* for *CAUSE DIE* may be marred by the thought of collection transformations gathering up semantic elements into a complex such as *CAUSE DIE BY UNLAWFUL MEANS AND WITH MALICE AFORETHOUGHT*, for which *murder* could be substituted. (The example is from Chomsky 1970a.) However, a difficulty for generative semantics does not necessarily constitute support for interpretive semantic theories. Standard and extended standard theory grammars must also represent the meaning of *murder*. Indeed, the greater role of the dictionary in a standard grammar means that it must be more complex, in its entries or its redundancy rules or both, than the dictionary of a GS grammar. Attention has only recently begun to be given to the details of a lexicalist treatment of derivational morphology and other systematic relations between words.

5.3. THE STRUCTURE OF
SENTENCE MEANINGS

Though there is disagreement about the way in which semantic representations should be structured, it is universally agreed that they must BE structured. Talk of SYNTACTIC structure is familiar, indeed the very word "syntax" incorporates the idea of an arrangement or configuration of elements. But while a sentence has a structure, it is not so immediately obvious that the MEANING of a sentence has a structure. In Section 2.6, we saw how Carnap's concept of intensional structure provided a way of individuating the meanings of logically equivalent sentences, which are otherwise not differentiated on a theory of meanings as necessary truth conditions. In linguistic semantics, there has been less concern with what meanings really are, and more with the development of adequate descriptive devices for meaning within formal grammars. But a similar evolution from unstructured to structured meaning representations can be discerned. This is such an important point that I will lay out the motivation for it in detail. I hope also that the discussion will illuminate some of the respects in which different linguistic theories have offered alternative solutions for fundamentally the same problem.

Note first that to say that the meaning of a sentence is structured is not to say that it must be represented diagrammatically rather than discursively, but to make a claim about the kind of information that must be specified, in whatever mode it is presented. The information that is carried by a syntactic phrase marker, a logical formula, or a structural diagram of a molecule can also be given discursively. In place of a phrase marker we could say: This sentence consists of a noun phrase followed by a verb phrase which in turn consists of a verb and . . . . But whether presented diagrammatically or in a lengthy English sentence, this specification identifies significant groupings of elements in the sentence, groupings which function in the prediction of a variety of properties of the sentence and its relations to other sentences of the language. Meaning specifications, in whatever notation they are couched, must also be structured in this sense. We have already argued that sentence meanings must be regarded as made up of smaller meanings (atomic concepts, components). Now we shall see that to specify only WHICH smaller meanings make up the meaning of a sentence is not sufficient; we must also state how these smaller meanings are grouped together and what relations hold between them.

Weinreich (1966) observed, in a criticism of the very early Katz and Fodor semantic theory, that if a meaning representation were to consist of an unordered, unstructured set of semantic markers, then synonymy relations would be predicted where none exist. A pair of sentences such as (6) and (7) would be assigned identical representations, since the meanings of both consist of the same atomic concepts.

(6) Cats chase mice.
(7) Mice chase cats.

The Katz and Fodor theory was not in fact open to this charge, since its readings consisted of sequences (ORDERED sets) of semantic markers and distinguishers. The elements in the readings for (6) and (7) would be differently ordered, and because of the difference in order the sentence readings would be distinct, as required. But the spirit of Weinreich's criticism was correct. The Katz and Fodor readings had no internal structure other than order, and it can be shown that ordering alone is not sufficient to capture all meaning differences.

One of the Katz and Fodor readings for the sentence (8) was (9).

(8) The man hits the colorful ball.
(9) [Some contextually definite] ⟶ (Physical Object) ⟶ (Human) ⟶ (Adult) ⟶ (Male) ⟶ (Action) ⟶ (Instancy) ⟶ (Intensity) ⟶ [Collides with an impact] ⟶ [Some contextually definite] ⟶ (Physical Object) ⟶ (Color) ⟶ [[Abounding in contrast or variety of bright colors] [Having globular shape]]

Notice that it is impossible to tell by examination of (9) which elements in the sentence reading represent the meanings of which constituents of the sentence. We cannot tell, for example, where the reading of the subject ends and the reading of the verb begins. Sometimes there may be clues: (*Male*) and (*Action*) are presumably incompatible markers, hence they could not both derive from the same lexical item or from an adjective-noun combination. But there is no guarantee that there will always be enough clues to define a unique 'parsing' of the reading. Yet a parsing is essential. If the reading of the subject is not distinguished formally within a sentence reading from the reading of the predicate, a pair of sentences such as (10) and (11) will be assigned identical readings.

(10) John's being in Cuba went on record.
(11) John's having gone to Cuba is on record.

This clearly cannot be permitted, since the two sentences are not synonymous—the concept of a change of state is part of the meaning of the predicate in (10) but part of the meaning of the subject clause in (11).

Another deficiency of the Katz and Fodor reading is that the scope of the definite articles is not well-defined. The reading for *the* is given as [*Some contextually definite*], which is presumably intended to express the fact that a definite noun phrase must have a unique referent. But we cannot tell from (9) whether what must be contextually definite is a physical object, a human physical object, a human, adult, male physical object, or even (were there such a thing) a physical object which is human, adult, male and an action. The scope of the reading of the first definite article in the sentence should be just those markers which make up the reading of *man*, but this fact is not expressed in (9) because these semantic markers are not formally separated off from the rest of the sentence reading.

This point is important, because a representation that does not contain this information cannot even predict correctly the truth conditions on sentences. A sentence containing a definite noun phrase is said to PRESUPPOSE the existence of a unique referent for that noun phrase. To use the familiar example, the sentence (12) presupposes that there is at present one and only one king of France.

(12) The present king of France is bald.

If this presupposition is met, i.e., if there IS exactly one king of France, then the sentence will be either true or false, depending on whether he is or is not bald. If the presupposition is not met, then the sentence is neither true nor false, i.e., it has no truth value.[1] A semantic representation which does not specify the scope of the definite article does not specify what the presupposition of the sentence is, and therefore does not specify under what conditions the sentence will have or lack a truth value.

The kinds of distinction that are needed in semantic representations appear to be very like the kinds of distinction made in syntactic phrase markers (e.g., noun phrases distinguished from verbs). It is therefore

---

1. It must be admitted that there is considerable disagreement, among both linguists and philosophers, over whether the concept of presupposition has any real justification, or whether the concept of entailment is sufficient to account for all the facts. There is a huge literature on presupposition. One recent work is Kempson (1975), which contains all the standard references.

tempting to try to use the syntactic phrase marker to structure the semantic representation. In Katz's theory, readings are attached to the deep structure phrase marker in a semantically interpreted underlying phrase marker (SIUPM). Weinreich complained that Katz and Fodor's projection rules "destroy the semantic structure," i.e., that their inputs are highly structured syntactic phrase markers but their outputs (readings) have virtually no structure at all. However, if we could take their output to be not just readings but SIUPMs, it might not matter that the readings themselves are unstructured, for they would be implicitly structured by the phrase marker to which they are attached. Though we still could not tell from the SENTENCE reading which markers represent the meaning of its subject noun phrase, we could get this information by looking down the SIUPM to the reading associated with the subject *NP* node.

Is this way of imposing structure on meaning representations feasible? Talk of using the underlying syntactic phrase marker to structure the semantic representation naturally brings generative semantics to mind. In a GS grammar, the tree diagram which represents the syntactic structure of a sentence simultaneously specifies its semantic structure. However, this approach is open only to a theory whose underlying syntactic phrase markers are very abstract, like those of generative semantics. It is NOT compatible with the level of deep structure defined by the standard theory. The reason is that there are sentences which are structurally distinct at the standard deep structure level but which are synonymous. Since their syntactic phrase markers differ, their semantically interpreted phrase markers will differ also. As long as synonymy is to be captured by identity of semantic representation, the semantic representations of the system cannot be equated with the SIUPMs, for this would fail to account for the synonymy of such pairs of sentences as (13) and (14), or (15) and (16).

(13) Bachelors are jolly.
(14) Unmarried men are jolly.
(15) The speeches preceded a buffet luncheon.
(16) A buffet luncheon followed the speeches.

Let us summarize our observations so far. Unstructured semantic representations are inadequate because the representations of sentences like (6) and (7), or (10) and (11) contain the same semantic elements and they therefore need to be differentiated by the relations between these elements. Semantic representations with the structure of standard deep structure phrase markers are incorrect because they are too highly structured; they predict that EVERY syntactic difference corresponds to a meaning difference, whereas in fact phrases such as *bachelor* and *unmarried man* are synonymous despite the fact that one is just a noun and the other is an adjective-noun combination.

Generative semantics has opted for using the syntactic phrase marker to structure the semantic representation and it can do so because it posits very abstract syntactic phrase markers in which many syntactic distinctions made in standard deep structures are not present. (Examples are given in Section 3.2.)

Weinreich (1966) opted for the other alternative of assigning more structure to the readings themselves, by elaborating the Katz and Fodor projection rules. Katz and Fodor proposed that there would be a different projection rule corresponding to each way in which constituents can be syntactically combined. However, the four projection rules they formulated were curiously similar. They differed in minor ways in their handling of distinguishers and selection restrictions; but basically, they all amalgamated readings by forming the ordered set consisting of the ordered set of markers in one constituent reading followed by the ordered set of markers in the other constituent reading. The possibility of having differently structured readings result from constituents with different syntactic structures was available in principle but not utilized in practice. Weinreich proposed enriching the theory by permitting both unordered sets of markers ("clusters") and ordered sets ("configurations"), as well as certain groupings ("impure linkings"). Though yet more ways of combining semantic elements might have been added had Weinreich lived to develop his system further, it appears that those which he actually proposed are still insufficient to distinguish the readings of all nonsynonymous sentences.

A third solution is the one that Katz has now adopted, that of introducing structure into sentence readings through the dictionary readings for particular lexical items (typically, though perhaps not only, the readings for verbs). The structural skeleton of the sentence reading is provided by the reading of its main verb, which contains categorized variables. All that the projection rule has to do is to insert the readings for other constituents into positions in the verb reading which are already determined by these categorized variables. Identical readings can then be ensured for synonymous but syntactically distinct sentences such as (15) and (16) above. The verbs *precede* and *follow* can be assigned identical readings in the lexicon—except that where one reading contains the categorized variable for the subject noun phrase, the other contains the categorized variable for the object noun phrase, and vice versa. In effect, the projection rule, governed by the categorized variables, 'transforms' the deep structures of (15) and (16) into an identical semantic representation.

Other formal devices have also been introduced into Katz's theory to articulate sentence readings more finely. These include HEAVY PARENTHESES, which surround the readings of referential noun phrases and thus define the presuppositions of a sentence, and DOUBLE PARENTHESES, which surround that part of a sentence reading which specifies the illocutionary force potential. (See Katz, 1972, Chapter 4).

All of this illustrates the point that there is more than one way of imposing the necessary structure on semantic representations. In the next sections, we will compare these alternative ways and try to determine to what extent they really differ, and which of them is the most adequate empirically. But we can clearly rule out, an empirical grounds, any theory that does not structure semantic representations at all. It was suggested in Section 5.1 that the representations of word meanings may be simpler than has been supposed. But the ways in which word meanings combine with each other do seem to demand a very rich representational system. The complexity of the semantic representations that have been proposed by linguists, though it may be formidable, is not gratuitous. (But see Section 5.6.)

5.4. KATZ'S THEORY AND GENERATIVE SEMANTICS COMPARED

We have been considering some of the kinds of information that semantic representations must contain. Obviously, those discussed in the last few pages do not exhaust the list. Current semantic theories have also been responsive to the scope relations between quantifiers, the semantic function of adverbs, and many other aspects of meaning. Each semantic phenomenon we observe adds to the empirical demands on an adequate system of semantic representation. We saw in the previous section how different theories have met these demands in different ways. Yet since the facts about meaning to which they are responsive are essentially the same in all cases, we might wonder to what extent the different styles of semantic representation of these theories COULD embody different empirical claims about language. Perhaps they simply make the same claims in different ways.

Resistance might be expected to such a suggestion. One issue that has generated some heat is whether the semantic representations of GS and of Katz's theory are, or are not, mere notational variants. Katz has argued that in many respects they are, and that where they are not, his own representations are more adequate. (This is part of his more general claim that the prelexical derivations of GS are merely inverses of the semantic derivations defined by the projection rules of his own theory. See Section 4.4.) Generative semanticists, on the other hand, have claimed that their semantic representations are formal objects of the same kind as syntactic phrase markers, that Katz's are not, and that therefore the two types of structure are significantly different.

I will not attempt to review all the arguments back and forth that appear in the literature on this topic. (Intrepid readers may consult Katz, 1970, 1971; McCawley, 1971; Katz, 1973). The complexity of the debate is due in large part to an unclarity about WHICH constructs in Katz's theory are to be compared with GS underlying phrase markers. The theory employs both readings and semantically interpreted underlying phrase markers (SIUPMs). Readings are sets of semantic markers, some of which may be internally structured, i.e., consist of parenthesized strings of other semantic markers. SIUPMs are standard deep structure phrase markers with readings associated with their nodes. Katz has referred at various times to both readings and SIUPMs as "semantic representations," and has compared both in various respects with GS underlying structures.

Two different kinds of comparison can be made between the structures of different linguistic theories. One is a comparison of FUNCTION, i.e., we seek to determine whether the two kinds of structure express the same facts about sentences. The other is a comparison of FORM, i.e., we ask whether the two structures express these facts in the same way.

One difference of FUNCTION between GS semantic representations and either the sentence readings or the SIUPMs of Katz's theory is that the former contain representations of focus, presupposition, etc., which Katz considers not to be truly semantic, and hence to have no place in semantic representations (see Section 3.3). But to renounce all functional comparisons between the semantic structures of the two theories on the basis of this one difference would be a tactical mistake, and we can easily set the difference aside by restricting the comparison to the underlying PHRASE MARKERS of generative semantics. The semantic properties which these represent appear to be just those which Katz agrees should be represented.

Katz's SIUPMs resemble GS underlying phrase markers in one important function. Both contain syntactic as well as semantic information about the sentence. (By contrast, Katz's sentence readings contain only semantic information.) Even here, however, there are differences. In a GS representation, one and the same branching configuration is used to represent both the semantic and the syntactic structure of the sentence simultaneouly. But as we noted in Section 5.3, the nature of STANDARD syntactic deep structures is such that Katz cannot identify the semantic structure of a sentence with its syntactic structure, and therefore the nodes of a SIUPM must dominate DISTINCT syntactic and semantic configurations.

Katz has implied that combining the syntactic and semantic structure in the fashion of generative semantics is just a notational trick. Certainly we could separate the two, and construct a modified GS representation which would then look somewhat like a SIUPM. Let us do this to Postal's representation for the sentence *Harry reminds me of Fred Astaire*, which we considered in Section 4.4. This is repeated here as (5-6).

(5-6)

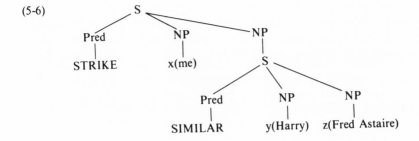

The modified form of (5-6) would be (5-7).

(5-7)

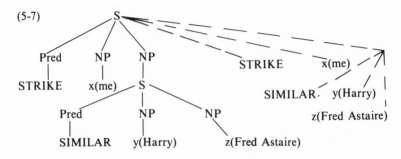

No generative semanticist has ever proposed representations like (5-7) and it is very unclear how transformational derivations from such structures would proceed. More importantly, such representations would not embody the fundamental principle of generative semantics that syntactic and semantic structure are one and the same. The format of (5-7) leaves open the possibility that the syntactic and semantic configurations might differ. By contrast, GS representations like (5-6) do commit the theory to this principle. They are therefore more than a trick—at the very least, they are a trick that can be played only within a theory embodying the GS principle and not within Katz's theory. Whatever the correct characterization of notational variance, this alone shows that SIUPMs and GS underlying phrase markers are not mere notational variants.

There are other important differences between SIUPMs and GS underlying representations. Synonymous sentences have identical GS representations, but as we noted in Section 5.3, if their standard deep structures are different, then they will necessarily have distinct SIUPMs. Similarly, a semantically ambiguous sentence with n distinct interpretations will have n distinct GS underlying phrase markers, but only one SIUPM (see Section

5.2). In other words, GS underlying structures correspond to sentence MEANINGS, while SIUPMs correspond to SENTENCES, where sentences are individuated only by their syntactic and lexical properties, not by their semantic properties.

In all of these respects, it is Katz's sentence READINGS which resemble GS underlying phrase markers most closely in function: each sentence reading also captures just one sentence meaning. The picture that emerges is that the syntactic part of a SIUPM is merely a skeleton on which readings, which are the true representations of meaning, are hung.

In Section 4.4, it was suggested that SIUPMs should be dropped from Katz's theory, together with the cumulative semantic derivations that generate them. Would anything be lost by this move? Katz and Postal (1964 Chapter 2) argued for SIUPMs in the following way.

> ... the semantic interpretation of a sentence is under the empirical requirement to characterize the meaning of EACH AND EVERY constituent (in the P-marker(s) whose nodes are assigned readings) of the sentence, and not to characterize the meaning for any substring of the sentence that is not one of its constituents. If a semantic theory failed to characterize the meaning of some constituent of a sentence, then since a speaker is able to determine meanings not only for whole sentences but also for their significant subparts, the theory would be to that extent incomplete. For example, the semantic interpretation of the sentence
>
> (9) the man hit the ball
>
> must represent the meanings of the constituents of this sentence, i.e., *the*, *man*, *hit*, *the*, *ball*, *the man*, *hit the ball*, and *the man hit the ball*. But it must not provide any meaning for such substrings of (9) as *the man hit* or *hit the*.

A natural way to satisfy this requirement is to set up semantic representations which consist of a syntactic phrase marker defining the constituents of the sentence, with a reading associated with each node that dominates a constituent, i.e., to take a semantic representation to be a SIUPM.

But this is a bad argument for SIUPMs. SIUPMs contain DEEP structure phrase markers; hence the subsentential constituents to which readings are assigned are the DEEP structure constituents of the sentence. But the Katz and Postal argument for providing meaning representations for constituents holds equally well for transformationally DERIVED constituents. English speakers are prepared to ask and answer questions about the meanings of phrases like *was hit by the man*, or *seemed to hit the ball*, as well as of phrases like *hit the ball*. The first two of these are transformationally derived constituents, not deep structure constituents, and SIUPMs will fail to contain readings for them.

We may conclude that even if Katz and Postal's requirement on grammars is correct, their way of meeting the requirement is not. A less direct way of specifying the meanings of subsentential constituents is needed. Given an account of sentence meanings, the meanings of phrases can be conceived as their contributions to the sentences in which they appear. For example, the meaning of *hit the ball* could be specified by determining what is common to the readings for the sentences in (5-8).

$$(5\text{-}8) \left\{ \begin{array}{l} \text{The man} \\ \text{John} \\ \text{I} \\ \text{No one} \\ \text{etc.} \end{array} \right\} \text{hit the ball.}$$

This approach is not limited to deep structure constituents. It is also not limited to a theory employing SIUPMs.

This argument for SIUPMs therefore fails. One further argument should be considered before we abandon SIUPMs altogether. Katz and Postal implied that SIUPMs are the domain for the definitions of the semantic properties and relations of sentences. These definitions apparently refer not only to readings, but also to the syntactic parts of SIUPMs. If this can be shown to be necessary, it would follow that NOT all the semantic information about a sentence is contained in its readings—some of it must reside in the syntactic part of its SIUPM, i.e., in its deep structure phrase marker.

In Section 4.4, we argued that this would not constitute valid motivation for the construction of SIUPMs. Even if there are semantic properties and relations of this kind, they could be defined equally well without SIUPMs and cumulative derivations, as long as their definitions are allowed accesss to intermediate stages in the derivation of sentence readings. But this point is probably little more than academic in any case, for though Katz may still allow in PRINCIPLE that semantic property definitions may refer to SIUPMs, there has been a trend in his PRACTICE towards definitions referring solely to readings. For example, an early definition of analyticity (Katz, 1964a) stated that a sentence is analytic if the meaning (reading) of its predicate is included in that of its subject, where the subject and predicate were defined over the deep structure phrase marker of the sentence. This has been superseded by a definition (Katz 1972, Chapter 4) stating that a sentence is analytic if what it asserts is included in what it presupposes, where what a sentence asserts and what it presupposes can be determined from its reading alone. (These are only informal renderings of Katz's definitions.)

As it happens, this trend in Katz's theory could have been predicted on general grounds, for a quite simple argument shows that semantic properties and relations MUST be defined over sentence readings. A semantic property of a sentence is presumably by definition a property that it has in virtue of its meaning. It follows that sentences with identical meanings must have identical semantic properties. But sentences with identical meanings are assigned identical sentence readings, and since these readings must be packed with sufficient meaning information to predict synonymy and nonsynonymy correctly, they will surely contain sufficient meaning information to predict other semantic properties and relations too. Reference to the syntactic parts of SIUPMs should therefore be unnecessary.[2] (It might conceivably be argued against this that some semantic property can be defined more SIMPLY over SIUPMs than over sentence readings alone. But since the SIUPMs of synonymous sentences can differ radically, this seems most unlikely.)

All of these considerations point to the conclusion that SIUPMs play no essential role in Katz's theory. Rather, they appear to be mere relics of a now outdated version of the theory. A highly compressed history might run thus. As we noted in Section 5.3, representations of sentence meaning must be internally structured. In early versions of Katz's theory, sentence READINGS had virtually no structure. SIUPMs, which were highly structured since they contained syntactic phrase markers, perhaps appeared to make just the structural distinctions that were needed to articulate meanings properly. When it was realized that the internal configurations of a meaning representation are NOT congruent with those of standard deep syntactic structures, highly structured verb and sentence READINGS were introduced instead. But for some reason, the SIUPMs lingered on.

The rejection of SIUPMs clears the field for a comparison of Katz's sentence readings with GS underlying semantic representations. It is the readings which seem to be the true meaning representations. We have already noted that sentence readings differ from GS representations in containing no syntactic information about sentences. But with respect to their SEMANTIC function, the two types of representation appear to be broadly equivalent; each is intended to be a complete specification of one

2. This argument needs one qualification. Readings will not fully determine those properties of a sentence which depend on its meaning but NOT ONLY on its meaning. An example is Katz's concept of semantic redundancy, which is in fact a RELATION between the meaning of a sentence and its lexical and syntactic structure. A phrase such as *male boys* is defined as redundant because both the adjective and the noun contribute the semantic marker (*Male*) to the reading for the phrase. But one of these instances of (*Male*) is deleted in the course of amalgamating the two constituent readings, so that *male boys* is assigned the same derived reading as (and is therefore defined as synonymous with) the nonredundant phrase *boys*. Of two phrases with the same meaning, one can be redundant and the other not. Whether some other conception of redundancy would be preferable to this might be debated, but at least on Katz's conception, redundancy is demonstrated to be not a PURELY semantic property. It would have to be defined over a combination of syntactic and semantic representations on any theory. So it does not disprove the claim that all information about the meaning, and meaning-properties, of a sentence is contained in its reading.

meaning of a sentence. We can therefore turn now to the question of whether the two theories specify the meanings of sentences in the same way.

To superficial examination, the semantic representations of the two theories are not at all alike. GS underlying structures are usually presented in the form of tree diagrams, like other syntactic phrase markers. Katz's sentence readings are usually presented in the form of parenthesized strings of semantic markers. But, as we have noted already, bracketed strings and tree diagrams can be equivalent (mere notational variants). A bracketed string such as (17) may be converted into an equivalent tree diagram by progressively substituting for each pair of brackets a node which dominates the bracketed elements, and for each label on a pair of brackets a label on the corresponding node. The conversion of (17) proceeds via (5-9i) and (5-9ii) to the tree diagram (5-9iii).

(17)   [[[a]   [b]]   [d]]
        E   C   A   B   D

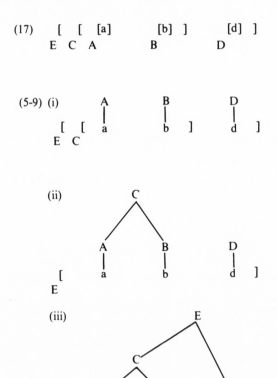

The tree diagram may be converted into the bracketed string by reversing the process.

Since tree diagrams tend to be easier on the eye, I shall present Katz's readings in tree form rather than convert GS phrase markers into string form. For comparison with Postal's underlying phrase marker (5-6) for the sentence *Harry reminds me of Fred Astaire*, Katz (1972, Chapter 8) offers the sentence reading (5-10).[3]

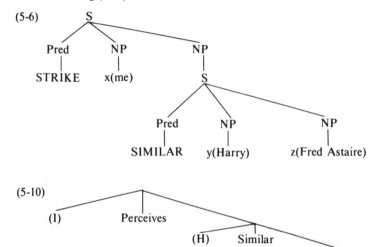

(I), (H) and (F) are abbreviations for the readings of the constituents *me*, *Harry*, and *Fred Astaire*, respectively.

Both (5-6) and (5-10) represent a decomposition of the meaning of the verb *remind* into two semantic predicates. One is a similarity predicate which expresses a relation between Harry and Fred Astaire; the other is some kind of perception predicate which expresses a relation between me (the speaker) and the similarity of Harry and Fred Astaire. (See footnote 6, page 135.)

3. Katz's parenthesized string version of (5-10) is *((I) Perceives ((H) Similar (F)))*. Note that the parentheses around PRIMITIVE semantic markers in a string do not convert into nodes in the corresponding tree diagram. The reason is that these parentheses are not used to indicate structure. Their function is simply to distinguish semantic markers from distinguishers, syntactic features, and other theoretical entities. The parentheses of a marker such as *(Male)*, for example, serve no function that could not equally well be served by writing *Male* in purple ink, or indeed by writing it in capital letters as is the practice in generative semantics. It is only the parentheses in COMPLEX semantic markers, which specify groupings of the semantic elements, that correspond to nodes in the tree diagram. (Notational consistency would seem to demand parentheses around *Perceives* and *Similar* in (5-10) too. But I will not stray too far from Katz's own conventions.)

Now that we have the representations of the two theories in a comparable format, we can examine the similarities and differences between them. One difference that has been debated in the literature concerns the labeling of nodes. The nodes of a GS representation, like those of any other syntactic phrase marker, are labeled with category symbols. By contrast, since the parentheses in the string formulations of Katz's readings have no labels on them, the corresponding tree diagrams must have unlabeled nodes.

It must be acknowledged that Katz has challenged this interpretation of his readings, and has argued that they do correspond to labeled trees, i.e., that they are LABELED parenthesized strings. Katz (1972, Chapter 3) gives the string (18) as the reading for the verb *chase*; Katz and Nagel (1974) give the tree diagram (5-11).

(18) (((Activity)(((Physical))((Movement)((Speed)$^{(Fast)}$(Following Y)))

((Purpose)((To catch Y))))) X)

(5-11)

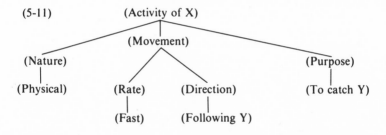

There are some irresoluble differences between these two representations, such as the absence of markers (*Nature*) and (*Direction*) in (18), as well as trivial mismatches such as between (*Speed*) and (*Rate*). So it is not quite (5-11), but something like (5-12) which should correspond to (18).

(5-12)

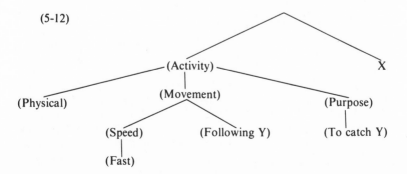

Notice, however, that the standard conversion algorithm will establish the equivalence of (18) and (5-12) only if the markers (*Activity*), (*Movement*) and (*Purpose*) in (18) are construed as labels on the parentheses that follow them, and (*Speed*) is construed as a label on (*Fast*). There is nothing in (18) to indicate that certain markers are to function as labels on parentheses, but this is apparently Katz's intention. In a more conventional notation, these labels would be made explicit, as illustrated in (19), which is the string version of the Katz and Nagel tree diagram (5-11).

With a variety of minor adjustments, then, the parenthesized string reading and the tree diagram reading can be STIPULATED to be equivalent. And the tree diagram certainly does have node labels, as a syntactic phrase marker does. Nevertheless, this does NOT mean that Katz's readings are formal objects comparable to syntactic phrase markers. This is because the categories and relations represented by a tree diagram such as (5-11) or (5-12) are of a very different type from those represented in a syntactic phrase marker of the usual kind, such as (5-13).

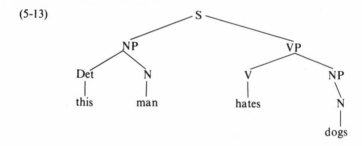

Syntactic phrase markers represent constituency relations, what Chomsky (1965) called "is a" relations. The syntactic phrase marker (5-13) says that the word *this* "is a" determiner, that *man* "is a" noun, that this determiner followed by this noun "are a" noun phrase, that a noun phrase followed by a verb phrase "are a" sentence, and so on. But a reading such as (5-11) does not appear to be consistently interpretable in a similar fashion. First a technical point. An "is a" relation is a set membership relation; for example, *man* is a member of the set of nouns. But a semantic marker is supposed to designate a concept. Thus, to interpret the domination relationships in (5-11) as "is a" relations would commit us to incoherent statements such as that the concept of being physical is a member of the concept of a nature. A concept is an individual, not a set, and therefore can have no members. Even if this objection can be overcome (by taking certain semantic markers, such as (*Nature*), to designate SETS of concepts), other worries remain. (5-11) indicates that the concept of X's chasing Y is composed of concepts of a nature, a movement and a purpose—but WHOSE movement and purpose is not specified. It WOULD be specified if we could interpret (5-11) as a paraphrase (in universal semantic vocabulary) of the form: 'X engages in an activity consisting of a certain movement and with a certain purpose.' But this has nothing to do with "is a" relations; it would apparently require (*Activity*), (*Movement*) and (*Purpose*), just like (*Physical*), (*Fast*), etc., to be terminal elements of the analysis, rather than labels on nonterminal nodes. Similarly, we might agree that for X to chase Y is for X to engage in a movement AT a certain rate, and IN a certain direction. But (5-11), with (*Movement*) as a node label rather than a terminal symbol, says instead that a concept of a rate and a concept of a direction (in that order?) CONSTITUTE a concept of a movement. This is a much more dubious claim. Thus, although the CONCEPTS which appear in (18) may be the correct ones for the analysis of the verb *chase*, the relations between these concepts become considerably less plausible if (18) is stipulated to be equivalent to a labeled tree with the same interpretation as a syntactic phrase marker.

Since construing the parenthesized string versions of Katz's readings as labeled tree diagrams like phrase markers does not seem to do justice to the semantic analyses they embody, it may be worthwhile to consider an alternative interpretation. Suppose we go back to (18), but do not assign any special status to the semantic markers (*Activity*), (*Movement*), (*Purpose*) and (*Speed*). Instead of taking them as labels, which would correspond to higher nonterminal nodes in a tree diagram, let us take these markers to be simply constituents of the reading along with markers like (*Physical*), (*Fast*), etc. Then (18) would correspond not to a LABELED tree diagram, but to the UNlabeled tree (5-14).

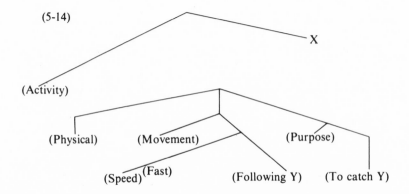

(5-14)

This, despite its lack of labels, is actually more like a phrase marker, and a GS semantic representation, than is (5-12). The semantic markers, representing primitive concepts, are terminal symbols in the tree; and their groupings and subgroupings constitute a 'parsing' of the complex concept of the act of chasing. Moreover, curiously enough, (5-14) contains special configurations which may be functionally equivalent to node labels.

What we observe is that some semantic markers in (5-14) have extra, nonbranching nodes above them; this is the case for (*Physical*) and (*To catch Y*). These extra nodes (which correspond to extra pairs of parentheses in the string (18)) need some explanation. Possibly the intention is that they should express MODIFICATION. For example, the marker (*To catch Y*) could be construed as a modifier on the marker (*Purpose*). This part of the tree would then express what we may paraphrase in English as 'with a purpose, which is to catch Y,' or 'with the purpose of catching Y.' The extra node/extra parentheses in Katz's reading would thus be functioning in much the same way as a node label like *PrepP* or *Adj* in a syntactic phrase marker.

In other words, there is an interpretation of Katz's readings on which they have no node labels, but nevertheless contain special configurations which can be used to carry some of the same information as node labels. In addition to the extra parentheses that we have taken to express modification, Katz's sentence readings contain heavy parentheses and double parentheses (see Section 5.3). How these latter styles of parenthesization could be coded into tree diagrams is unclear, but it IS clear that a system of unlabeled trees is not necessarily weaker in expressive power than a system of labeled trees.[4] Whether or not we have correctly divined Katz's intentions, this is an important observation. It underlines the moral that judgments of equivalence between theories must not rely on superficial appearances. Notational devices are ten a penny; it is their interpretation that counts.

---

4. In fact, neither brackets (branching structure) nor labels are especially privileged representational devices. For example, much of the information in a labeled tree such as (i) is conveyed by the logical formula (ii).

(i)

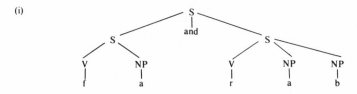

(ii) Fa & Rab

But (ii) contains neither brackets nor labels; it uses a contrast between upper- and lower-case letters, and is subject to certain scope conventions which define the internal groupings of symbols.

Let me review the conclusions of this long series of arguments (though Katz and perhaps even generative semanticists may disagree with some of them). Katz's SIUPMs seem to be otiose; his sentence readings are complete specifications of meaning. These are formal structures which are either labeled but not phrase markers, or phrase markers but not labeled. On the latter interpretation they nevertheless exhibit structural distinctions which could convey the same kind of information as labeling distinctions. These observations by no means prove Katz's semantic representations and those of generative semantics to be functionally equivalent in ALL details. What I have attempted to show is (i) that the comparison is a more difficult and subtle one that has often been implied in the literature, and (ii) that despite their obvious superficial differences, the two kinds of semantic representation are, in some respects, equipped to express the same facts about the internal structures of meanings.

Certain differences remain. For example, in (5-6) above the predicates precede their arguments, while in (5-10) the predicates appear in second position in their clauses. In Section 3.5 it was suggested that this difference is more than notational. It does not affect the range of meanings that can be expressed in the two systems, but it probably can be cashed in terms of different psychological predictions about the form of mental representations of meanings. In addition, both Katz and generative semanticists have argued, on internal LINGUISTIC grounds, for the superiority of their own representations.

Katz has argued that it is incorrect for node labels in semantic representations to be SYNTACTIC category names, since this implicitly claims that the members of each syntactic category share significant semantic properties, which is false. But is it false? Certainly the traditional attempts to relate syntactic class and semantic function were never very successful. The identification of a noun, for example, as the name of a person, place or thing is obviously much too crude. But these traditional characterizations concerned what we would now call SURFACE STRUCTURE syntactic categories, and these bear only a very indirect relation to the syntactic categories of GS DEEP STRUCTURES. The noun *procrastination* is not the name of a person, place or thing, but then it is not dominated by the node *N* in GS deep structures. The failure of traditional definitions therefore does not preclude successful definitions within the framework of generative semantics.

McCawley (1971a) has proposed characterizing the semantic content of the node labels *S*, *NP* and *V* (which are all that appear in GS underlying phrase markers) indirectly, by relating them with the concepts of predicate logic. He suggests that:

> S corresponds to the use of 'sentence' in the terms 'closed sentence' (= 'proposition') and 'open sentence' (= 'propositional function'), V to 'predicate' (taken as including 'operator'), and NP to 'argument'.

A standard modal predicate calculus recognizes a class of quantifiers (corresponding roughly to *all* and *some* in English), a class of sentential connectives (roughly *and*, *or*, *if-then*), and a class of sentential operators (*not*, *necessarily*, *possibly*); all of these classes are formally distinguished from the class of predicates (corresponding roughly to ordinary verbs and adjectives like *walked*, *pretty*, *kill*, etc.). Generative semantics classifies all of these elements together, and labels them all *V*. Which classification is correct for the description of natural languages might be debated. Nevertheless, there seems to be nothing in principle against an identification of the GEN-ERAL kind that McCawley has proposed, i.e., a semantic identification of syntactic categories in terms of the role that the members of a category play in determining the truth conditions and other semantic properties of sentences.

To motivate the inclusion of syntactic node labels in semantic representations would thus require a demonstration that the labels facilitate the operation of inference rules or the definitions of anomaly, analyticity, and so on. It may well turn out that they do not. For example, the node label *NP* may prove to be redundant if every *NP* node (and no other node) dominates only a referential variable, as in McCawley (1972). But whatever the outcome, this is at least the proper basis for the debate.

A frequent argument for the superiority of GS semantic structures over Katz's readings is a simplicity argument, which turns on the interdependence of structural representations and rules in a grammar. The GS semantic representation for a sentence is a syntactic phrase marker, and is thus formally similar to the more superficial syntactic structures with which it must be related by the rules of the grammar in the derivation for the sentence. These rules can therefore be expected to be simpler and more homogeneous than the rules needed on Katz's theory. This is argued at length in Postal (1972). It is an important but also a very difficult issue, which obviously connects with the topics discussed in Chapter 4.

We want to find out what semantic rules are like. A natural research technique is to compare them with syntactic rules, which at present we know much more about. If the similarities are very close, a strong general hypothesis would be that the rules are of formally IDENTICAL types. A variety of specific predictions about semantic rules would immediately flow from this identification, for the semantic rules must meet ALL the general formal conditions that syntactic rules are known to meet. However, a homogeneous grammar is correct only if the facts are homogeneous. If they are not, if semantic rules and representations do differ in general formal respects from syntactic rules and representations, then the theory that we want is one that identifies these differences (and ultimately explains them). As a theory of semantic structure, this latter might be less specific and more exploratory than the homogeneity theory; the observed differences between semantic and syntactic rules which originally led to the hypothesis that they differ fundamentally, might very well not add up to a full specification of what semantic rules ARE like. Further research would be necessary to complete the picture. Nevertheless, from the fact that a theory is methodologically inconvenient, it does not follow that it is incorrect.

If generative semantics is wrong about the homogeneity of semantic and syntactic structures, then its claim to a simpler mapping between these structures would presumably collapse on further examination. Although structures with syntactic node labels would not have to be mapped onto structures without syntactic labels, as in Katz's theory, other complications might arise. For example, it might turn out to require very long and complex derivations in order to ensure that semantic representations are abstract enough for each syntactic node label at that level to identify a uniform semantic function. On the other hand, if generative semantics is right, we can expect the thesis that semantic patterning is essentially the same as syntactic patterning to offer solutions to many specific semantic phenomena, solutions that would be missed on the standard theory.

5.5. JACKENDOFF'S THEORY

Jackendoff (1972) defines semantic representations as collections of four distinct structures. These are: a FUNCTIONAL STRUCTURE, which is an unlabeled parenthesization of semantic primitives and which "represents relations in the sentence induced by the verbs, including such notions as agency, motion, and direction"; a MODAL STRUCTURE, which is also an unlabeled parenthesization of semantic primitives and which specifies the relative scopes of the various elements of the sentence; a TABLE OF COREFERENCE, which lists pairwise the referring terms in the sentence and specifies for each pair whether the terms are coreferential or non-coreferential; and a representation of FOCUS AND PRESUPPOSITION, which specifies "what information in the sentence is intended to be new and what is intended to be old."

The structural properties of the representation of focus and presupposition will not be discussed here. If we set this representation aside, the other three partial semantic representations taken together obviously serve essentially the same semantic function as the underlying phrase markers of generative semantics, and the sentence readings of Katz's theory. Yet they appear to differ considerably from the semantic representations of the other theories in their formal properties. Jackendoff (1972, Chapter 7) has given three arguments, and hinted at a fourth, against integrating all the semantic information about a sentence into a single structural representation. But before examining these arguments, let us consider why a general preference for non-unified semantic representations could be expected on the extended standard theory.

Unlike Katz's theory, the extended standard theory claims that more than one syntactic structure in the derivation of a sentence contributes to its meaning. Unlike generative semantics, its response to this observation is to posit a set of interpretive rules which apply to the relevant syntactic structures and derive semantic structures for the sentence. Different aspects of the meaning of a constituent are determined by different interpretive rules. The simplest situation would be for these interpretive rules to operate independently, each generating a self-contained representation of some of the semantic properties of the constituent. The grammar would almost certainly be more complex if in addition it had to integrate the output of all the interpretive rules into a single semantic structure.

Consider the sentence (20)

(20) A friend of mine told Joe that I hated him.

This must have a functional structure which specifies that the source of the telling is designated by *a friend of mine*, that the goal of the telling is designated by *Joe*, and so on. The functional structure is to be assigned on the basis of the lexical items and the DEEP syntactic structure of (20). Coreference relations between the noun phrases in (20) would be determined by other interpretive rules, which apply to certain DERIVED structures in the derivation. The coreference rules must specify that the noun phrase *a friend of mine* is not coreferential with *Joe*, that on one reading of (20) the pronoun *him* is coreferential with *Joe*, and so on. These rules would presumably be much simpler if this were ALL that they had to do, than if in addition they had to identify the representations of the noun phrases within the functional structure, and then add some distinguishing marks (e.g., referential indices) to encode the information about coreference relations.

In addition to this simplicity argument, and at least as important, is the fact that interpretive rules building up unified semantic representations for sentences would be GLOBAL rules, rules whose input consists of two or more structures in the derivation of the sentence. The input to the coreference rules, for example, would have to be both the derived syntactic structures which determine possible coreference relations and the functional structures to which coreference information is to be added. Global rules of the kind that appear in GS grammars have been criticized by proponents of the extended standard theory as too powerful a theoretical device. (Among other things, they undercut the need for the interpretive semantic rules that are characteristic of the extended standard theory. See Section 3.3.) But this criticism would obviously have no force if the interpretive rules of the extended standard theory must themselves be global rules. The defense of the EST would have to be that the global rules which it permits are much more highly constrained than those of generative semantics, and are to that extent less objectionable.

It is almost certainly no accident that the four partial semantic representations advocated by Jackendoff correspond very closely to the different derivational stages at which the interpretive rules apply. Functional structures are the output of rules interpreting deep syntactic structures. Representations of focus and presupposition result from the interpretation of surface structures. The table of coreference is derived by interpreting end-of-cycle structures (i.e., the interpretive rules apply within each syntactic cycle, after all the syntactic transformations). Modal structures are derived by interpretation of deep structures and surface (or perhaps end-of-cycle) structures.

Only the last two cases presuppose a procedure for 'adding up' semantic information derived from two or more syntactic structures into a single semantic structure. (For a sentence containing more than one clause, the end-of-cycle interpretation rules will apply to more than one phrase marker in the syntactic derivation.) For the table of coreference, this procedure is probably trivial; the table of coreference is simply a list, and new entries can be added to the list without disturbing the entries already present. But for the modal structure, which is a complex configuration of semantic elements, the 'adding up' procedure may present more problems. For example, the position of a quantifier in the modal structure represents its scope relative to other elements of the sentence. Its position relative to VERBS is determined by the rules that interpret DEEP structures, but its position relative to other QUANTIFIERS is determined by the rules that interpret SURFACE (or end-of-cycle) structures. (Examples are given later in this section.) Exactly how information from these two sources will interact to determine the eventual position of a quantifier in a modal structure has not yet been specified by Jackendoff, but our arguments above suggest that the necessary interpretive rules are likely to be complicated, and will certainly be global. Perhaps the nature and power of these global rules can be narrowly circumscribed. If not, we can guess that a further breakdown of semantic representations will be made—the modal structure will be replaced by a number of partial modal structures, each derivable from one phrase marker in the derivation of the sentence.

Having seen why non-unified semantic representations are desirable for the extended standard theory, let us now consider whether they are possible. The four partial semantic representations must not be completely independent of each other. It is easy to demonstrate that cross-identification of constituents operated on by the various interpretive rules is essential. For one of the interpretations of the sentence (20) above, the table of coreference would be (5-15).

(5-15)	*a friend of mine*	−coref	*Joe*
	a friend of mine	−coref	*I*
	a friend of mine	+coref	*him*
	Joe	−coref	*him*
	I	−coref	*Joe*
	I	−coref	*him*

But for the sentence (21), the table of coreference cannot be simply (5-16).

(21) A friend of mine told a friend of mine that I hated him.

(5-16)	*a friend of mine*	−coref	*a friend of mine*
	a friend of mine	−coref	*I*
	a friend of mine	+coref	*him*
	I	−coref	*him*

Table (5-16) would exclude the interpretation of (21) on which the pronoun *him* refers to someone not mentioned elsewhere in the sentence, but it would not distinguish between the interpretation of *him* as referring to the person doing the telling and the interpretation of *him* as referring to the person who is told.

Obviously, the table of coreference must indicate WHICH of the two noun phrases *a friend of mine* in the functional structure of (21) is to be taken as the antecedent of the pronoun. Notice that it is not sufficient to identify this noun phrase as the first (or the second) in the sentence, for the order of noun phrases in the derived structure, over which the coreference rules operate, may be different from their order in the deep structure, over which the functional structure interpretive rules operate. In sentence (21), the two orders are the same, but in the sentence (22) they are reversed—the first noun phrase *a friend of mine* specifies the person told and the second specifies the teller.

(22) A friend of mine was told by a friend of mine that I hated him.

A general procedure for identifying the same noun phrase across different derivational stages cannot be based on grammatical relations, either, for these may also change between deep and derived structures. For example, in the derived structure of the sentence (23), the teller is specified not by the subject of *tell* but by the subject of *appear*.

(23) A friend of mine appears to have told a friend of mine that I hated him.

In fact, there is NO reliable way of identifying the same constituent at two different stages of a derivation other than by tracing that constituent through all the changes it undergoes in the course of the derivation. To interpret two different stages of a derivation is in this sense to interpret the WHOLE of the derivation.

Jackendoff (1972, Chapter 6) has proposed that each node in the deep structure of a sentence should be assigned an IDENTIFICATION INDEX, which it will retain throughout the transformational derivation.[5] These indices render derivations cumulative in at least some respects. They encode into a phrase marker certain information about its relations to earlier phrase markers in the derivation. Therefore, instead of actually having to track through the whole of the derivation, the interpretive semantic rules could identify the same constituent at different derivational stages by simply referring to its identification index.

Once identification indices are introduced to correlate different occurrences of the same constituent in a SYNTACTIC derivation, they could also be carried over into the semantic representations that result from interpretation of the syntactic derivation. They would indicate which syntactic constituent is being assigned which semantic properties, and would also serve to cross-index the four partial semantic representations with each other. It would then be unnecessary to integrate the four representations into a single structure. For example, the sentence (21) could be assigned an indexed functional structure of the form (24) and the indexed table of coreference (5-17).

(24) TELL (FRIEND OF MINE$_i$, FRIEND OF MINE , (HATE $(I_k, HIM_l)))$

(5-17)	a friend of mine$_i$	+coref	him$_l$
	a friend of mine$_j$	−coref	him$_l$
	a friend of mine$_i$	−coref	a friend of mine$_j$
	I_k	−coref	him$_l$
	I_k	−coref	a friend of mine$_i$
	I_k	−coref	a friend of mine$_j$

Together, these representations will carry the same information as a more familiar unified representation with REFERENTIAL indices, such as (25).

(25) TELL (FRIEND OF MINE$_a$, FRIEND OF MINE$_b$, (HATE $(I_c, HIM_a)))$

The cross-indexing of partial semantic representations is a very powerful device. Though it has not yet been fully explored, it is hard to imagine any semantic fact about a sentence that could be expressed in a unified semantic representation but not in separate but cross-indexed partial semantic representations.

One might doubt whether the separate but cross-indexed representations are an ECONOMICAL way of presenting semantic information. Jacken-

---

5. Note that this identification index is not the same as a referential index. Verbs and other nonreferential constituents must have identification indices. And two noun phrases in a sentence will have distinct identification indices even if they are interpreted as coreferential.

doff's table of coreference includes representations of noun phrases which are already represented in the functional structure; and the modal structures Jackendoff gives repeat almost all of the elements in the functional structure, though in different configurations.[6] But the redundant overlap between the various partial representations can perhaps be avoided. For example, the table of coreference might be revised to contain ONLY identification indices, without any representation of the internal content of noun phrases. The suspicion that Jackendoff's representation system will complicate the inference rules, and other rules which apply to semantic representations to determine semantic properties and relations of sentences, may likewise be unfounded. The definitions of synonymy, ambiguity, redundancy, entailment, etc., appear to be rather simply reformulable so as to apply to the divided semantic representations.

If this is so, Jackendoff's system of semantic representation may be threatened instead by the other horn of the inevitable dilemma in linguistics. If his semantic representations express the same kinds of information about sentence meanings as the unified semantic representations of competing theories, could they possibly constitute any real theoretical advance? Are they not merely notational variants of these other styles of semantic representation? Jackendoff has argued that there are some real differences, and that they militate in his favor. His arguments take the form of criticisms of the formalism of standard quantificational logic, and hence of the various extensions of this formalism that have been incorporated into semantic representations by linguists. (See the discussion of Lakoff's treatment of quantifiers in Section 4.3.) These formalisms are claimed to be inadequate to the task of representing the meanings of sentences of NATURAL languages.

It is characteristic of the familiar quantificational representation system, and is usually regarded as one of its assets, that one single formula can simultaneously represent the association of predicates with their arguments (functional structure), the relative scope of operators (modal structure), and the coreference relations between noun phrases. For example, the sentence (26), on one of its possible readings, would be assigned a quantificational representation of some such form as (27).

(26) One boy wrote his name on each page.
(27) $(\exists x)(\forall y)(boy_x$ wrote x's name on page$_y)$

Corresponding to the noun phrase *one boy* in (26), the quantificational representation contains TWO elements, a quantifier and a variable. The position of the quantifier indicates the scope of the noun phrase; on this reading, *one boy* has scope over *each page*, so that it must be the same boy

6. It is to be assumed that the vocabulary for all these representations consists of universal semantic elements, rather than language-specific lexical items, though Jackendoff's modal structures are not always so formulated.

that wrote on each page. The position of the variable relative to the verb *wrote* indicates the functional role of the noun phrase; *one boy* designates the agent of the writing. The fact that the variable for *boy* is identical with the variable in *x's name* indicates a coreference relation between *one boy* and *his*—the boy wrote his own name. The important fact about such representations is that the quantifier and the variable that correspond to a single noun phrase can vary their positions independently (subject only to the condition that the quantifier is to the left of the variable it binds). In (27), the first quantifier happens to bind the variable which is the first argument of the verb. But the system can also accommodate interpretations on which the scope relations and the functional relations do not coincide. For example, (26) has another interpretation, on which it leaves open the possibility that a different boy may have written on each page; this would be represented by (28), in which it is the second quantifier that binds the first argument of the verb.

(28) $(\forall y)\,(\exists x)\,(\text{boy}_x$ wrote x's name on page$_y$)

Jackendoff does accept one fundamental characteristic of these representations, which is that quantifier ambiguities are represented as SCOPE ambiguities. That is to say, a quantifier can have two different interpretations only when it co-occurs with another quantifier (or with some other modal element such as negation or an opaque verb). The quantifier is not ambiguous in itself, but only in its relations with other constituents. In this respect, it is quite unlike ambiguous lexical items such as the noun *bank*. The word *bank* is ambiguous in ANY context—except those that specifically disambiguate it (e.g., *My bank pays 7% on savings accounts*). But a quantified noun phrase like *one boy* is unambiguous in a simple sentence like (29), which contains no other quantifier, negation, opaque verb, etc.; it has two scope interpretations in a sentence like (26), which contains two quantifiers; it has six scope interpretations in a sentence like (30), which has three quantifiers; and so on.

(29) One boy wrote his name.
(26) One boy wrote his name on each page.
(30) One boy wrote many names on each page.

For a sentence with four quantifiers, there would be 24 different scope interpretations, though by then it is beyond the linguistic intuitions of most speakers to keep track of them all. These facts about the ambiguity of a quantifier cannot be accounted for by assigning it a different decomposition into semantic features for each of its readings, as we might for *bank*. However many different semantic feature analyses we were to assign it, too many readings would be predicted for some sentences and too few for others. The ambiguity of quantifiers can be explained only if it is recognized to be inherently relational. This is the case in standard logical formulae, which require a proper ordering of quantifiers relative to each other. There is only one way of ordering a single quantifier, there are two ways of ordering two quantifiers, six ways of ordering three quantifiers, 24 ways of ordering four quantifiers, and so on.

Jackendoff uses a similar representational device in his modal structures. If we continue to disregard focus and presupposition, the sentence (31) would on one of its readings be assigned the three partial semantic representations in (32).

(31) John wants to catch a fish.
(32) (a) functional structure: WANT (JOHN, (CATCH (JOHN, FISH)))
     (b) modal structure: John, a fish, want (catch)
     (c) table of coreference: *John* – coref   *a fish*

Sentence (31) exhibits a scope ambiguity, since it contains both the quantified noun phrase *a fish* and the opaque verb *wants*. The reading represented by (32) is the specific reading, according to which there is some particular fish that John wants to catch. For the nonspecific reading of the sentence, the semantic representation would be (33), which is exactly like (32) except that in the modal structure the quantified phrase *a fish* now appears to the right of, and hence within the scope of, the opaque verb. (The specific/nonspecific distinction is discussed in Section 4.3.)

(33) (a) functional structure: WANT (JOHN, (CATCH (JOHN, FISH)))
     (b) modal structure: John, want (catch, a fish)
     (c) table of coreference: *John* – coref   *a fish*

Observe that instead of representing the various semantic properties of the phrase *a fish* by using two different elements, a quantifier and a variable, in the same formula, Jackendoff achieves a similar effect by placing *a fish* in different positions in the functional and modal structures. In the functional structure its position indicates that it is the object of the verb *catch*. It is in the modal structure that its position specifies its scope.

One of Jackendoff's objections to standard quantificational representation systems is that for some sentences they appear to predict incorrect meanings. The verb *try* is opaque, and so the sentence (34) shows the characteristic ambiguity between a specific and a nonspecific interpretation for the indefinite noun phrase in its complement clause.

(34) Bill is trying to find a pretty girl.

Quantificational representations would distinguish the two readings by the position of the quantifier with respect to the opaque verb, as in (35) and (36).

(35) $(\exists x)$ (Bill is trying (Bill find a pretty girl$_x$)) [specific reading]
(36) Bill is trying $((\exists x)$ (Bill find a pretty girl$_x$)) [nonspecific reading]

Reading the existential quantifier as 'there is something such that . . . ,' Jackendoff observes that the representation (36) predicts that the sentence is synonymous on its nonspecific reading with some sentence such as (37).

(37) Bill is trying $\left\{ \begin{array}{l} \text{for there to be} \\ \text{to cause there to be} \end{array} \right\}$ a pretty girl such that he finds her.

But he also contends that sentences like (37) entail that Bill is trying to make a pretty girl exist, while the original sentence (34) clearly has no such entailment. If Jackendoff's judgments are correct, then the quantificational representation (36) must therefore be rejected. Since his own semantic representation for the sentence would not contain any existential quantifier, there is no danger of this error in his system.

This objection is not a conclusive one. There are several ways around it. In characterizing the representation system we can STIPULATE the interpretation of the existential quantifier, and we are under no compulsion to identify it with 'there is something such that . . . .' In fact there is no obligation to correlate it unambiguously with ANY particular phrase of English; it is sufficient to specify its role in determining truth conditions, synonymy, anomaly, etc., and to supply the grammatical rules which relate sentences of the language with representations containing the quantifier. But in any case, there are natural interpretations of the quantifier which are not open to Jackendoff's objection. If we read it as "something is such that . . . ," then the nonspecific reading of sentence (34) would be analyzed as 'Bill is trying for something to be both such that it is a pretty girl and such that he finds it.' This may not be a syntactically elegant paraphrase of (34), but as a semantic analysis it has the advantage of not implying that Bill is trying to bring a pretty girl into existence. (For it might be that Bill is trying for something such that it is a pretty girl to be both such that it is a pretty girl and such that he finds it.)

Yet another way out of the problem would be to deny that the quantifier whose scope disambiguates specific and nonspecific readings of an opaque construction like (34) is the EXISTENTIAL quantifier. It is the STRUCTURAL properties of the quantifier that allow it to capture the relevant scope distinctions, not the fact that it is existential. So we could propose a different, non-existential, quantifier for representing specificity distinctions, and retain the existential quantifier for overtly existential constructions in English such as sentence (38).

(38) Bill hopes that there is a pretty girl in his section.

Finally, we could cope with example (34) by ACCEPTING (37) as a paraphrase. If we do this, then we must find some way of ruling out the inference from (37) to the conclusion that Bill is trying to make someone exist. That is, we must explain why the deletion of a modifying clause like *such that he finds her* does not produce a valid inference for a sentence like (37), even though a similar deletion is valid in many other cases, for example in the inference from (39) to (40).

(39) There are pretty girls that Bill hasn't met.
(40) There are pretty girls.

The explanation is not hard to find. Unlike (39) and (40), (37) is an opaque construction. It is the defining property of opaque constructions that they do not permit certain inferences which are valid in transparent contexts. The failure of substitutivity discussed in Section 2.6 is just one example of this general phenomenon. The occurrence of nonspecific noun phrases is another, for what it amounts to is the invalidity of the inference pattern known as 'existential generalization.' Indefinite noun phrases in transparent contexts support the inference to overtly existential sentences; (41) entails (42).

(41) John caught a fish.
(42) There is (was) a fish that John caught.

But in an opaque construction such as (43), existential generalization is not valid; (43) does not entail (44), because the noun phrase *a fish* in (43) may be nonspecific.

(43) John wants to catch a fish.
(44) There is a fish that John wants to catch.

We now see that the deletion of a modifying phrase is likewise restricted to transparent contexts. It is valid for (39) but not for (37), and in general not for any opaque construction; (45), for example, does not entail (46).

(45) Bill would hate there to be any pretty girls that he hasn't met.
(46) Bill would hate there to be any pretty girls.

Opaque constructions are semantically very complex, and we are far from a complete understanding of all their complexities. (See J. D. Fodor, 1970, for more extensive discussion.) Even where there is agreement about the data, there are very often disagreements about its proper analysis. What is needed is a complete specification of the inference patterns that are blocked in opaque contexts, and, ultimately, some unified explanation of WHY these inferences are blocked. In the meantime, as we have seen, there are several different analyses that may be worth exploring.

Another of Jackendoff's objections to semantic representations which make use of the quantifiers and variables characteristic of standard logical formulae rests on the claim that some sentences with only two quantifiers have more than two distinct scope interpretations. In a quantificational system, as we have seen, the relative scope of quantifiers is captured formally by their relative order (or by their relative height in GS representations, see Section 4.3 above). Since there are only two distinct ways of ordering two quantifiers, this apparently predicts only two readings for a sentence like (47), which contains the two quantifiers *three* and *many*.

(47) I told three of the stories to many of the men.

But Jackendoff observes that with appropriate stress and intonation, sentence (47) can have THREE different interpretations: (i) the same group of many men heard all three stories; (ii) each story may have been told to a different group of many men; there is no single group of many men that heard all three stories; (iii) each member of a particular group of many men heard three stories, but it is not claimed that all of them heard the same three stories.

In this case, the standard quantificational notation comes off rather well. In fact, it even PREDICTS that the sentence (47) has just these three interpretations. For it is clear from Jackendoff's own paraphrases that reference is being made in (47) both to SETS (of stories and of men), and to the MEMBERS of these sets. So, even though they do not show up clearly in the SURFACE form of (47), there must actually be FOUR quantifiers in the semantic structure of the sentence—one for the set of stories, one for its members, one for the set of men, and one for its members. Four quantifiers could in principle be ordered in 24 different ways. But the well-formedness conditions and inference rules of a standard logic are such that only three out of these 24 orderings produce formulae which are both well-formed and logically distinct. These three formulae turn out to be just the representations of readings (i)–(iii) above. (Uniform paraphrases of these three readings are: (i) there is a set of three stories and a set of many men such that I told each man in the set all of the stories in the set: (ii) there is a set of three stories such that for each story in the set there is a set of many men such that I told that story to each man in the set; (iii) there is a set of many men such that for each man in the set there is a set of three stories such that I told each story in the set to that man.)

A third argument against the standard, unified, quantificational representations is that there are coreference relations in natural language which these representations cannot capture. In particular, there can be anaphora across sentence boundaries, as in (48), as well as within sentence boundaries, as in (49).

(48) John caught a fish. Sam ate it.
(49) John caught a fish and Sam ate it.

Using quantifiers and variables in the standard fashion, we can capture the anaphora of (49) with the representation (50).

(50) $(\exists x)((\text{John caught a fish}_x) \And (\text{Sam ate } x))$

But in standard systems of quantificational logic, the binding of variables by quantifiers may not extend across the boundaries of formulae. There is no well-formed representation for the two-sentence sequence (48). The only natural candidate would be (51), but here the variable in *Sam ate x* is not properly bound by the quantifier, and hence has no interpretation (or at least, not the interpretation intended).

(51) $(\exists x)$ (John caught a fish$_x$)   (Sam ate x)

Again, there is more than one way of meeting this objection. We might simply play the trick of inserting a conjunction between separate sentences, so that the conjoined formula (50) could serve as the representation for both (48) and (49). These hypothetical conjunctions do not always show up in surface structures, it is true, but all we would need is a transformation to delete them in certain circumstances. This solution may not have much positive motivation, but it does appear to be feasible. The complementary move would be to admit a representation like (51) as well-formed, by relaxing the usual constraints on the binding of variables. This certainly would constitute a revision of quantificational logic, though apparently not a revision which demands separate representations for the different semantic properties of a sentence, as in Jackendoff's theory.

Coreference does raise more serious problems, however, when it is combined with opacity. Jackendoff presents some examples (similar to those discussed in G. Lakoff, 1970a) which appear to illustrate some very non-standard kinds of variable binding in English.

The sentence (52) exhibits the usual ambiguity between specific and non-specific readings of the indefinite noun phrase *a fish* in the subordinate clause.

(52) It is possible that John caught a fish.

On the specific reading, this noun phrase may be followed by a pronoun which is coreferential with *a fish*, even though the pronoun is not itself within the scope of the opaque predicate *is possible*.

(53) It is possible that John caught a fish, and certain that he ate it.

But the pronoun *it* in (53) CANNOT be coreferential with the phrase *a fish* in the first conjunct if *a fish* is read as NONspecific. Unless a specific fish is being referred to in the first conjunct, there is nothing for the pronoun in the second conjunct to refer to. As it happens, this fact is neatly captured by constraints on variable binding in standard logical formulae. The quantificational representation of (53) on its nonspecific reading will be (54), in which the quantifier is inside the scope of the opaque predicate in the first conjunct, and hence is also INSIDE the scope of the CONJUNCTION.

(54) (It is possible that $((\exists x)$ (John caught a fish$_x$))) & (it is certain (that he ate it))

The quantifier that binds *a fish* therefore does not, on this reading, have scope over the second conjunct of the sentence, and it thus may not bind a variable in the second conjunct. The pronoun *it* therefore may not be represented in (54) by the variable x. It follows that the pronoun cannot be coreferential with *a fish*. The noncoreference relation in (53) is thus automatically predicted by the formal properties of the representational system.

The problem arises when we turn sentence (53) around into (55).

(55) It is certain that John caught a fish and possible that he ate it.

Here, apparently, there CAN be coreference between the pronoun and the indefinite noun phrase, EVEN if the noun phrase is read as nonspecific. That is, (55) can be taken to mean: 'it is certain that John caught some fish or other, and possible that he ate whatever fish he caught.' Structurally, the quantificational representation of (55) will be exactly parallel to (54). Therefore, just as in (54), the pronoun *it* must not be represented by the same variable as *a fish*. A semantic theory which used standard quantificational representations would thus fail to account for the fact that (55) does have a nonspecific but coreferential interpretation. If, on the other hand, we were to relax the constraints on the binding of variables, in order to permit the coreferential representation of sentence (55), we would then no longer have an explanation for the impossibility of the corresponding reading for sentence (53).

The contrast between (53) and (55) makes it clear that coreference relations depend in part on the meanings of the PREDICATES in a sentence, as well as on its syntactic structure. A nonspecific noun phrase in the scope of *certain* behaves differently from a nonspecific noun phrase in the scope of *possible*. No allowance is made for this in standard quantificational logic or in the modifications of it that have been used by linguists. Jackendoff's table of coreference, distinct from and supplementary to the representation of modal structure, does offer one solution to the problem.

Suppose, for example, that we do loosen the constraints on variable binding, so that the nonspecific but coreferential reading of (55) can be represented. The corresponding representation of (53) will then also meet all the STRUCTURAL conditions on well formedness. The fact that its variables cannot after all be identical, because of their interaction with the PREDICATES in the sentence, would then have to be separately recorded. A table of coreference appended to the quantificational representation could serve just this purpose.

Alternatively, suppose we retain the standard constraints and continue to rule out the representations of both (53) and (55) as ill-formed. The existence of a coreferential reading for (55) would then constitute a special case in need of explanation. It would seem to be attributable to the fact that even on a nonspecific interpretation, the clause *it is certain that John caught a fish* happens to entail (because *certain* is a factive predicate) that there is a fish that John caught—and hence a fish that can be referred to by the pronoun in the second conjunct. The explanation thus lies in the inferential apparatus of the system (including the meaning postulates for *certain*). But if it is deemed necessary that coreference relations should be explicitly specified in semantic representations, then once again it would follow that semantic representations must contain something very like a table of coreference to supplement the quantificational representation.

It hardly needs stressing that our understanding of these matters leaves much to be desired. The semantics of quantifiers and opacity is obviously very different from the internal semantic analysis of lexical items which occupied generative linguists in the early years of semantic research. Now that we are beginning to catch up with the logicians, it is important to test their systems against the facts of natural languages, as Jackendoff has done. Because of the different goals for which these systems were developed, some modifications of their formulae will surely prove necessary if they are to be given a role in the grammars of natural languages. If nothing else, we must presumably recast the formulae of logic into structures of a kind that we have some evidence that the human language mechanisms can manipulate. Lakoff's analysis of quantifiers as the predicates of superordinate clauses in phrase markers is one way in which this might be achieved. To what extent Jackendoff's representations meet this requirement it is hard to say at present.

Whatever modifications may turn out to be necessary, something at least as rich as the standard logical apparatus for quantifiers clearly must form part of the semantic representation system for natural language. Indeed, it has long been recognized that standard logics are not rich enough. A greater variety of quantifiers must be accommodated (e.g., *several, most, seventeen*). And, as we have seen, the interaction of quantifiers with opaque contexts places very heavy demands on a representation system, demands that might be met in one of several different ways. Recently, Hintikka (1974) has argued that there are sentences of English which (though they look harmless enough—e.g., *Some relative of each villager and some relative of each townsman hate each other*) demand a very powerful ('finite partially-ordered') quantificational logic, a logic which is not open to all of Jackendoff's objections to standard systems.

This discussion has focussed on Jackendoff's treatment of scope and coreference. His treatment of focus and presupposition, which is an elaboration of Chomsky's approach discussed in Section 3.3 above, is given in Jackendoff (1972, Chapter 6). His analysis of functional structure, which bears some resemblance to Gruber's semantic system discussed in Section 3.4 above, is in Jackendoff (1972, Chapter 2).

5.6. ARE SEMANTIC REPRESENTATIONS NECESSARY?

This section is frankly speculative, an exploration of some ideas provoked by the most obvious difference between Jackendoff's semantic representations and those of Katz's theory and generative semantics.

In a Jackendoff grammar, a sentence is assigned a SET of semantic representations, each of which specifies PART of the meaning of the sentence. Every entailment (or at least, analytic entailment) of a sentence constitutes a PART of its meaning. Perhaps—and this is a big perhaps—these two notions of part-meaning can be identified with each other. Then the semantic interpretation rules of the grammar could be regarded as inference rules generating entailments, rather than as derivational rules generating semantic representations.

This is a very different picture from the one that has guided most semantic theory construction to date. The usual assumption, shared by theories which differ on other matters, has been that there MUST be a level of semantic representation such that (i) each sentence of the language has a representation at this level, which is correlated, by the grammatical derivation, with syntactic and ultimately phonological and phonetic representations of the sentence; and (ii) inference rules apply to this semantic representation to determine the (possibly infinite) set of entailments of the sentence. But Jackendoff's departures from the standard theory suggest an even more radical revision, which would do without the intermediate stage of semantic representations entirely. Instead, there would be just the syntactic derivation for a sentence, together with a set of inference rules applying to one or more of the phrase markers (deep, surface, end-of-cycle, etc.) in this derivation to generate the entailments of the sentence.

This approach would obviously undercut most of the familiar debates about the properties of semantic representations and the kinds of rules that generate them. It is quite unclear at present what implications it may have for the characterization of intensional isomorphism, for the explanation of 'syntactic' constraints on semantic rules, for the direction of derivation between syntax and semantics, and for a host of other matters which the better established semantic theories have contended with. It is, however, very much in keeping with the shift from lexical decomposition to meaning postulates discussed in Section 5.1. As we observed there, meaning postulates determine entailments without providing any REPRESENTATION which could be substituted for a word in a sentence as a way of making explicit its meaning. The idea of doing without semantic representations is, in general, an extreme instance of the growing emphasis on entailment in linguistic semantics. A grammar without semantic representations, but with a suitable body of inference rules, could apparently do everything that has traditionally been demanded—as long as it is the case that all the significant semantic properties and relations of a sentence can be captured by reference to its entailments. I will discuss in detail just one example, the definition of semantic anomaly, which has shown an interesting course of development in recent years.

The original Katz and Fodor semantic component included semantic selections restrictions. These acted as constraints on the projection rules, blocking certain amalgamations, with the result that an anomalous expression was assigned no reading (semantic representation) at all. It has since been noted (in McCawley, 1968b, and Jackendoff, 1972, Chapter 1) that anomalous expressions MUST be assigned semantic representations. The reason is that an anomalous expression can appear as a constituent of a nonanomalous sentence;[7] the sentence (56) is anomalous, but (57) and (58) are not.

(56) Colorless green ideas sleep furiously.
(57) It is nonsense to talk of colorless green ideas sleeping furiously.
(58) Max insists that he has proved that colorless green ideas sleep furiously.

Therefore semantic anomaly cannot be identified, as it is in Katz's theory, with meaninglessness in the literal sense of a total lack of meaning. If it were, all anomalous sentences would be represented as meaning the same (i.e., nothing), and (58) would be predicted, incorrectly, to be synonymous with (59).

(59) Max insists that he has proved that sincerity admires John.

The conclusion is that semantic anomaly does not consist in the absence of a meaning, but rather in some defect of the meaning. We might therefore attempt a definition of anomaly in terms of some incompatibility relation

7. All the convincing examples appear to have the anomalous constituent within an opaque context.

between the semantic elements that make up the semantic representation of the sentence. Jackendoff (1972) proposes certain well-formedness conditions on semantic representations, and thus seems to take a position of essentially this kind. However, McCawley (1971) has argued for removing the treatment of anomaly out of the semantic component entirely, and into the inferential system—the logic—associated with the grammar. He maintains that anomaly consists in the incompatibility of certain entailments or presuppositions of the sentence.

To attribute anomaly to a property of semantic representations, and to attribute it to a relation between entailments, MIGHT come to the same thing. The two proposals would not really differ if sentences which shared an entailment always had some part of their semantic representations in common. Such a condition is implied by Katz's definition of (analytic) entailment as the INCLUSION of the reading of the entailed sentence within the reading of the entailing sentence (Katz, 1972, Chapter 4). Two sentences with an entailment in common will both have readings which include the reading of the sentence they entail. The entailments of a sentence will thus correspond in fairly direct fashion with parts of its semantic representation; and if anomaly can be defined over the entailments of the sentence, then it could presumably equally well be defined over the semantic representation. However, Katz also admits some cases of entailment that apparently cannot be captured by reading inclusion, i.e., cannot be determined simply by inspection of the reading itself. For example, (*Aesthetic Object*) is said to entail (*Aesthetic Object*) v (*Social Activity*); and *all* entails *some*, even though there appears to be no possible DECOMPOSITION of the meaning of *all* into a set of smaller meanings that includes the meaning of *some*. If entailments of this kind can be captured only by means of inference rules applying to semantic representations, (and if entailments of this kind are relevant to semantic anomaly), then semantic anomaly cannot be defined over semantic representations. Rather, as McCawley argues, it must be defined over the entailments which are drawn from the semantic representations by the inference rules of the logic associated with the grammar.

A further motivation for characterizing anomaly in terms of entailments is that it would unify the two roles of selection restrictions in more traditional treatments. Selection restrictions have been used to predict the anomaly of a sentence like (60) which contains an impermissible combination of semantic elements. They have also been used, for nonanomalous sentences such as (61), to fill out the meaning of the sentence.

    (60) Sincerity admires John.
    (61) This one admires John.

In (61), the subject noun phrase is not specified for animateness, so there is no direct conflict with the selection restriction on the verb *admire* which requires its subject to be animate (or more precisely, to be capable of higher psychological functions). But the selection restriction on the verb induces an interpretation of the subject as if it WERE an animate noun phrase. Katz (1972, Chapter 3) employs a special mechanism in such cases, which will transfer the semantic markers in the selection restriction for the verb into the reading for the subject. The sentence reading will then contain the marker (*Animate*), even though this is not present in the readings of any of the lexical items in the sentence. But notice that both of these functions of the selection restriction will be reflections of the same underlying principle, if the information in the selection restriction is regarded instead as an entailment of the sentence. When this entailment conflicts with others, the sentence will be anomalous; when it does not, it merely contributes to the content of the sentence.

The inferential approach to anomaly does, however, present certain problems which have yet to be resolved satisfactorily. One is that there seem to be different degrees of anomaly (see Drange, 1966). Assuming, as seems reasonable, that there are not different degrees of contradictoriness, anomaly cannot be attributed without further comment to a contradiction between entailments. Moreover, semantically anomalous sentences such as *The king is axiomatic* must be distinguished in some fashion from straightforwardly contradictory sentences such as *The king is female*. The solution to both of these problems may lie in some notion of the DEPTH of a contradiction within the meaning of a sentence—the more 'embedded' the contradiction, the more anomalous the sentence. *The king is female* contains a direct contradiction, but in the anomalous sentence *The king is axiomatic*, the contradiction is more distant; axiomaticity entails abstractness, which entails inanimacy, and it is this which is directly inconsistent with the meaning of *king*.

It may be considerations of this kind that led McCawley to characterize anomaly in terms of a contradiction between PRESUPPOSITIONS rather than straightforward entailments. (See Section 5.3 and Chapter 6 on presuppositions.) An anomalous sentence rests on a contradiction without actually asserting a contradiction. Certainly anomaly, like presupposition and unlike regular entailment, seems to be preserved under negation. Sentence (63) has at least one interpretation on which it is quite as anomalous as (62).

(62) My afterimage is waterproof.
(63) My afterimage is not waterproof.

Thomason (1972) argues that anomalous sentences exhibit truth value gaps (i.e., are neither true nor false), just like sentences with failed logical presuppositions.[8] However, the converse does not seem to be true. Sentences

8. Thomason's theory is actually a REFERENTIAL theory of anomaly. The sentence *This tree is lefthanded* is anomalous, but so is the sentence *This is lefthanded* when it is used of a tree. Jackendoff (1972, Chapter 1) makes a similar point.

like (64) and (65), which have false or contradictory presuppositions, do not strike us as semantically anomalous in anything like the way that (62) is.

(64) The present king of France is bald
(65) My childless brother loves my son more than he does his own.

Thus, the presuppositional approach to semantic anomaly could probably stand some further attention. But if it can be made to work, it will provide an illustration of how at least one semantic property of sentences can be defined in a theory which does not admit semantic representations.

Another move away from semantic representations as they have traditionally been conceived was made some years ago by McCawley (1968b), who suggested giving up the usual assumption that semantic representations must stand in a one-to-one correspondence with meanings, i.e., that all (and only) sentences which are synonymous with each other must share the same semantic representation. In a discussion of the formal similarities between semantic representations and syntactic phrase markers, McCawley questioned whether the ordering of constituents in semantic representations is significant, as it is in syntactic phrase markers. In some cases it appears not to be. The sentences (66) and (67) are logically equivalent, even synonymous.

(66) Roses are red and violets are blue.
(67) Violets are blue and roses are red.

If synonymy has to be captured by identity of semantic representation, as has usually been assumed, then (66) and (67) MUST be assigned the same semantic representation, and the two conjuncts in this semantic representation must therefore presumably be unordered. The alternative is to assign the sentences distinct (and less abstract) representations, in which the conjuncts are ordered as in the respective surface structures. Then it would have to be stipulated somehow that these two representations are semantically equivalent. This could be done by means of a bidirectional entailment rule of the form p and $q \equiv q$ and p. It is this latter treatment that McCawley opts for.

The significance of this proposal is that meaning (even identity and difference of meaning) is no longer to be characterized by semantic representations alone. Instead it is captured by the interaction of semantic representations with the inferential mechanisms for the language. Synonymy is not explicitly REPRESENTED at any LEVEL of the grammar. Sentences are defined to be synonymous just in case they have identical entailments.

This approach might be extended to a number of other cases in which semantic representations very far removed from surface structures have previously had to be posited in order to meet the condition that synonymous sentences should have the same semantic representation. As just one example, it has been claimed (perhaps falsely) that sentences related as (68) and (69) are synonymous.

> (68) The man who shouted at the meeting was asked to leave.
> (69) A man shouted at the meeting and the man was asked to leave.

On the assumption that these sentences must have identical semantic representations, it has been argued that (68) must be represented as a conjunction. (See Thompson 1971. I leave it to the reader to see why conjunctions cannot be represented as relative clauses.) This analysis does perhaps make the meaning of (68) more explicit, but it also inflates the syntax-semantics mapping rules of the grammar. McCawley's suggestion opens up the possibility of shifting this work into the logic. The rules of the grammar would assign (68) and (69) distinct semantic representations, each quite similar configurationally to the corresponding surface structure. Then we would add to the logic an inference rule stating (roughly) that a relative clause construction entails both of its clauses, in addition to the standard inference rule stating that a conjunction entails both of its conjuncts.[9]

Once the assumption is challenged that semantic representations must stand in a one-to-one correspondence with meanings, it is a short step to the idea that semantic representations are not necessary at all—as long as the grammar is supplemented by a rich enough logic. (Under a psychological interpretation, this theory would imply that the on-line processing of a sentence to derive its underlying structure is less elaborate than it has been thought to be; many entailments of a sentence could be extracted, at greater leisure and perhaps only if needed, by applying the rules of the logic.) Whether this is the way things are remains to be established, but it is at least interesting to see that a semantic theory without semantic representations is not a contradiction in terms.

---

9. If it is true that (68) and (69) are not quite synonymous, the inferential approach would actually be superior, since it offers more degrees of freedom. For example, it could state that the relative clause is presupposed rather than entailed.

6
Current Trends

For readers interested in pursuing any of the topics raised in the previous chapters, there is no substitute for tackling the current research literature. All I can do here is to indicate some of the directions in which noses are pointing. As will be seen, this includes most points of the compass. What follows is a more or less random survey of the main trends, interspersed with critical comments at a very general level, and cross-referenced with topics discussed earlier in the book. The criterion for inclusion in this chapter is not simply date of publication but reflects (my estimate of) how influential these developments are likely to be on the course of future research.

Chomsky, and many of his students and former students, have continued to develop the extended standard theory, with particular emphasis on the search for constraints on linguistic rules. (See Chomsky, 1973; Fiengo, 1974; Wasow, 1972; and references therein.) As Chomsky has often observed, children acquire natural languages very rapidly and with little or no explicit tuition. It is concluded that the language learner selects his hypotheses about the structure of the language to which he is exposed from among a small set of alternatives which are all that are compatible with his innate knowledge of what a human language is like. (If "knowledge" sounds too grandiose, one may think of the child's brain as a machine which, just like a tomato-canning machine or a computer, is limited by its structure or at least its basic programming, to certain kinds of operation.) What is innate must presumably be universal. Since rather few grammatical rules are themselves universal, what must be ascribed to the infant is rather a set of constraints on possible rules and their mode of application.

We have already touched on one respect in which these concerns bear on semantics. As noted in Section 3.3, certain previously accepted syntactic transformations have been recast in the extended standard theory as semantic interpretation rules. This shift of labor from the syntactic to the semantic component permits the imposition of tighter constraints on possible syntactic transformations—for example, that they may not appeal to command relations between constituents (though semantic rules may). This shift has been objected to on the grounds that, without a concomitant tightening of the characterization of semantic rules, the freedom of a grammar as a whole is not reduced but is simply transferred from one component to another. The implied boundary between syntax and semantics has also been criticized. Consider sentence (1).

(1) The girl washed himself.

If (1) is generated by the syntactic rules, and is marked as deviant only by the interpretive rule which seeks an antecedent for the reflexive pronoun, then we might expect the sentence to strike speakers as syntactically well-formed though semantically uninterpretable. In fact, many speakers consider it to be syntactically ill-formed.

One reply to this objection is that intuitions of unacceptability do not come clearly labeled with the source of the unacceptability, so they cannot be the arbiter in such decisions. For example, (1) can be viewed EITHER as an ill-formed expression of the meaning properly carried by *The girl washed herself*, OR as a well-formed expression of the inconsistent proposition that the girl washed some male identical with herself. In ordinary conversation, of course, the former is the much more likely mistake. But this is surely not a fact that should be stated in the grammar; it has to do with the way people are made, and the fact that in real life slips of the tongue are more common than slips of the logic. The discussion of semantic anomaly in Section 5.6 suggests that the grammar should generate the surface form (1) and associate it with the anomalous meaning. On the other hand, the use of (1) with the intention of asserting that the girl washed herself need not be accounted for in the grammar, for it would fall under supplementary principles of the kind proposed by Katz (1964b) for treating 'semigrammatical' sentences in terms of how their derivations deviate from those licensed by the grammar.

Thus although (1) is most strikingly an instance of an ungrammatical but semantically impeccable sentence, it may nevertheless be proper for the grammar to characterize it as well-formed but incoherent. Would this leave us on the brink of a slippery slope? Surely SOME combinations of words are to be ruled out on syntactic grounds as simply not sentences at all; (2) is a likely candidate.

(2) After if envelopes paper tearing.

But if so, where is the line to be drawn between examples like this and examples like (1)? One suggestion would be to identify the semantics/syntax distinction with the distinction between word sequences which are so structured that the rules of the grammar can apply to assign them an interpretation, however bizarre, and sequences which are so ill-formed that no interpretation principles exist for them at all. But, as observed in Section 3.5, the application of this distinction to particular cases is not always easy to motivate. On which side of the line, for example, should we put (3), which has no antecedent at all for its reflexive pronoun?

(3) Themselves are waiting.

Certainly it is difficult to think up any interpretation, even an anomalous one, for (3); and this suggests that (3) should be excluded on syntactic grounds. However, the most economical treatment in an EST grammar would be to allow the phrase structure rules and transformations to generate (3) and to exclude it by means of the interpretive rule which assigns an antecedent to a reflexive pronoun in acceptable sentences. This rule would then have a double function—it would assign a semantic interpretation to some sentences, and filter out others as ill-formed. G. Lakoff (1970) has cited a number of examples of this kind, and has argued that only generative semantics, which does not distinguish separate syntactic and semantic components to a grammar, can successfully explain the double function of such rules. A better understanding of the nature of filters and their status relative to 'constructive' rules (see Section 4.1) may help to clarify this debate. In the meantime, questions about the degree to which syntax is autonomous from semantics seem to be inextricably entwined with the question of whether certain word sequences are to be assigned aborted derivations or no derivations at all.

In Section 3.3, passing reference was made to a revision of the extended standard theory which has direct bearing on semantics. In recent work by Chomsky (1973, 1975) and Fiengo (1974), it is observed that the constraints on movement transformations mirror those on the binding of variables by quantifiers. The condition on the movement of a constituent from one position in a phrase marker to another is: if a quantifier were in the new position, it could bind a variable in the old, pre-movement position. This constraint automatically excludes lowering transformations (see Section 4.2) and many types of rightward movement rules; for a quantifier can typically bind only those variables which are to its right and no higher than it in the phrase marker.

This constraint is incorporated into the extended standard theory by having movement rules leave behind a TRACE of the moved constituent in its original position. The trace (which is present in surface structures but has no phonological realization) is regarded as BOUND by the moved constituent, just as a variable is bound by its quantifier. These traces effectively encode into a surface structure certain information about previous stages of the transformational derivation—in particular, information about the deep structure relations of surface constituents.

We have already discussed the global rules of generative semantics (Section 3.3), the cumulative function of Katz's projection rules (Section 4.4), and Jackendoff's use of identification indices (Section 5.5). All of these mechanisms serve, in their different ways, to relate structural representations at distinct and otherwise nonadjacent stages of a derivation. In a defense of traces, Chomsky has observed that cumulative devices are far from new; the familiar syntactic transformations preserve many of the configurations and node labels of a phrase marker throughout its derivation. The issue, then, is WHAT needs to be preserved. For semantics, the interest of the trace theory is Chomsky's claim that the trace-augmented surface structures which are motivated by consideration of constraints on syntactic rules constitute just the structures that are needed for semantic interpretation. The move has been from the interpretation of deep structures alone (as in Katz's theory), *via* the interpretation of deep and surface structures (as in Jackendoff's theory), to the interpretation of surface structures alone. Some semantic interpretation rules are still necessary; even with traces, surface structures do not provide distinct representations for scope-ambiguous sentences like *Everyone saw an opossum*, in which no movement or other syntactic transformations differentiate the derivations for the two interpretations. But the interpretive rules are apparently to be limited to dealing with scope relations, anaphora and related phenomena. How, or even whether, lexical decomposition is to be accomplished is not clear.

Generative semantics has also been moving further and further from the original standard theory of Katz and Postal (1964) and Chomsky (1965), though in a different direction from the extended standard theory. In generative semantics the emphasis has tended to be on phenomena which demand MORE powerful descriptive devices. It should be noted that this is not necessarily incompatible with the concern of the EST to restrict the power of the theory, even though many GS proposals have as a matter of fact been rejected by standard theorists. A theory can be simultaneously too powerful and not powerful enough. To put it loosely, earlier linguistic theories may have had power in the right amount but in the wrong place. A 'sideways' shift of the theory would therefore be in order, with some of the older limitations lifted and some new ones imposed.

Generative semantics admits global rules and derivational constraints. In this framework, what have been called 'transformations' can be seen as simply a special case of derivational constraints—they are those constraints which happen to be LOCAL in the sense that they determine permissible relations between two ADJACENT phrase markers in a derivation. Indeed, G. Lakoff (1974) and others no longer regard generative semantics as a variety of transformational grammar; transformational grammar is considered a preliminary and overly restricted approach to language, standing in much the same relation to generative semantics as taxonomic linguistics does to transformational linguistics.

It is uncertain just which current developments should be counted as contributions to the theory of generative semantics, but certain recent proposals form a natural constellation and probably could be explicitly integrated into a single consistent theory of language.

Perlmutter and Postal have argued against one of the earliest restrictions that Chomsky imposed on transformations, the restriction that the structural description of a transformation must be expressible as Boolean conditions on analyzability. (See Postal, 1974; and Perlmutter and Postal, to be published.) It is claimed that many syntactic processes require reference to grammatical relations (e.g., to the SUBJECT of a verb rather than merely to the noun phrase which directly precedes the verb), and that there are universal generalizations about possible types of rules which can be captured only in these terms. Since grammatical relations clearly are relevant to semantics, this position seems to be very much in keeping with the generative semantics rejection of a sharp distinction between syntactic rules and semantic rules.

Ross (1972, 1973a, 1973b, 1974, 1975) has developed a "squishy" approach to grammar, which rejects other restrictive assumptions of the standard theory, such as that a constituent must either be a member of a certain category or not. Category membership is a matter of degree, and different syntactic transformations may differ in the degree of membership they demand. For example, the sentences (4)–(7) represent a declining degree of acceptability.

(4) It's strange that you are so embarrassed.
(5) It's strange for you to be so embarrassed.
(6) It's strange your being so embarrassed.
(7) It's strange your embarrassment.

Extraposition is fully acceptable in (4), which has the most sentence-like complement clause, and is least acceptable in (7), which has the most noun-like complement.

In a similar vein, though with more direct relevance to semantics, G. Lakoff (1972) has applied the theory of 'fuzzy sets' to natural language data. Instead of assuming, for example, that anything must either be a bird or not be a bird, the concept of 'birdiness' is defined by a function which permits degrees of membership in the set of birds. Robins enjoy full membership, chickens and penguins a lesser degree, and cows don't belong at all. Phrases which Lakoff calls "hedges" interact with such words and directly exploit their fuzziness. Sentence (8) is claimed to be only partly true, but the hedged sentence (9) is fully true, and the hedged sentence (10) is completely false.

(8) A penguin is a bird.
(9) Strictly speaking, a penguin is a bird.
(10) A penguin is a bird par excellence.

This approach is designed to offer a more realistic account of word meaning than the more traditional assumption that precise necessary and sufficient conditions for set membership can always be given. (We will return to this topic below.)

A very general trend in generative semantics has been away from the competence/performance distinction and the concern with formalism which figured so prominently in early work in generative grammar. It has been complained that by shunting a number of important phenomena into the siding called 'performance,' linguists have been able to ignore them and to develop spuriously tidy formal descriptions of the facts that remain. (See G. Lakoff, 1974; and R. Lakoff, 1974.) Other linguists (e.g., Dougherty, 1975; and Katz and Bever, 1976) have accused generative semantics in return of being taxonimic, empiricist, and/or behaviorist.

Chomsky's original demarcation was intended as an instance of 'divide and conquer.' The expected result was a narrowly constrained theory of language structure, which could then be meshed with a separate theory of language use, or perhaps with a number of different theories dealing with production and perception processes, stylistic preferences, pragmatic constraints, and so on. Generative semanticists consider that such compartmentalization is impossible, and that far from simplifying grammatical description by abstracting linguistic facts from these other matters, it can be shown that they all form one complex indivisible system. Facts about the world, about speakers' and hearers' beliefs about the world, about their relative social status, and so on, must all be fed into the grammar which determines the form-meaning correlations for the language.

One argument to this effect comes from Lakoff's study of hedges. Lakoff argues that it is not sufficient for the grammar to specify only the meaning of a word, if this is taken to include just those properties which are normally relevant to truth conditions on sentences. The dictionary must also include a specification of the pragmatic properties of the word, such as its connotations. This is because in hedged sentences, its connotations may have a bearing on truth conditions. It is irrelevant to the truth conditions of sentence (11) that typical bachelors tend to behave freely and look unkempt but cheerful.

(11) John is a bachelor.

But Lakoff claims that such facts do make a difference to the truth of the hedged sentence (12), which attributes to John the typical rather than the analytic properties of bachelorhood.

(12) John is a regular bachelor.

Lakoff draws the general moral that semantics is not independent from pragmatics.

On the other hand, many observations that have often been taken to support this view are equally compatible with the 'divide and conquer' approach. For example, R. Lakoff (1971) has noted that a conjoined sentence is judged acceptable to the extent that its conjuncts share a common topic or other connection in content. For a sentence like (13), enormous ingenuity is needed to detect any common topic, and the sentence is therefore a strange one.

(13) Boys eat apples and Mary threw a stone at a frog.

For the sentence (14), the connection will be obscure, and the sentence consequently unacceptable, to anyone who does not know that Peking Duck is served with Hoisin sauce, or at least that both are items of Chinese cuisine.

(14) John wants to make Peking Duck, and I know that the A&P is having a sale on Hoisin sauce.

In the sentence (15), the connection is a temporal and causal one that can probably be appreciated by most contemporary English speakers.

(15) The police came into the room and everyone swallowed their cigarettes.

The important point is that the intelligibility of a conjoined sentence depends not only on the hearer's linguistic knowledge, but also on his knowledge about the world.

Lakoff's examples are not unlike some which Grice (to be published) has used to motivate a distinction between meaning in a strict sense, and pragmatically determined connotations or implicatures. (See Section 2.3.) It has often been asserted that the connectives of formal logic do not fully capture the meanings of the corresponding English words *and*, *or* and *if . . . then*. Grice argues that they do, and that the apparently richer meanings of the English words are due to conversational implicatures. The sentence (16) and (17) notoriously convey quite different sequences of events, though the corresponding logical formulae would have no temporal implications and would be logically equivalent.

(16) Joe took off his boots and went to bed.
(17) Joe went to bed and took off his boots.

But there is no need for the temporal implications of English *and* to be specified in the dictionary; they can be derived from the conversational maxim "Be orderly," which enjoins the speaker to relate events in the order of their occurrence (unless there is good reason to the contrary).

The temporal implication of *and* does not amount to a strict entailment, as is shown by the fact that, like other examples of conversational implicature, it can be 'cancelled' without self-contradiction. Someone might utter (17) and then add, for the benefit of the horrified landlady, "But I hasten to assure you, madam, that he removed his boots first." In other contexts the implicature does not even arise, because the maxim is overridden by other considerations. In response to the question: "What are the most important things Joe did today?", the order of conjuncts in (17) could be construed as indicating degree of importance rather than sequence. The general picture that emerges from Grice's work is that the meanings of sentences can be distinguished from the overlays of significance that attach to them when they are put to use in conversational exchanges.

Presupposition is another (and related) phenomenon which may be regarded either as within the domain of the grammar, or as governed by extra-grammatical principles which relieve the grammar of responsibility for certain data. After some years of general confusion, a distinction has been recognized between two kinds of presupposition (see Keenan 1971). LOGICAL or semantic presuppositions are relevant to the truth conditions on sentences (strictly speaking, on statements); if a sentence S has the logical presupposition L, and L is false, then S has no truth value. PRAGMATIC presuppositions are relevant to the appropriateness of an utterance in a context; if S has the pragmatic presupposition P, and P is not among the beliefs shared by speaker and hearer, then the utterance of S is inappropriate in that conversational context. The sentence (18), discussed in Section 5.3, exhibits a failure of reference, and such sentences seem to provide the strongest examples of logical presupposition.

(18) The present king of France is bald.

Many people judge that (18) cannot strictly be called false, for to call it false would be to accept that there IS a king of France while denying that he is bald. Since (18) is obviously not true either, it exhibits a 'truth value gap.' Another familiar example is (19), which presupposes that Smith has beaten his wife.

(19) Smith has stopped beating his wife.

An example of pragmatic presupposition would be any French sentence containing the second person pronoun *tu*; this could be used appropriately only if it is agreed (at least implicitly) by the speaker and the addressee that their relationship is of a kind to allow such familiarity. Another example that has been proposed is (20).

(20) John isn't here yet.

The presupposition that John is expected to arrive is claimed to be pragmatic rather than logical. It is claimed that (20) is true just as long as John is not now present, and that it suffers not from a truth value gap but only from strangeness if John is neither present nor even expected to be present.

This distinction having been drawn, and accepted by some linguists if not by all, attention now centers on which sentences exhibit which kinds of presupposition, and, more fundamentally, on whether both kinds actually occur in natural language. It is logical presupposition which has come under heaviest attack. Many linguists (e.g., Karttunen, 1973, 1974; and Kuroda, MS.) reject intuitive judgments of truth value gaps. Putative examples of logical presupposition are reduced to pragmatic presuppositions—a sentence like (18) is judged to be false but inappropriate. Certainly the strangeness of (18) in normal conversational contexts would be so severe as to make judgments of truth value difficult, and there could be many reasons for our reluctance to CALL it false that do not exclude its actually BEING false.

But there are also defenders of logical presupposition (see Katz and Langendoen, 1976), and the dispute is not over yet. Its outcome is relevant for the scope of semantics, for the logical presuppositions of a sentence must feature in any account of its truth conditions, and it is widely agreed that anything which affects truth conditions must be dealt with by the grammar. By contrast, pragmatic presuppositions, which do not bear on truth conditions, might be treated by some extra-grammatical component or theory which takes grammatical derivations as its input, and generates appropriateness conditions for sentences in context as its output. Complicating the picture, however, is a distinction which Grice has drawn between conventional and nonconventional implicatures (conversational implicatures being a subset of the latter). The temporal implications of *and*, discussed above, are derivable from the maxims of conversation together with just the simple truth conditions on conjunction that apply also in formal logics. (In support of this conclusion, it is claimed that any other word with the same truth conditions as *and* would give rise to the same conversational implicatures.) If this is right, the dictionary entry for *and* could simply give these truth conditions and need contain no further information about temporal sequence. Conventional implicatures, on the other hand, depend on specific words or constructions. Unlike *and*, the word *but* carries certain implications of contrast or unexpectedness—even though, in some strict sense, *and* and *but* seem to mean the same. So a dictionary for English apparently MUST explicitly record the special connotations carried by *but*.

G. Lakoff (1969) has pointed to another kind of interaction between presuppositions and the grammar. He observes that a sentence like (21) will be acceptable only to an English speaker who classes cats among the higher animals.

(21) My cat, who is hungry, is scratching at the larder door.

The use of *who* in (21), rather than *which*, will strike other speakers as ungrammatical. Clearly the *who/which* contrast is a linguistic matter and must be characterized in any adequate grammar of English, but it appears to be bound up with pragmatic considerations. Lakoff's point has sometimes been taken to constitute an argument in favor of making information about speakers' beliefs available to the formal mechanisms of the grammar. Grammars are required to predict grammaticality, and (21) seems to show that judgments of grammaticality depend on a person's beliefs about nonlinguistic matters. But, as Lakoff himself observed (see also Chomsky 1972a), this does not prove that the grammar itself must take account of speakers' beliefs. The grammar could simply pair sentences with specifications of their presuppositions, and leave it to other principles (rather obvious ones in this case) to establish that all and only those people who believe the presuppositions to be true will judge the sentences to be acceptable. Here again, the argument seems to hinge on the question of whether or not an unacceptable sentence should be generated by the grammar. Beliefs about the world affect the operation of the grammar only if a sentence like (21) is assumed to have no derivation at all in the grammar of a person who does not anthropomorphize cats.

In Section 2.8, it was noted that many of the most recent concerns in linguistic semantics reflect the influence of developments in philosophy. One important example is the growing interest in Montague grammar, briefly mentioned in Section 2.5. While Montague was alive, linguists were at first ignorant and then largely sceptical about his contributions to the study of natural lanague. A fundamental tenet of his approach is that in natural languages, as in the artificial languages constructed by logicians, every syntactic rule makes a specific semantic contribution. As each syntactic rule combines constituents, a semantic rule computes the meaning of the resulting expression by combining the meanings of its parts. This is reminiscent of the early Katz and Fodor projection rules (though these applied in a block after all the syntactic rules of the base component). However, in Montague's syntax there is no transformational derivation, and no level of deep structures distinct from surface structures. The syntactic part of the grammar consists entirely of tree-building rules (working from the bottom up), though these rules are much more powerful than the phrase structure rules which construct underlying phrase markers in generative grammars. (This is a very rough picture. For details, see Montague, 1974, and Partee, 1975, 1976.)

To many linguists, this kind of grammar has seemed hopelessly inadequate for the description of natural languages—the whole point of the 'transformational revolution' in linguistics was precisely that a nontransformational syntax cannot do the job of distinguishing grammatical from ungrammatical sentences. To standard theorists believing in the 'autonomy of syntax,' the assumption that syntactic and semantic rules are inherently associated has been particularly unacceptable. Nevertheless, Cooper and Parsons (1976) have demonstrated an equivalence between a Montague grammar, a standard theory grammar, and a generative semantics grammar for a small fragment of English, suggesting that the differences between them may have been exaggerated. In particular, the Montague rules which combine constituents can mimic some transformational operations. Partee (1975) and others have shown how other transformations (e.g., Reflexive, Passive, *Tough*-Movement) can be added to a Montague grammar. Thomason (1974, 1976), Bennett (1976), and others have explored the alternative possibility of doing without many of the standard transformations by enriching the semantics of the system instead. This move is similar in spirit, though perhaps not in motivation, to developments in the extended standard theory. The synonymy of active and passive sentences, or of sentences like *I expect to win* and *I expect myself to win* has for many years been taken to demand deep structures distinct from surface structures, and a transformational derivation to relate the two levels. But in some such cases, it is arguable that the SYNTACTIC relation between the sentences has been overestimated, and that all the grammar need do is assign them the same meaning. This can be done by the inference rules and meaning postulates of a suitable intensional logic.

Montague grammar has probably had its greatest influence on linguistics in introducing the formal machinery of intensional logic into semantic descriptions. The semantic part of Montague's grammar makes use of a translation of English sentences into the formulae of a rich logic in which quantification, attributive adjectives, necessity, opaque constructions with 'psychological' verbs, and a variety of other traditional sources of semantic problems become amenable to formal treatment. Even linguists who still reject Montague's approach to grammar have been coming to recognize the importance of relating sentences to objects and states of affairs in the world, and thus to accept the need for model theoretic interpretations for natural languages of at least the general kind that Montague developed.

Finally, we must return to the problem of word meanings raised in Section 5.1. We questioned there whether word meanings can be decomposed to any appreciable extent. The word *bachelor* rather obviously means 'unmarried man,' and the meaning of *man* can perhaps be decomposed into 'male' and 'human.' But at some point, decomposition has to stop, and the assignment of meaning to the semantic primitives must be accomplished by some other means. A second and deeper worry was whether, at the point at which decomposition stops, there is anything more to meaning than merely extension.

These doubts have been pressed by philosophers, notably Putnam and Kripke. (See Putnam, 1970, 1973, 1975, and Kripke 1972; also Stampe, 1972, and McCawley, 1975, which are written primarily for linguists.) Important and interesting questions are raised, particularly about logical necessity, which I will not go into here; but the general idea is this. A word like *tiger* is a "natural kind term." To know the meaning of *tiger* is simply to know something about tigers and to know that they are called tigers. The common noun *tiger* refer to tigers in much the way that the proper noun *Noam Chomsky* refers to Noam Chomsky.

We acquire a proper name by learning what person it attaches to. If he is conveniently to hand, we may be taught by direct ostension: "Noam Chomsky is that man over there." If he is not, then he must be identified by means of some description, e.g., "Noam Chomsky is the author of *Syntactic Structures*," or "Noam Chomsky is the Ferrari P. Ward Professor of Linguistics." Of course, the name *Noam Chomsky* doesn't MEAN (isn't synonymous with) 'the Ferrari P. Ward Professor'; we use the description only because we must somehow indicate the individual, and ANY description which served this purpose would be equally good.

In a similar fashion, the theory goes, we acquire a common noun like *tiger* by learning to attach it to a certain kind of animals. WHICH kind of animals may be indicated to us by ostension—we are shown a tiger, and this stands as an exemplar of its kind. Or we may be given a description, e.g., "Tigers are large, fierce cats with yellow and black stripes." But once again, the description is not a definition of the word, is not intended to be synonymous with the word, but merely serves to indicate its extension.

Both for proper nouns and common nouns, one's knowledge of the referent may be extensive or quite fragmentary. One may even have to rely on more expert members of the language community to fill in gaps, to show how to distinguish tigers from leopards or Chomsky from Halle, and perhaps even to back up one's belief that they differ at all. But though I may be hopelessly ignorant about tigers, my word *tiger* still refers to tigers, because I acquired it from someone who acquired it from someone who . . . acquired it from someone who does know how to attach it to the world. The chain of communication (some kind of causal chain) ultimately reaches all the way back to the original event of 'baptism' in which tigers were given their name.

The important point is that none of this produces any ANALYTICITIES. Most of us have a theory about tigers: we know (or at least believe) that tigers are animals, members of the cat family, carnivorous, striped, fierce, usually to be found in jungles. But these are facts (or beliefs) about tigers, not facts about the word *tiger*. The arguments for this claim lie in the game that philosophers play of imagining what we would say in the face of various bizarre discoveries. If it were to turn out that what we have been calling tigers are really a kind of short-necked giraffe, or even that they are robots and not animals at all, then our theory of tigers would have to be drastically revised. But, it is claimed, we would still call these things tigers, and the meaning of the word *tiger* would still be just as it was.

But does it make any sense to talk about the MEANING of the word *tiger* if this theory is correct? The analogy with proper names suggests that it does not, for the usual claim is that proper names have reference but no meaning. However, there is an important difference between *Noam Chomsky* and *tiger*. To be in command of the word *tiger* means knowing that it applies equally to tigers one has never met, tigers no one knows the existence of, future tigers, and even possible tigers. So there has to be some way of EXTENDING the extension of *tiger* to tigers other than those particular animals which were present when tigers were baptized, or which serve as the samples for children learning the word. How is this done?

Putnam and Kripke hold that for a word like *tiger*, nature does it for us, i.e., that the answer to "Is this a tiger?" follows from the nature of the animals so christened, together with the laws of biology or physics which determine the natural class to which these animals belong. Something is a tiger just in case it is the same kind of thing as (i.e., has the same 'essence' as) these things that we have called tigers. (There are questions here that I must leave hanging. One is what happens when the original samples are heterogeneous, mistakenly drawn from a mixture of several natural classes. Another is how the level of classification is determined. Tigers are representative of felines, animals, and physical objects as well as of tigers. Wittgenstein wanted to know how to point to the COLOR of a vase, and much the same question applies to the 'tigerhood' of tigers. A sample of NON-tigers might help resolve such ambiguities. So might the use of superordinate terms in ostensive definition; we say "Blue is the COLOR of this vase," "A tiger is an ANIMAL like this." It is then an interesting question whether these definitions support the analyticity of *Blue is a color, A tiger is an animal*.)

This account of how the potentially infinite extension of *tiger* is determined is a radical one, for it entails that the linguistic competence of a speaker in command of the word does NOT determine the extension. What determines the extension of a word is a certain causal connection between the use of the word and the things that it is used of, together with whatever laws determine which other things are of the same kind. As Putnam puts it, either meaning is not in the head, or meaning does not determine extension. Certainly I may have in my head a concept (or "stereotype") of tigers, but this may have very little relation to the actual class of tigers; it is the facts, not my stereotypes or beliefs, that decide what really is a tiger. (Notice that this goes far beyond the familiar observation that my knowledge of the meaning of *tiger* does not guarantee that I can RECOGNIZE every tiger as a tiger.)

The causal theory provides a ready explanation of the familiar observation that we are more confident and consistent about the central cases of the extension of a word than about peripheral cases. (See Berlin and Kay, 1969; and Heider, 1971, 1973, for psychological studies of color terms.) A traditional concept of meaning as that which determines extension is most at ease when the extensions of terms have sharp boundaries. If the meaning of a word can be given as a set of criterial properties, then anything which has those properties is in the extension of the word, and anything which does not is not. Special allowance has to be made for fuzzy concepts. They may be assigned a cluster of weighted criteria; or some of the criteria, as on Lakoff's treatment, may be continuous—the more of the property something has, the more central its membership in the extension of the word. Analyses along these lines often turn out to be very complicated. The causal theory offers a simpler solution. Fuzziness of extension may reflect only our present ignorance (which scientific progress can cure) about which things are of the same kind as the exemplars with which the word was originally connected when it was introduced into the language or transmitted to new speakers in language learning. Lakoff's sentence *A penguin is a bird* is just straightforwardly true (if contemporary zoologists can be trusted), even though some English speakers may not realize it. Lakoff's claim that it is only partly true seems to rest on the view that the word *bird* IN FACT applies to whatever competent English speakers BELIEVE it applies to, and that their criteria for 'birdiness' may be many and vague and can be satisfied to greater or lesser degree.

But does the causal theory exaggerate the extent to which the referents of common nouns are genuine natural kinds? A realistic view of natural language surely must recognize that ordinary people often do use the word *bird* without intending to include penguins, or use the word *fish* intending to include whales. To what extent do we really care, in our everyday conversation, whether the words we use carve nature at its joints?

The natural kind analysis has been defended for nouns which name plant and animal species, chemical elements and compounds. It may be adaptable to certain verbs, adjectives and other parts of speech. (e.g., *cough, choke, sneeze, hiccup*; *acidic, magnetic, radioactive*). Perhaps in these cases the intention of English speakers IS to pick out genuine natural classes of objects or actions, despite our ignorance as to exactly where the boundaries of these classes lie. That is, it seems as a matter of fact that when there IS a natural kind to be referred to, the implicit intention very often is that the word should pick out that natural kind. There clearly is SOME tendency to adjust the use of a word like *fish* in response to empirical discoveries about fish and whales. In a world which relies heavily on scientific knowledge, this may even have some survival value. But surely the language—or the members of the language community—has some freedom here. Even when there is a natural kind in the offing, we might intend (as perhaps we do intend for *bird* in at least one sense) to pick out a class of referents which is at odds with the lines of classification provided by physics or genetics. And there are many words for which no physically natural kind seems to be forthcoming at all. The word *chair*, for example, does not refer to a physically definable class; the FUNCTION of chairs is more important than their physical composition. Even for *telephone* we must allow that two coffee cans joined by a piece of string may be more of a telephone than a public address system is.

Whether the causal theory can do justice to the full range of lexical items in natural languages depends on the answers to a number of questions. Must EVERY word pick out a kind, i.e. a class of referents which share an essence? If so, we need to know how many different kinds of kinds there are, and what they are. We have seen that if only PHYSICAL kinds are admitted, a great many familiar words will thereby be excluded as defective. The principles which unify the extensions of words seem to include sameness of function (e.g., *chair*), sameness of aesthetic effect (e.g., *beautiful*), sameness of role (e.g., *nurse*), and perhaps many more.

Another important question is whether there can be fuzzy kinds. For, whatever we say about *bird*, there are some words which are INHERENTLY fuzzy, for example the word *bald* as demonstrated by the old paradox: a man with no hair is bald, a man with only one more hair than a bald man is bald, therefore all men are bald. Even some words that appear to be natural kind terms might conceivably turn out to be truly fuzzy, rather than fuzzy only given the present state of our knowledge. It might turn out, contrary to our present beliefs, that there is a continuum of animals intermediate between tigers and leopards. In this eventuality, would we have to conclude that the word *tiger* strictly speaking has no extension at all—that nothing really is a tiger because tigers are not a kind? If so, then the stereotypes associated with words will have to bear the weight of explaining how we can manage to communicate using words like this, and in apparently much the same fashion as we communicate with nondefective words.

Until more is determined about kinds and essences, the full implications of the causal theory for the description of natural language vocabulary will not be entirely clear. Linguists may detect prescriptive overtones in the theory, and may find it harder to swallow that there exist limits on the intentions of members of a language community to stipulate extensions for the words they use, or that intuitions about these extensions are fallible. If so, some compromises might be struck with more traditional linguistic approaches to word meaning. Real world samples can serve to attach words to things, but they might be combined with dictionary entries not too far removed from traditional definitions in terms of properties. Perhaps something is a vase just in case it is sufficiently like some standard vase in shape, in size, in origin, in function, and so on. These properties would be specified in the lexical entry for *vase*, but instead of fully defining the shape, size, function, etc. of a vase, their only role would be to define relevant dimensions of similarity to the sample. The sample would provide the anchor points, much as a conventional reference dictionary often resorts to pictures of typical referents in order to supplement verbal definitions. This minimal modification of the traditional linguistic notion of a definition would at least explain the powerful hold of patently inadequate definitions, such as the definition of *chair* as 'something with a seat, legs, a back . . .' (see Section 5.1). For though this will not do as an account of the analytic properties of ALL chairs, it is not at all implausible as a verbal characterization of TYPICAL (or stereotypical) chairs.[1]

It may be appropriate at this point to remember that natural languages do contain some (though perhaps not many) words like *bachelor* or *quotient*, which characteristically are taught not by ostension but by verbal definitions which do support semantic decomposition. These words may be utterly unlike kind terms; or they may perhaps be at one extreme, and *tiger* at the other, with a range of words in between whose extensions are constrained to varying degrees by analytic properties. This would allow for words like *require* and *permit* (see Section 5.1), which seem to exhibit partial analytic connections of the kind that meaning postulates can express. Furthermore, as many of the examples of Chapter 2 illustrate, at the level of phrases and sentences (which have internal structure) there is often a striking difference between meaning and extension, even if the two fall together at the word level to a greater degree than has been supposed. Stampe's discussion raises the question of how to provide different semantic representations for nonsynonymous sentences (e.g., *I saw a tiger* and *I saw a toenail*) if the words they contain are assigned an extension but not anything that would count as a meaning.

In the face of sceptical attacks on meaning, it is understandable that linguists should have been concerned first and foremost to show that meaning cannot be ignored in the description of natural languages—that there do exist synonymous expressions, analytic sentences, semantic entailments between sentences, and so on. These concepts have now been accorded a place. But we may have pushed them too far in aiming at precise analytic relations for the characterization of meaning at all levels, and attributing to word meanings the sorts of internal structure characteristic of phrases. Perhaps in the future we will have more attention to spare for the special properties of kind terms, and for the possibility that these properties are not so very special after all but reveal themselves throughout the language.

---

1. Putnam (1975) himself suggests a reversion to the format of the early Katz and Fodor dictionary entries, in which a word meaning is represented with just one or two semantic markers, and it is the distinguisher which contains a detailed description of the referent. As observed in Section 5.1, much of the information in the earliest distinguishers was subsequently extracted and represented independently by semantic markers. This was necessary because, for Katz, the properties given in the lexical entry must be analytic properties of the word, and must be made fully explicit so that they are accessible to the theory's definitions of synonymy, anomaly, entailment, etc. But for Putnam, the properties specified by the semantic markers and the distinguisher would not be analytic, but would only define the stereotype associated with the word.

Bibliography

NOTE: Listed below are the books and articles referred to in the text. For further readings in semantics, see Hofmann (1974) and Partee, Sabsay, and Soper (1971).

Alston, W. P. (1968). Meaning and use. In Parkinson, ed. Shorter version in *Philosophical Quarterly*, 1963, **XIII**, 107–124; also in Feigl, Sellars, and Lehrer, eds., and in Rosenberg and Travis, eds.

Anderson, S. R. (1970). On the linguistic status of the performative/constative distinction. In Report No. **NSF-26,** The Computation Laboratory of Harvard University. Also Indiana Univ. Linguistics Club (1971).

Anderson, S. R. and Kiparsky, P., eds. (1973). "A Festschrift for Morris Halle," Holt, New York.

Austin, J. L. (1962P. "How to Do Things with Words," Oxford Univ. Press, New York.

Bach, E. (1968). Nouns and noun phrases. In Bach and Harms, eds.

Bach, E. and Harms, R. T., eds. (1968). "Universals in Linguistic Theory," Holt, New York.

Bailey, C.-J. N. and Shuy, R., eds. (1973). "New Ways of Analyzing Variation in English," Georgetown Univ. Press, Washington, D.C.

Bennett, M. (1976). A variation and extension of a Montague fragment of English. In Partee, ed.

Berlin, B. and Kay, P., (1969). "Basic Color Terms: their University and Evolution," Univ. of California Press, Berkeley, California.

Black, M., ed. (1965). "Philosophy in America," Allen and Unwin, London.

Bolinger, D. (1965). The atomization of meaning. *Language*, **41**, 555–573. Also in Jakobovits and Miron, eds.

Bresnan, J. (1971). Sentence stress and syntactic transformations. *Language*, **47**, 257–281.

Brown, R. (1973). "A First Language: The Early Stages," Harvard Univ. Press, Cambridge, Massachusetts.

Carnap, R. (1947). "Meaning and Necessity," Univ. of Chicago Press. Chicago, Illinois. Enlarged edition 1956.

Chomsky, N. (1957). "Syntactic Structures," Mouton, The Hague.

Chomsky, N. (1964). Current issues in linguistic theory. In Lunt, ed. Revised version in J. A. Fodor and Katz, eds., and published by Mouton, The Hague, 1964.

Chomsky, N. (1965). "Aspects of the Theory of Syntax," MIT Press, Cambridge, Massachusetts.

Chomsky, N. (1970a). Deep structure, surface structures, and semantic interpretation. In Jakobson and Kawamoto, eds. Also in Chomsky (1972b).

Chomsky, N. (1970b). Remarks on nominalization. In Jacobs and Rosenbaum, eds. Also in Chomsky (1972b).

Chomsky, N. (1972a). Some empirical issues in the theory of transformational grammar. In Peters, ed. Also in Chomsky (1972b).

Chomsky, N. (1972b). "Studies on Semantics in Generative Grammar," Mouton, The Hague.

Chomsky, N. (1973). Conditions on transformations. In Anderson and Kiparsky, eds.

Chomsky, N. (1975). "Reflections on Language," Pantheon Books, New York.

Cohen, D., ed. (1972). "Papers from the University of Wisconsin—Milwaukee Linguistics Group First Annual Symposium: Limiting the Domain of Linguistics," Milwaukee, Wisconsin.

Cole, P. and Morgan, J., eds. (1975). "Syntax and Semantics, Vol. 3," Seminar Press, New York.

Cooper, R. and Parsons, T. (1976). Montague grammar, generative semantics, and interpretive semantics. In Partee, ed.

Cresswell, M. J. (1973). "Logics and Languages," Metheun, London.

Darden, B. J., Bailey, C.-J. N. and Davison, A., eds. (1968). "Papers from the Fourth Regional Meeting of the Chicago Linguistic Society," Univ. of Chicago, Chicago, Illinois.

Davidson, D. (1967). Truth and Meaning. *Synthese*, **17**, 304–323. Also in Rosenberg and Travis, eds.

Davidson, D. and Harman, G., eds. (1972). "Semantics of Natural Language," Reidel, Dordrecht.

Davidson, D. and Harman, G., eds. (1975). "The Logic of Grammar," Dickenson Publishing Co., Encino, California.

Dougherty, R. (1970). A grammar of co-ordinate conjoined structures: I. *Language*, **46**, 850–898.

Dougherty, R. (1975). Generative Semantic Methods: A Bloomfieldian counterrevolution. *International Journal of Dravidian Linguistics,* **III**, 255–286.

Drange, T. (1966). "Type Crossings," Mouton, The Hague.

Feigl, H. and Sellars, W., eds. (1949). "Readings in Philosophical Analysis," Appleton-Century-Crofts, New York.

Feigl, H., Sellars, W. and Lehrer, K., eds. (1972). "New Readings in Philosophical Analysis," Appleton-Century-Crofts, New York.

Fiengo, R. W. (1974). Semantic conditions on surface structure. (Ph.D. Dissertation), Massachusetts Inst. of Technology.

Fiengo, R. and Lasnik, H. (1973). The logical structure of reciprocal sentences in English. *Foundations of Language*, **9**, 447–468.

Fillmore, C. J. (1968). The case for case. In Bach and Harms, eds.

Fillmore, C. J., Lakoff, G., and Lakoff, R., eds. (1974). "Berkeley Studies in Syntax and Semantics, Vol. I," Department of Linguistics and Institute of Human Learning, Univ. of California, Berkeley, California.

Fillmore, C. J. (1971). Entailment rules in a semantic theory. In Rosenberg and Travis, eds.

Fillmore, C. J. and Langedoen, D. T., eds. (1971). "Studies in Linguistic Semantics," Holt, New York.

Fodor, J. A. (1975). "The Language of Thought," Crowell, New York.

Fodor, J. A., Bever, T. G., and Garrett, M. F. (1974). "The Psychology of Language: An Introduction to Psycholinguistics and Generative Grammar," McGraw-Hill, New York.

Fodor, J. A. and Katz, J. J., eds. (1964). "The Structure of Language: Readings in the Philosophy of Language," Prentice-Hall, Englewood Cliffs, New Jersey.

Fodor, J. D. (1970a). Formal linguistics and formal logic. In Lyons, ed.

Fodor, J. D. (1970b). The linguistic description of opaque contexts. (Ph.D. Dissertation), Massachusetts Inst. of Technology.

Fodor, J. D., Fodor, J. A., and Garrett, M. F. (1975). The psychological unreality of semantic representations. *Linguistic Inquiry*, **VI**, 515–531.

Fraser, B. (1971). An examination of the performative analysis. Indiana Univ. Linguistics Club.

Frege, G. (1892). Uber Sinn und Bedeutung. *Zeitschrift für Philosophie und Philosophische Kritik*, **100**, 25–50. Translated as On sense and nominatum, in Feigl and Sellars, eds., and as On sense and reference, in Geach and Black, eds.

Fujimura, O., ed. (1973). "Three Dimensions of Linguistic Theory," TEC Co., Tokyo.

Geach, P. and Black, M., eds. (1952). "Translations from the Philosophical Writings of Gottlob Frege," Blackwell, Oxford, England.

Grice, H. P. (1957). Meaning. *Philosophical Review*, **LXVI**, 377–388. Also in Rosenberg and Travis, eds.

Grice, H. P. (1968). Utterer's meaning, sentence-meaning, and word-meaning. *Foundations of Language*, **4**, 225–242. Also in Searle, ed.

Grice, H. P. (1975). Logic and conversation. In Davidson and Harman, eds. (1975).

Grice, H. P. "Logic and Conversation: The William James Lectures, Harvard University, 1967," Harvard Univ. Press, Cambridge, Massachusetts: to be published.

Gruber, J. S. (1965). Studies in lexical relations. (Ph.D. Dissertation), Massachusetts Inst. of Technology.

Gruber, J. S. (1967). Look and see. *Language*, **43**, 937–947.

Gunderson, K., ed. (1975). "Minnesota Studies in the Philosophy of Science, Vol. 7," Univ. of Minnesota Press, Minneapolis, Minnesota.

Halle, M. (1959). "The Sound Pattern of Russian," Mouton, The Hague.

Harman, G. (1970). Deep structure and logical form. *Synthese,* **21,** 275–297. Also in Davidson and Harman, eds. (1972).

Harris, Z. S. (1952). Discourse analysis. *Language,* **28,** 1–30. Also in J. A. Fodor and Katz, eds.

Heider, E. (1971). "Focal" color areas and the development of color names. *Developmental Psychology,* **4,** 447–455.

Heider, E. (1973). On the internal structure of perceptual and semantic categories. In Moore, ed.

Hintikka, J. (1974). Quantifiers vs. quantification theory. *Linguistic Inquiry,* **II,** 153–177.

Hofmann, T. R. (1974). "Bibliography on the Semantics of Human Language," Univ. of Ottawa Press, Ottawa.

Jackendoff, R. (1972). "Semantic Interpretation in Generative Grammar," MIT Press, Cambridge, Massachusetts.

Jackendoff, R. (1975). Morphological and semantic regularities in the lexicon. *Language,* **51,** 639–671.

Jacobs, R. A. and Rosenbaum, P. S., eds. (1970). "Readings in English Transformational Grammar," Ginn, Waltham, Massachusetts.

Jakobovits, L. and Miron, M., eds. (1967). "Readings in the Psychology of Language," Prentice-Hall, Englewood Cliffs, New Jersey.

Jakobson, R. and Kawamoto, S., eds. (1970). "Studies in General and Oriental Linguistics Presented to Shiro Hattori on the Occasion of His Sixtieth Birthday," TEC Co., Tokyo.

Kant, I. (1781). "Critik der Reinen Vernunft," J. F. Hartknoch, Riga. Translated as "Critique of Pure Reason," by N. K. Smith, 1929, Humanities Press, New York.

Karttunen, L. (1973). Presuppositions of compound sentences. *Linguistic Inquiry,* **IV,** 169–193.

Karttunen, L. (1974). Presupposition and linguistic context. *Theoretical Linguistics,* **1,** 181–194.

Katz, J. J. (1964a). Analyticity and contradiction in natural language. In J. A. Fodor and Katz, eds. Also in Rosenberg and Travis, eds.

Katz, J. J. (1964b). Semi-sentences. In J. A. Fodor and Katz, eds.

Katz, J. J. (1966). "The Philosophy of Language," Harper, New York.

Katz, J. J. (1970). Interpretive semantics *vs.* generative semantics. *Foundations of Language,* **6,** 220–259.

Katz, J. J. (1971). Generative semantics IS interpretive semantics. *Linguistic Inquiry,* **II,** 313–331.

Katz, J. J. (1972). "Semantic Theory," Harper, New York.

Katz, J. J. (1973). Interpretive semantics meets the zombies. *Foundations of Language,* **9,** 549–596.

Katz, J. J. and Bever, T. G. (1976). The fall and rise of empiricism. In Katz, Bever and Langendoen, eds.

Katz, J. J., Bever, T. G. and Langendoen, D. T., eds. (1976). "An Integrated Theory of Linguistic Ability," Crowell, New York.

Katz, J. J. and Fodor, J. A. (1963). The structure of a semantic theory. *Language, 39,* 170–210. Also in Fodor and Katz, eds.

Katz, J. J. and Langendoen, D. T. (1976). Pragmatics and presupposition. *Language,* to be published. Also in Katz, Bever and Langendoen, eds.

Katz, J. J. and Nagel, R. I. (1974). Meaning postulates and semantic theory. *Foundations of Language,* **11,** 311–340.

Katz, J. J. and Postal, P. M. (1964). "An Integrated Theory of Linguistic Descriptions," MIT Press, Cambridge, Massachusetts.

Keenan, E. L. (1971). Two kinds of presupposition in natural language. In Fillmore and Langendoen, eds.

Keenan, E. L. (1972). On semantically based grammar. *Linguistic Inquiry,* **III,** 413–461.

Keenan, E. L. (1975). "Formal Semantics of Natural Language," Cambridge Univ. Press, New York.

Kempson, R. M. (1975). "Presupposition and the Delimitation of Semantics," Cambridge Univ. Press, New York.

Klima, E. S. (1964). Negation in English. In J. A. Fodor and Katz, eds.

Kripke, S. (1972). Naming and necessity. In Davidson and Harman, eds. (1972).

Kroch, A. S. (1974). The semantics of scope in English. (Ph.D. Dissertation), Massachusetts Inst. of Technology.

Kuroda, S.-Y. (1974). Description of presuppositional phenomena—from a nonpresuppositionalist point of view. Unpublished MS, University of California at San Diego.

La Galy, M., Fox, R. and Bruck, A., eds. (1974). "Papers from the Tenth Regional Meeting of the Chicago Linguistic Society," Univ. of Chicago, Chicago, Illinois.

Lakoff, G. (1965). On the nature of syntactic irregularity. (Ph.D. Dissertation), Indiana University. Also Report No. **NSF-16,** The Computation Laboratory of Harvard University, 1965. Published as "Irregularity in Syntax," Holt, New York, 1970.

Lakoff, G. (1966). A note on negation. In Report No. **NSF-17,** the Computation Laboratory of Harvard University.

Lakoff, G. (1968). Instrumental adverbs and the concept of deep structure. *Foundations of Language,* **4,** 4–29.

Lakoff, G. (1969). Presupposition and relative grammaticality. In Todd, ed. Also as Presupposition and relative well-formedness, in Steinberg and Jakobovits, eds.

Lakoff, G. (1970a). Counterparts, or the problem of reference in transformational grammar. In Report No. **NSF-24,** the Computation Laboratory of Harvard University. Also Indiana Univ. Linguistics Club.

Lakoff, G. (1970b). Global rules. *Language,* **46,** 627–639.

Lakoff, G. (1970c). Linguistics and natural logic. *Studies in Generative Semantics, No. 1,* Phonetics Laboratory, Univ. of Michigan. Also *Synthese,* (1970) **22,** 151–271, and in Davidson and Harman, eds. (1972).

Lakoff, G. (1971). On generative semantics. In Steinberg and Jakobovits, eds.

Lakoff, G. (1972). Hedges: a study in meaning criteria and the logic of fuzzy concepts. In Paranteau, Levi, and Phares, eds.

Lakoff, G. (1974). Interview with Herman Parret. In Fillmore, G. Lakoff, and R. Lakoff, eds.

Lakoff, R. (1971). If's, and's, and but's about conjunction. In Fillmore and Langendoen, eds.

Lakoff, R. (1974). Pluralism in linguistics. In Fillmore, G. Lakoff, and R. Lakoff, eds.

Lehrer, A. and Lehrer, K., eds. (1970). "Theory of Meaning," Prentice-Hall, Englewood Cliffs, New Jersey.

Lewis, D. (1970). General semantics. *Synthese,* **22,** 18–67. Also in Davidson and Harman, eds. (1972).

Linsky, L., ed. (1952). "Semantics and the Philosophy of Language," Univ. of Illinois Press, Urbana, Illinois.

Locke, J. (1689). "An Essay Concerning Human Understanding," Thomas Basset, London. Also Dutton Paperbacks, New York, 1971-72, (J. W. Yolton, ed.), and Oxford Univ. Press, New York, 1975, (P. H. Nidditch, ed.).

Lunt, H. G., ed. (1964). "Proceedings of the Ninth International Congress of Linguistics, 1962," Mouton, The Hague.

Lyons, J., ed. (1970). "New Horizons in Linguistics," Penguin, Harmondsworth, Middlesex, England.

Mates, B. (1952). Synonymity. In Linsky, ed.

McCawley, J. D. (1968a). Lexical insertion in a transformational grammar without deep structure. In Darden, Bailey, and Davison, eds.

McCawley, J. D. (1968b). The role of semantics in a grammar. In Bach and Harms, eds.

McCawley, J. D. (1970). English as a VSO language. *Language,* **46,** 286–299.

McCawley, J. D. (1971a). Interpretive semantics meets Frankenstein. *Foundations of Language,* **7,** 285-296.

McCawley, J. D. (1971b). Prelexical syntax. In *Monograph Series on Languages and Linguistics,* No. **24,** Georgetown Univ., Washington, D.C. (R. S. O'Brien, ed.).

McCawley, J. D. (1971c). Tense and time reference in English. In Fillmore and Langendoen, eds.

McCawley, J. D. (1972). A program for logic. In Davidson and Harman, eds. (1972).

McCawley, J. D. (1973). Syntactic and logical arguments for semantic structures. In Fujimura, ed.

McCawley, J. D. (1975). The role of lexicographic information in dictionary definitions. Presented at the annual conference of the International Linguistic Association, New York, March 8.

Montague, R. (1974). "Formal Philosophy: Selected Papers of Richard Montague", edited and with an introduction by R. H. Thomason, Yale Univ. Press, New Haven, Connecticut.

Moore, T., ed. (1973). "Cognitive Development and the Acquisition of Language," Academic Press, New York.

Olshewsky, T. M., ed. (1969). "Problems in the Philosophy of Language," Holt, New York.

Parkinson, G. H. R., ed. (1968). "The Theory of Meaning," Oxford Readings in Philosophy Series, (Warnock, G. J., ed.), Oxford Univ. Press, New York.

Partee, B. (1975). Montague grammar and transformational grammar. *Linguistic Inquiry*, **VI**, 203–300.

Partee, B., ed. (1976). "Montague Grammar," Academic Press, New York: to be published.

Partee, B., Sabsay, S. and Soper, J. (1971). Bibliography: Logic and Language. Indiana Univ. Linguistics Club.

Peranteau, P. M., Levi, J. N. and Phares, G. C., eds. (1972). "Papers from the Eighth Regional Meeting of the Chicago Linguistic Society," Chicago Linguistic Society, Chicago, Illinois.

Perlmutter, D. M. (1971). "Deep and Surface Structure Constraints in Syntax," Holt, New York.

Perlmutter, D. M. and Postal, P. M. "Relational Grammar": to be published.

Peters, S., ed. (1972). "Goals of Linguistic Theory," Prentice-Hall, New York.

Postal, P. M. (1970). On the surface verb 'remind.' *Linguistic Inquiry*, **I**, 37–120. Also in Fillmore and Langendoen, eds.

Postal, P. M. (1972). The best theory. In Peters, ed.

Postal, P. M. (1974). "On Raising: One Rule of English Grammar and its Theoretical Implications," MIT Press, Cambridge, Massachusetts.

Putnam, H. (1970). Is semantics possible? *Metaphilosophy*, **1**, 187–201.

Putnam, H. (1973). Meaning and reference. *Journal of Philosophy*, **70**, 699–711.

Putnam, H. (1975). The meaning of meaning. In Gunderson, ed.

Quine, W. V. O. (1953a). "From a Logical Point of View," Harvard Univ. Press. Revised edition 1961. Reprinted by Harper, 1963.

Quine, W. V. O. (1953b). Reference and modality. In Quine (1953a).

Quine, W. V. O. (1953c). Two dogmas of empiricism. In Quine (1953a).

Rosenberg, J. F. and Travis, C., eds. (1971). "Readings in the Philosophy of Language," Prentice-Hall, Englewood Cliffs, New Jersey.

Ross, J. R. (1967a). Constraints on variables in syntax. (Ph.D. Dissertation), Massachusetts Inst. of Technology.

Ross, J. R. (1967b). On the cyclic nature of pronominalization. In "To Honor Roman Jakobson: Essays on the Occasion of His Seventieth Birthday, Vol. II," Mouton, The Hague.

Ross, J. R. (1969). Auxiliaries as main verbs. In Todd, ed.

Ross, J. R. (1970). On declarative sentences. In Jacobs and Rosenbaum, eds.

Ross, J. R. (1972). The category squish: Endstation Hauptwort. In Peranteau, Levi and Phares, eds.

Ross, J. R. (1973a). A fake NP squish. In Bailey and Shuy, eds.

Ross, J. R. (1973b). Nouniness. In Fujimura, ed.

Ross, J. R. (1974). There, there, (there, (there, (there, ...))). In La Galy, Fox and Bruck, eds.

Ross, J. R. (1975). Clause-matiness. In Keenan, ed.

Schlick, M. (1936). Meaning and verification. *Philosophical Review,* **XLV,** 339–369. Also in A. Lehrer and K. Lehrer, eds.

Searle, J. R. (1965). What is a speech act? In Black, ed. Also in Rosenberg and Travis, eds., and in Searle, ed.

Searle, J. R. (1969). "Speech Acts: An essay in the Philosophy of Language," Cambridge Univ. Press, New York.

Searle, J. R., ed. (1971). "The Philosophy of Language," Oxford Univ. Press, New York.

Searle, J. R. (1975). Indirect speech acts. In Cole and Morgan, eds.

Sebeok, T. A., ed. (1966). "Current Trends in Linguistics, Vol. 3," Mouton, The Hague.

Stampe, D. W. (1972). On the meaning of nouns. In Cohen, ed.

Steinberg, D. D. and Jakobovits, L. A., eds. (1971). "Semantics: An Interdisciplinary Reader in Philosophy, Linguistics and Psychology," Cambridge Univ. Press, New York.

Tarski, A. (1944). The semantic conception of truth. In "Symposium on Meaning and Truth," *Philosophy and Phenomenological Research,* **IV.** Also in Feigl and Sellars, eds., Linsky, ed., and Olshewsky, ed.

Thomason, R. H. (1970). "Symbolic Logic: An Introduction," Collier-Macmillan, London.

Thomason, R. H. (1972). A semantic theory of sortal incorrectness. *Journal of Philosophical Logic,* **1,** 209–258.

Thomason, R. H. (1974). Some complement constructions in Montague grammar. In La Galy, Fox and Bruck, eds.

Thomason, R. H. (1976). Some extensions of Montague grammar. In Partee, ed.

Thompson, S. A. (1971). The deep structure of relative clauses. In Fillmore and Langendoen, eds.

Todd, W., ed. (1969). "Studies in Philosophical Linguistics I," Great Expectations, Evanston, Illinois.

Wasow, T. (1972). Anaphoric relations in English. (Ph.D. Dissertation), Massachusetts Inst. of Technology.

Weinreich, U. (1966). Explorations in semantic theory. In Sebeok, ed.

Wittgenstein, L. (1953). "Philosophical Investigations," translated by G. E. M. Anscombe, Blackwell, Oxford, England.

Zwicky, A. (1972). Remarks on directionality. *Journal of Linguistics,* **8,** 103–109.

INDEX

*Bold numbers indicate section numbers.